Collector's Guide to
INDIAN
PIPES

Identification
and Values

LAR HOTHEM

COLLECTOR BOOKS

A Division of Schroeder Publishing Co., Inc.

Searching for a Publisher?

We are always looking for knowledgeable people considered to be experts within their fields. If you feel that there is a real need for a book on your collectible subject and have a large comprehensive collection, contact Collector Books.

Front cover:

Bird effigy pipe, steatite, Hogan Gallery Inc., Naples, Florida. $250.00.
Deer effigy pipe, steatite, H. B. Greene II collection, Florida. Museum quality.
Catlinite effigy pipe, wolf (?) or other animal, Bob Johnson, Eagle Eye Gallery, Schenectady, New York. Museum quality.
T-shape pipe, catlinite and lead, Hogan Gallery Inc., Naples, Florida. $850.00.
Human head effigy pipe, black steatite, Hogan Gallery Inc., Naples, Florida. $1,200.00.

Back cover:

Crow effigy pipe, black steatite, H. B. Greene II collection,.. Florida. Museum quality.
High-bowl keeled pipe, steatite, H. B. Greene II collection, Florida. $850.00.
Effigy platform pipe, woodland buffalo (?), sandstone, Hogan Gallery Inc., Naples, Florida. $1,675.00.
Effigy catlinite pipe, raccoon on fish, Eye Gallery, Schenectady, New York. $750.00.

Cover Design   Book Design
Terri Stalions   ←→   Joyce Cherry

Collector Books
P.O. Box 3009
Paducah, Kentucky 42002-3009

CONTENTS

Acknowledgments

The author would like to thank all those who helped make this book possible. Contributors of photographs are credited by name throughout the book. They have kindly presented many fine pipe examples from across North America, and in fact have made this book possible. Special thanks are also due those who helped with large numbers of photographs, and these include Len and Janie Weidner (Midwestern pipes), Larry Lantz (Catlinite pipes), and several others who requested anonymity. Iron Horse collection contributed hundreds of photographs of fine Northeastern pipes. Finally, appreciation to Larry Garvin for suggesting this book idea.

Author's Note

Rather than simply a price guide, this is a book about Indian pipes that also includes values or a value range. This helps round out information, but please keep in mind that values are sometimes the least important aspect of the item being collected. Values can vary in different parts of the country as can a person's concept of how good something is, or even the authenticity of any one pipe. For these and other reasons neither the author nor the publisher will be responsible for losses incurred as a result of consulting this book.

Lar Hothem

Introduction

Even someone only casually knowledgeable about North American Indian artifacts is likely to be aware of pipes. Along with tipis and canoes and moccasins, pipes were (and are) basic to many Native American lifeways. Indians are thought to be the first people in the world to make and use instruments for smoking various substances including tobacco, and pipe use extended for more than 3,000 years.

The earliest known pipes began with simple tubular forms in the Upper Mississippi Watershed region. This was during the Late Archaic period, sometime before 1000 BC, say ca. 1500 BC. Pipe design developed into other styles, such as basic, realistic, and abstract effigy forms in Woodland times, 1000 BC – AD 800. Amerind pipes flowered in the Mississippian period to produce many different forms when almost any object was depicted. And, depending on the section of the country, Indian-made pipes had largely disappeared by ca. AD 1650.

As to distribution, all parts of North America had pipes of one or more kinds. Regional designs arose and faded, with some styles made for a brief period, while others were popular for hundreds of years. Materials used to make pipes depended on the best stones available, plus pottery and even wood, antler, and bone.

Collectors and students have long been interested in acquiring pipes, and some remarkable collections have been put together. Though there are few all-pipe or mainly pipe collections today that compare with some old-time collections, they do exist. And a large number of general American Indian artwork and artifact collections have at least a few representative specimens.

In terms of other ancient artifacts, like points or knives, there are fewer pipes available. Still, there are many thousands of pipe examples in dozens of types and hundreds of varieties. Pipes have been picked up on village and camp sites for over 350 years and specimens are still found today. Agriculture lands are usually the hunting grounds for the lucky finder, though pipes have also come from construction sites and stream beds and the shores of reservoirs.

For the collector, pipes have always had a certain aura or presence not shared with more common Indian artifacts. There has always been something special about them, this perhaps having to do with pipes being highly personal and well made and important and even somewhat mysterious.

Relative scarcity coupled with collector demand means that even average pipe examples have become valuable in recent years. Along with increased appeal and interest the problem of fake pipes developed. This of course is not unique to pipes, for fake Indian artifacts have been made for well over a century. The real concern is that pipe fakers are getting better and so are their fraudulent products.

As in many worthwhile collecting fields, knowledge and experience are often more important than money in identifying and acquiring good pipes. Those who have good pipes in their collections are to be commended, for such collectors have an appreciation as keen as that of the ancient artisans who made the pipes. Via such well-put-together and documented collections, important objects from the past are being preserved for the future.

How Pipes Were Made

Once the raw material (usually stone of some kind) was obtained, there is little doubt as to how pipes were made. There are many pipe examples — from roughed-out blanks to nearly completed pipes — that illustrate the step-by-step process. While unfinished pipes do not often receive the attention they might deserve from collectors, they are still prime examples of primitive art and industry.

The first step was selecting the raw material, the basic stone for the pipe-to-be. In some cases, a piece of the appropriate size was located in the glacial drift or from nearby bedrock. In the drift this was merely a matter of picking up a few likely stones and checking for flaws or inclusions of inferior material. In glaciated regions this process concentrated on stones like banded slate, various hardstones, even quartzite.

At other times and other areas, pipe material was quarried from deposits near the surface. Familiar examples would be steatite, catlinite, and various colorful and relatively soft pipestones. In such cases the material was encountered in layers or masses and first had to be mined or quarried. At times the material was removed in sheets or blocks which had to be broken or reduced in size, even chipped as with some slates. This made the pipe material smaller and more manageable and easier to transport.

Shaping the pipe had three stages after the original material had been selected and acquired. First was the preform or roughed-in-stage, when the mass was reduced to a bit larger than the desired, final form. This was accomplished by the pecking process, whereby a hammerstone was repeatedly struck against the stone. Done at the right place and with just enough force, each blow removed a small spray of tiny stone fragments.

Often hammerstones are found on and near village sites, and some of them may have been used to shape preliminary pipe forms. Hammerstones tend to be rounded, and this was caused by the worker's rotation of the hammerstone so that the smallest area was constantly being used for the striking surface or impact point. For durability, hammerstones were usually made of ultra-hard stone such as flint or chert, even quartzite and hematite or iron ore.

Once the preform had been worked down to slightly larger than the desired pipe shape in all dimensions, grinding took place. Long or large sections of the pipe — the platform bottom or the exterior of tube pipes — could be ground against sandstone slabs. Smaller pipe surface areas could be worn away using hand-held pieces of sandstone of the proper size. Then sandstone sections could even be used as saws to flatten such places as the bowl top. Some pipes were actually made of sandstone itself, but in such cases a coarser-grain sandstone could be used for tools.

Grinding did two things. It removed peck-mark traces, the characteristic small, shallow pits, and evened the surface of the pipe. It also brought the pipe into the final form, size-wise. While occasional slight peck-marks might be seen here and there on some examples, the grinding process left other marks. These were very slight abrasions or scratches from silica grains.

In a few cases, such as Hopewell platform pipes worked in pipestone, the marks of unusual tools can be seen. These have been reported by many students of prehistoric artifacts, and the marks resemble those left by a modern metal file. This scoring or very slight plowing was probably made by specialized knives mounted with shark-tooth blades, teeth the Hopewell are known to have imported from the southeast coastal areas or the Gulf of Mexico. Such tools scratched or gouged away the surface, especially in otherwise hard-to-reach places.

The final stage of pipe manufacture was polishing. Just as grinding removed most signs of pecking, polishing took away most signs of grinding. Many materials accepted a high polish, like pipestone, and retained it long centuries after the pipe was made. This of necessity and logically was the last thing done to prepare the surface of pipes.

Polishing made the pipe even more attractive, giving a sheen or surface luster to the object, enhancing the content or color of the stone. A soft piece of leather and finely ground stone particles mixed with animal fat would have done the job nicely. It should be noted that not all stone took a high polish, and, some stone did not hold the polish well once it was put on. Weathering or soil chemicals removed or diminished some of the polish over the centuries.

Once the pipe had been finished on the exterior, interior work was required for true completion. Drilling in fact sometimes took place between pecking and grinding or between grinding and polish. The reason for such "early" drilling was simple. If a problem developed during the painstaking drilling process, one that essentially ruined the pipe, less time and energy had been wasted. Also, for some pipe types drilling was more easily accomplished in the preform stage when the blank was still thick and there was some material margin for error.

This is especially valid for long, narrow tube pipes. Simply put, a thick cylinder was easier to drill than a slender cylinder, partly because it was easier to hold or secure. The drill hole could meander off-center slightly and still be more or less centered by reshaping the outside of the tube. Some tubular pipes, however, were drilled after grinding and before polishing.

Depending on time period and region, four different kinds of drilling could be used. These are, wand, cane, flint, and copper.

Wand drilling was the use of a solid hardwood stick with fine sand as the cutting agent. As the sand became worn and rounded it was replaced with fresh, sharp-edged sand or grit. When the wand wore down it was simply replaced with a new hardwood stick.

Cane drilling was similar, except that reed or cane was hollow and the grit-assisted cut made a circle, leaving a central column of stone. This eventually was broken off and, in a few cases, was itself drilled to make a long bead. Both wand and cane drilling made fairly large holes, often for the pipe bowl interior.

Flint drills made different-sized holes depending on the size and shape of the drill head itself. Some were finger turned while others were hand twirled or bow-string driven. Some drills previously used to hole pipes have their tips and sides worn smooth and for some reason were never resharpened. Some slender drills were mounted on narrow shafts so they could make smaller, short, stem holes or at least start the holes.

The three drilling types described made suitable holes, but these holes could be enlarged as needed. The big southern medicine tubes and massive Great Pipes often had the bowl interior portions enlarged by reaming, scraping, or gouging. Marks left on the pipe interior walls suggest that flint or chert tools were used.

The fourth and final drill type was a thin native copper awl or cylinder-like form, very narrow and at least several inches long. In a way, this is solid-wand drilling with slender metal instead of heavier wood, producing long holes of much smaller diameter. Copper-assisted

drilling was used by the Hopewell Indians (Middle Woodland) and probably also by Late Woodland pipe makers.

Some pipes, though shaped, polished, and drilled, were still not considered to be complete. Some Hopewellian effigy pipes, with fine details put in with flint gravers, had inset pearls for eyes. The Great Pipes often had shell or mother-of-pearl eyes. A few pipes with traces of red ochre suggest that some pipes were even painted.

One question about Indian pipes that occasionally arises is, who made the pipes? That is, did each user make his or her own, or did certain skilled workers or even a class of artisans engage in pipe making? The answer probably is, it depends. Very high-grade pipes of certain kinds certainly required greater than average knowledge and skill. Some of the more common forms, like bowl-type pipes from Mississippian times, could easily have been made by individual owners. Whoever did the work, the result was often an artistic marvel.

Drill holes in pipe stems were once considered to be a means of determining whether a pipe could be dated to historic or prehistoric times. Historic, of course, inferred the use of metal drill bits and thus at least indirect association with tools not made by Indians. Two classes of drill holes were thought by some students to be beyond the technical capability of Indian craftspeople. One was very narrow hole, ⅛" or less in diameter. Another was a very long drill hole of whatever size. Both of course were sometimes done by Indians.

Drills probably used to bore pipes are rather scarce, but one such was mentioned as coming from the Pratt Site in south-central Kansas. This drill had a pointed end and a rounded end. (Gunnerson, James H. *Archeology of the High Plains.* USDA Forest Service, Rocky Mountain Region. 1987, p 93.)

Some common-sense thinking about unfinished pipes suggest the progression of work steps. "A study of such unfinished forms gives a clue as to how the finished specimens were made. In general they were rough pecked into form, and then drilled or reamed out. The polishing was usually done after the drilling. This would seem to indicate that the drilling was rather a crucial test of the material of the pipe, and that if it broke while being drilled before polishing, the work of polishing was thus not lost." (Funkhouser, W. D. and W. S. Webb, *Ancient Life in Kentucky.* 1928, p 256.)

A platform pipe with an oval (1¼ x 1½") bowl gives an idea of the steps in making this kind of pipe. The steatite example, 4½" long, was finished except for drilling. The bowl was undrilled, while the stem hole was just started and reached a depth of ¹¹⁄₁₆". At least in this case the stem hole was drilled first, to be followed by the larger bowl opening. (Matthews,

James J. "Unfinished Curved Base Monitor Pipe," *Central States Archaeological Journal*. Vol. 36 No. 4 October 1989, p 191.)

Some tubular pottery pipes, in regions as far removed as Pennsylvania and the Southwest, had the elongated pipe bowl shaped quickly and easily. Pipe fragments prove that the pipe was molded around sections of corn cob, which were probably left in place. When the pipes were fired the cob burned away and the pipes retained the cavity to be used as the bowl.

A large kneeling human effigy pipe in quartzite from Monroe County, Arkansas, had the pipe bowl drilled in an unusual manner. Several small drill holes were first made, then the material between them was broken out to form the large bowl in the body of the figure. This hole was 1⅜" across and the pipe was 7" long. (McGuire, Joseph D. "Pipes and Smoking Customs of the American Aborigines," *Report of U. S. National Museum*. 1897, p 539.)

Stem holes for the Iroquois type pottery pipes were made in an ingenious manner. "Probably the majority have had the hole punched through the stem while the clay was yet plastic but there are many specimens that show that the clay was rolled or modeled over a small reed, straw, or wisp of twisted grass. When the clay was burned the reed or grass burned out and left the stem hole." (Parker, Arthur C. *The Archeological History of New York, Part 1*. 1922, p 151.

A stone elbow pipe with handle-knob extension beneath the bowl was found in Jersey County, Illinois. Two holes were drilled in the stem, as the first failed to contact the base of the smoking chamber. The second hole contained the remains of a bone stem liner or mouthpiece. (*Central States Archaeological Journal*. Vol. 14 No. 3. July 1967, p 107.)

Small-hole drilling of curved-base platform pipes was probably accomplished early in the manufacturing process. "An unfinished pipe from Jefferson County, is of diorite, 4" long. It is interesting as demonstrating that a specimen was at first rudely blocked out, then drilled, after which it was ground down and polished. This would indicate that the wonderful skill accredited to the aborigines in drilling through a thin plate of stone was not always due them, nor, as is often asserted, was a metal drill a necessity in the successful performance of the work." (West, George A. "The Aboriginal Pipes of Wisconsin," *The Wisconsin Archeologist*, Vol. 4 Nos. 3 & 4. April – August 1905, p 123.)

The manufacturing steps for some pipe types, from examination of unfinished examples, can be determined. For tubes: "As noted in reference to other tubes, those of the hourglass form appear to have been originally drilled by means of solid points, the perforation being subsequently enlarged by gouging out each end, and leaving a narrow hole or channel connecting the two bowls or ends." (McGuire, Joseph D. "Pipes and Smoking Customs of the America Aborigines," *Report of U. S. National Museum*. 1897, p 398.)

Precisely when the drilling was done or at what stage of completion for some of the long tubular pipes is uncertain. Some Adena forms were worked almost into final shape before drilling, indicating that making the long stem hole was nearly the final step. Other Adena pipes, especially shorter examples, have been completed and polished, but remained undrilled for some reason. At least for this particular artifact class drilling required great precision and care. This seems to hold true whatever the pipe material, ranging from sandstone to pipestone. However, some tubular pipes that were otherwise finished have been only partially drilled. It is then possible that drilling went part way into a semi-finished tube, the exterior was then shaped and/or polished, and drilling then was either resumed or abandoned. More studies are needed in this particular area.

A very large steatite Mississippian elbow pipe, found in 1911 in Tennessee, had a bowl size of 2½ x 3½". The stem-drilling method is of great interest. "The stem was crafted by the stick and sand method of drilling in three states, from ¾" to ¼" into the bowl. The first 1½" shows wear where a hollow shaft was projected as a mouthpiece." (Hart, Gordon, "Jolly's Island Pipe," *The Redskin*. Vol. 7 No. 3. 1972, p 86.)

Unfinished elbow pipe, prehistoric Plains Indian culture, material a fine-grained red sandstone. The pipe preform measures 1¼ x 3" and was found in the western Oklahoma area. Collection of and photograph by Larry G. Merriam, Oklahoma. Unlisted.

Unfinished elbow pipe made of high-grade pink and black hardstone. It measures 1⅜" high and 1½" long, and evidences completion to the grinding and polishing stage. Undrilled, the Ft. Ancient pipe is from northern Kentucky. Patrick Welch collection, Ohio. $50.00.

Elbow pipe, probably Mississippian period, red catlinite. It is 3½" high and 3¾" long, and is from Holt County, Missouri. The pipe is completed except that it is drilled only about 1½" in each hole. Mike George collection, Missouri. $200.00.

A pipe in the making, this example has the bowl hole drilled but the stem hole is unfinished. Note the peck marks on the side of the bowl surface and polish on the stem. This interesting example is 3⅜" long and is from Richland County, Ohio. Larry Garvin, Back to Earth, Ohio. $165.00.

Gray steatite pipe, prehistoric, 3⅛" long. The pipe was nearly finished, as the bowl was hollowed out but the stem was not drilled. Owasco tradition and ca. AD 1000 – 1300, the pipe was found near the Susquehanna River, Pennsylvania. Richard Savidge collection, Pennsylvania. $250.00.

Mountain lion effigy, possibly an unfinished pipe or preform, 2½" high. This image is very well made in a dark green Pennsylvania pipe-stone infused with black spots. Very attractive and unusual, the piece is from Juniata County, Pennsylvania. Richard Savidge collection, Pennsylvania. Museum grade.

Great Pipe, Woodland-Mississippian period, 8½" long. The material is attractive porphyry with dark gray and cream phenocysts. This piece lacks finished drilling, but both stem and bowl holes were just started. Other than drilling, the pipe is complete, including polish. Belmont County, Ohio. Private collection. Museum grade.

Preform pipe with top hole just begun, possibly effigy form with mouth hole only pecked. It is made of gray hardstone and measures 2" high and 1⅛ x 3¾" wide. Augusta County, Kentucky. Bill Mesnard collection, New Jersey. $100.00.

Hopewell unfinished platform pipe, preform state and undrilled, #A13. CA 500 BC – AD 500, the pipe is made of light brown stone and has peck marks and some polish. The platform measures 3¼" long and the bowl is 1¾" high. Onondaga County, New York. Iron Horse collection. $250.00 – 350.00.

Among the rarest objects (not necessarily the most valuable except from a scientific viewpoint) shown in this book are these two. One is the stem end of a Hopewell platform pipe made of pipestone. The other, measuring 3½" long, is a tapered cylinder made of copper. Found in close proximity, the copper object once drilled the stem hole. Ohio. Len and Janie Weidner collection, Ohio. Unlisted.

How Hopewell (Middle Woodland) pipe stem holes were probably drilled: "Just what was used as a drill for producing these long, yet small, stem bores, is a matter not wholly resolved. We know that the bore was started by the use of a very slender flint drill. This must have been followed up by an instrument that was strong and not flexible. There is good reason to believe that it was made of copper." (West, George A. *Tobacco, Pipes and Smoking Customs of the American Indians, Part I*, Text. 1934, p 157.) Len and Janie Weidner collection, Ohio. Unlisted.

Catlinite Pipes

Certainly the best-known and widest-used material for stone historic-era pipes of the Great Plains region, catlinite was also widely distributed elsewhere. Exportation went north into Canada, west to the Rockies, south to Oklahoma and Arkansas, and east to the Great Lakes. Catlinite, the red pipestone, was instantly recognized wherever it was traded and used.

In several respects, catlinite was, and is, the perfect pipe-making material. In the quarry it exists in thin layers, and once the overburden of soil and rock is removed, it can be readily quarried. Catlinite pipe blanks can be roughly outlined with a saw and further shaped with knives. Catlinite drills easily and polishes nicely.

This red pipestone is highly resistant to heat in normal use and retains basic color from earth to pipe. Catlinite has solid color ranges from light to dark red and varieties have different shades of color in layers and spots. Some of the more pleasing catlinite combinations include a darker ground sprinkled or speckled with lighter spots.

Catlinite material has been used since prehistoric times, and selection for Mic-mac and disc pipes was fairly common. It is, of course, the classic stone for long-stemmed Plains pipes, and sometimes both the bowl and stem were made of catlinite.

The extended and complex story of catlinite pipes continues into the present. Pipes are still being made by Native American craftspeople at the original quarry site, now Pipestone National Monument. Founded in 1937, personnel at the Monument can be contacted at P.O. Box 727, Pipestone, MN 56164-0727. The phone number is (507) 825-5464.

For travelers in the upper eastern Midwest, this is a highly recommended place to visit. While the area has certainly changed since it was first written about by George Catlin, the basic quarrying steps and pipe-making processes remain nearly the same.

Catlinite (red Minnesota pipestone) was a favorite material for late prehistoric and especially historic pipes of many kinds. One type is called a disc or sun-disc pipe and it is found over much of the eastern United States. An example from Adair County, Missouri, had a disc approximately 1½" in diameter and pipe was about 3" long. Such pipes are believed to be Oneota culture, ca. AD 1350 into historic times. (*CSAJ/The Archaeology of Missouri and Greater St. Louis.* Vol. 37 No. 4 1990, p 123.)

Many examples of Great Lakes area pipes and stems were similar to those of the Eastern Plains, especially the Sioux Indians. Catlinite, sometimes lead-inlaid, was used in common. (King, J. C. H. *Smoking Pipes of the North American Indian.* 1977, p 18.)

Catlinite pipes have long been treasured, though not all such historic pipe heads were necessarily Indian-made. "Red catlinite pipes were made by the Indians as early as the late 1400s. The red pipestone became so popular that white traders fashioned and engraved many pipes for trade purposes. A popular white man made trade shape was the pipe tomahawk. These types are often designed with floral patterns on the blade. They were probably produced between 1870 and 1920." (Baldwin, John. "Red Pipe Tomahawks," *Artifacts.* Vol. 5 No. 3 1975, p 23.)

As has been noted, many pipes of Minnesota pipestone were turned out by whites in the late 1800s. One aspect of this is that power-operated equipment was often used, such as lathes and drills. This means that any late Plains-type pipe with extensive rounded surfaces or long drilled sections might well have been a white-made product.

Catlinite is probably the most famous pipe-making material in North America, at least to the average person and for historic-era pipes. "The better catlinite is found in the extreme southwest corner of Minnesota near the city of Pipestone. This deposit is of the highest quality from the standpoint of workability, color, and texture. Other deposits are found in the United States and Canada but are of inferior quality. Catlinite occurs in several colors, but that from Pipestone is red, probably stained by hematite iron." (Erickson, Clifford S. "Catlinite," *Central States Archaeological Journal.* Vol. 13 No. 4 October 1966, p 133.

Three different historic Plains pipes are here listed from the pages of a major early Indian artifact dealer; bowls are all red catlinite except for one. "L-shape bowl, 2⅛ x 2⅜", round wood stem, 17½" overall, fine — $3.25. V-shape bowl, 2 x 2", beveled edges, wood stem partly covered with colored quillwork, 14" overall — $3.25. T-shape bowl, polished black stone, 3¼ x 6½", square edges partly beveled, round wood stem, 23" overall, fine — $6.00." (Grutzmacher, A. D. Clearing Sale Catalog/Season 1926 – 1927. p 19.)

Catlinite was sometimes used for pipes made by Europeans. "Many pipes, including the Calumet, were produced during the 1800s and were crafted by white man's tools or by the white man himself then traded to Indians. The Northwest Fur Company, which consisted of Canadian merchants, produced both stems and pipes using metal drills and other modern methods." (Hart, Gordon. "Calumets and Their Pipes," *Prehistoric Art/Archaeology '80.'* Vol. 15 No. 1. 1980, pp 26 – 29.)

Catlinite Plains type bowls were made in three different ways. There were Indian-made with prehistoric tools and methods, Indian-made with white-manufactured metal tools, and, white-made with white-manufactured tools.

Disc or disk pipes have an unusual design and, though far from common, are much admired by collectors and students of Amerind lifeways and objects. "Catlinite disk pipes (...) are generally considered a horizon marker for the late prehistoric – protohistoric Oneota culture, and occur on Oneota sites in Iowa, Missouri, Minnesota, and other Midwestern states near the catlinite quarries." (Rice, Orleans L. Jr. "A Catlinite Disk Pipe Find," *Central States Archaeological Journal.* Vol. 21 No. 2, 1974, p 166.)

Lead inlay on Catlinite pipes was done in the period late 1700s to early 1800s; eventually the technique became widely known and was copied by others.

Catlinite was selected for pipe-making for several reasons, one of which was aesthetic. "Constant handling of these artifacts add a high polish and a soft lustrous patina produced by contact with natural body oils." (Berner, John F. "Catlinite Pipe Making Spanned 1700 Years," *Prehistoric Artifacts.* Vol. 19 No. 1. 1985, p 13.)

The material used for making a pipe-tomahawk collected in 1880 at LeVorn, Minnesota, was catlinite. The pipestone was dark red and the pipe head was 5½" high. (West, George A. "The Aboriginal Pipes of Wisconsin," *The Wisconsin Archeologist.* Vol. 4 Nos. 3 & 4, April – August 1905, p 67.)

Being probably the best-known historic pipestone in North America, catlinite from southwestern Minnesota is described at the quarry itself: "The thickest layer of the stone is about the middle of the vein, from which, while only 2" thick at most, plates of this thickness may be obtained of almost any size. In boring this stone a jasper or quartzite drill point answers very well. A wood shaft used with dry sand is equally serviceable." (McGuire, Joseph D. "Pipes and Smoking Customs of the American Aborigines," *Report of U. S. National Museum.* 1897, pp 571 573.)

Today Plains style pipes, the bowl and stem sets, are quite valuable. Such was not the case more than half a century ago. "Sioux Indian red stone peace pipe, old, used, genuine. I have a nice lot recently purchased, complete with stems and name of Indian who owned it. Each $2.50 – $5.00." (H. T. Daniel/1941 Catalog and Price List. Hot Springs, Arkansas. 1941, p 19.)

For whatever stylistic reasons, Plains pipes of catlinite often have a platform projecting beyond the bowl, which in early examples was small. Also, the stem leading to the bowl is often longer than the bowl itself.

Thomas E. Gilcrease, founder of the famous Gilcrease Museum in Tulsa, Oklahoma, had various collections and many of the objects were fine examples of American Indian art. For example, a pipe collection obtained from Willis Tilton of Topeka, Kansas, was housed in a building behind the museum. It contained over one thousand catlinite pipes. (Fecht, William G. "They Are Gone But Not Forgotten," *Central States Archaeological Journal.* Vol. 37 No. 2. April 1990, pp 101 – 102.)

Just after the Civil War, apparently, there was a brisk business in white-made catlinite pipes. "There are thousands of 'red pipestone' pipes disseminated in the museums of the world, which were made by whites. (...) the Northwest Fur Company made 2,000 of these pipes between 1865 and 1868, selling them to the Indians on the upper Missouri for furs." (Winchell, N. H. The *Aborigines of Minnesota.* The Minnesota Historical Society. 1911, p 486.)

While the process of making a pipe from catlinite is well known, just how a final polish was put on is not in agreement. Methods mentioned for doing this include rubbing with grease, rubbing with plant material having silica, polishing with beeswax, buffing with ashes and leather or fine grit and leather. Burnishing with water-worn pebbles and pieces of bone has been suggested. Ppprobably all methods would impart a gloss or sheen of some kind.

Many people believe that pipestone is easier to work when first quarried, but this may not be the case. "Catlinite has by some writers been said to be soft when taken from the quarries and to become harder on exposures to the atmosphere; but the writer's experience in working this stone would indicate that the difference in working fresh or dry stone is insignificant, as pieces which have dried for years are yet nearly as soft as commercial soapstone." (McGuire, Joseph D. "Pipes and Smoking Customs of the American Aborigines," Report of U. S. National Museum. 1897, p 572.)

T-shape late historic pipe bowl, 2 x 4". The catlinite is exceptional in being a deep, dark red, and
there are lead or pewter inlays. This is one of the
few pipes where there is a near balance of inlay
and stone. Dodge County, Wisconsin. Larry
Lantz, First Mesa, Indiana. $750.00.

Double-bowl catlinite platform pipe,
ca. 1890 – 1910. This is a scarce style,
4½" long with the bowl 1¾" and 1¼"
high respectively. This artifact was collected at an Indian auction in San
Diego, California, in 1989. J. Steve and
Anita Shearer collection, California.
$550.00.

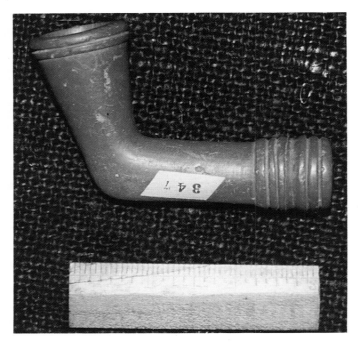

Obtuse-angle elbow type catlinite pipe, ca. AD 1700 –
1750, formerly in the Leslie W. Hills collection of Ft.
Wayne, Indiana. With stem 2½" long and bowl 2"
high, #347 was pictured in Moorehead's *The Stone
Age in North America,* Vol. II, p 49. Iron Horse collection. $350.00 – 450.00.

Vase-shaped catlinite pipe bowl, 1¼ x 2⅛"
well carved in a deep red stone. Bowl top has
radiating lines from center while the sides
have a line running from bottom to top.
Unusual and attractive. Leelanau County,
Michigan. Larry Lantz, First Mesa, Indiana.
$385.00.

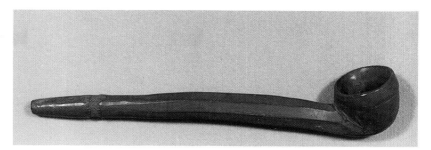

Chippewa catlinite "Voyager" type carrying pipe, 6½" long. Both bowl and stem are delicately carved on this early piece which has a warm patina and good polish. Larry Lantz, First Mesa, Indiana. $395.00.

Biconical pipe made of unusual material, catlinite. The piece has very smooth, flowing lines and measures 1⅞ x ¹³⁄₁₆" and is 1⅛" high. Nicely polished, this is from Wisconsin. Bill Mesnard collection, New Jersey. $300.00.

Pipe, historic period, catlinite, with broken stem area. It measures 2" high and 2¼" long. This pipe was found in east-central Nebraska on a Pawnee site. Richard Krueger collection, Iowa; Sandra Krueger photograph. $75.00 – 150.00.

Miniature catlinite pipe, only 1⅛" long and ⁹⁄₁₆" high. This was a personal find of the owner on an Oto-Missouri site in east-central Nebraska. Lewis and Clark, on their great cross-country expedition, met Indians from this village. Richard Krueger collection, Iowa; Sandra Krueger photograph. $150.00.

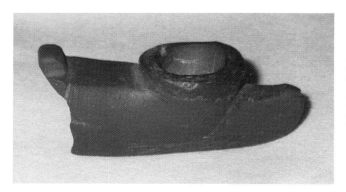

Historic pipe, catlinite, ⅝ x 1½" long. This pipe with several small nicks was picked up in east-central Nebraska on a Pawnee site. Richard Krueger collection, Iowa; Sandra Krueger photograph. $150.00.

Block-type catlinite pipe, early historic and ca. AD 1600 – 1750. This scarce style pipe is 2¼" long and 2" high. Material is mottled orange-red catlinite. Plains to Great Lakes region. Len and Janie Weidner collection, Ohio. $450.00.

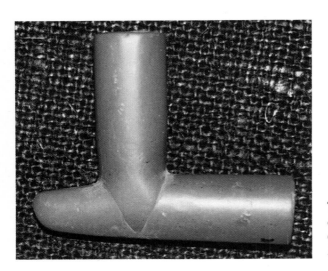

Historic-era catlinite pipe, 1½" x 2½". The base and sides have line engraving in cross-hatch design, and the bowl has radiating lines. The pipe has a small suspension hole. This pipe came from Knox County, Indiana. Larry Lantz, First Mesa, Indiana. $385.00.

T-shaped high bowl pipe, ca. AD 1650 – 1750, red catlinite. #106\A has a 3" stem with bowl 2½" high. Chautauqua County, New York. Iron Horse collection. $300.00 – 375.00.

T-shaped historic pipe with squirrel effigy and a base that changes from squared to rounded. This is a large Sioux pipe, 3¾" high and 6¾" long. Ex-collection John F. Neil. Jim Frederick collection, Utah. $750.00.

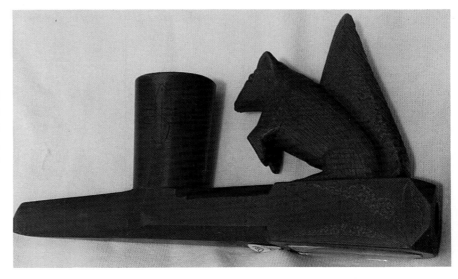

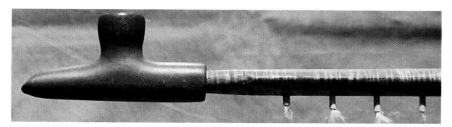

T-shaped red pipestone (catlinite) pipe with original wooden stem. It is historic period, with pipe size 2 x 4" and bowl diameter of 1". The stem is 15¾" long. This set came from Trumbull County, Ohio, and is ex-collection Pickenpaugh. Collection of and photograph by Larry G. Merriam, Oklahoma. $700.00 – 900.00.

Catlinite L-shape pipe, Great Lakes type, fin or crest with two holes, ca. AD 1700 – 1750. This pipe, #P-42, has a round bowl 1¾" high and the squared stem is 2¾" long. Van Buren County, Michigan. Iron Horse collection. $350.00 – 450.00.

L-shape Plains type catlinite pipe, 2½ x 4". This is probably an early piece, plain yet expressive, done in orange-red material. It came from the St. Paul area, Minnesota. Larry Lantz, First Mesa, Indiana. $550.00.

L-shaped catlinite pipe, ca. AD 1650 – 1775, #106/B. This small pipe has a stem 1½" long and bowl height 1⅜". Chautauqua County, New York. Iron Horse collection. $300.00 – 400.00.

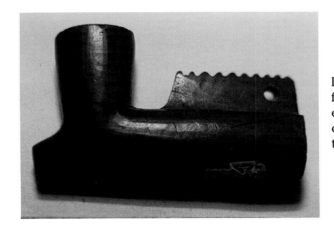

L-shaped catlinite pipe, 2⅜" long. This fine example with high serrated ridge is ex-collections Dresslar and Swann and came from Wisconsin. Larry Garvin, Back to Earth, Ohio. $650.00+.

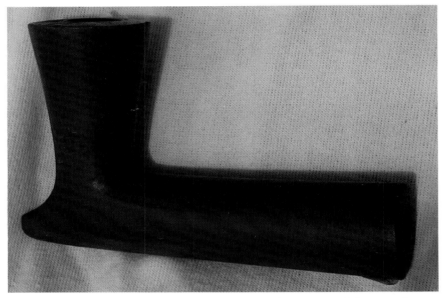

L-shaped historic catlinite pipe, Sioux, with flared bowl. It is early, ca. 1790 – 1810, and measures 5" long and 3" high. Ex-collection Tom Davis. Jim Frederick collection, Utah. $1,000.00.

L-shaped catlinite pipe, mid-1800s. This pipe measures 2⅝" long and 2¼" high, with ring decorations. The pipe is a maroon color, ex-collections Newton and Bovis, and is Great Lakes area or Eastern Prairie. Len and Janie Weidner collection, Ohio. $525.00.

L-shaped pipe, Eastern United States, marked with "oo" on the bowl. This is a nicely shaped and polished historic pipe, ex-collections Fruit and Pickenpaugh. The bowl is 2½" high and 1½" in diameter at the top. Ca. late 1800s. Collection of and photograph by Larry G. Merriam, Oklahoma. $350.00 – 450.00.

Iroquois Great Lakes type pipe, catlinite, double fins or crests, ca. 1720 – 1750. #RJ/BT has a stem 4¾" long and bowl height is 1½". Lancaster County, Pennsylvania. Iron Horse collection. $500.00 – 750.00.

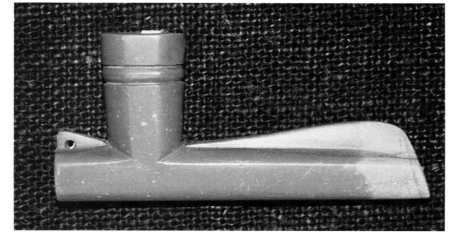

Iroquois catlinite T-pipe, stem and base canoe-shaped plus fin with hole, ca. 1700 – 1750. Overall length of #RJ-95 is 4" and bowl height is 1¼". The pipe came from the east end of Chautauqua Lake, Chautauqua County, New York. Iron Horse collection. $500.00 – 750.00.

High-bowl keeled pipe, canoe-shaped, ca. 1400 – 1750. Nicely made of catlinite and with incised decorations, it measures 2¼" high and 8⅝" long. It was found in Colbert County, Alabama. H. B. Greene II collection, Florida. $850.00.

War bundle pipe in platform style, Pawnee, ca. 1860 – 1870. Made of deep red catlinite it is 4" long, 1¼" high, and 2¼" in disc diameter. This pipe was traded with a Chicago dealer in 1995. J. Steve and Anita Shearer collection, California. $1,300.00.

Plains pipe set, late 1800s, made of speckled Catlinite. The V-shaped bowl is 5" high, and the bent stem is 7¼" long. Private collection. $1,350.00.

Plains Catlinite pipe set, turn-of-century, with V-shaped pipe and bent stem. In order for the pipe to be fully drilled, both bowl and stem, there is a plugged hole at the stem base which allowed drilling between the two. Bowl is 5½" high while the stem is 9" long. Private collection. $1,000.00 – $1,300.00.

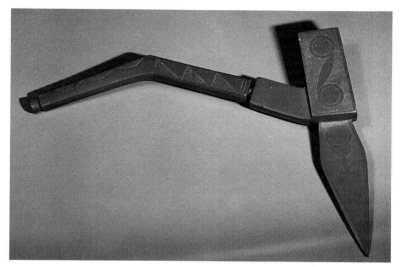

Catlinite pipe and stem with German or Scandinavian styling, the set ca. 1890 – 1920. The bowl upper extension is 2¼" high and the stem is 6" long. This set was collected at an antiques show in Buena Park, California, in 1984. J. Steve and Anita Shearer collection, California. $750.00.

Catlinite pipe and stem with European styling, ca. 1890 – 1910. The flange below the bowl bears a likeness to the spontoon-type pipe-tomahawk of the mid-1800s. The stem is 6" long while the pipe portion above the flange is 2¾" high. A fine pipe, this has the elaborate bowl design. The set was collected in Brimfield, Massachusetts in 1995. J. Steve and Anita Shearer collection, California. $850.00.

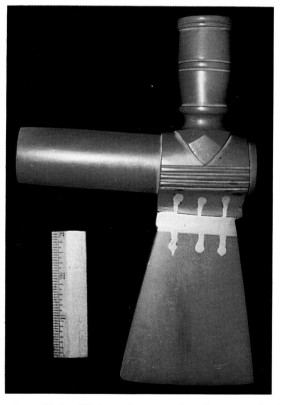

Catlinite flared-blade pipe-tomahawk head, ca. 1900, 7½" high. The engraved florals are well done, and the type often comes from the Wisconsin-Minnesota region. Private collection. $800.00.

Historic catlinite Plains pipe-tomahawk pipe inlaid with pewter, #RKR/27. The bowl and blade of this pipe, ca. 1890 – 1910, are 8½" high while the stem is 6¼". This piece was obtained at a gun show in Ohio, 1982. Iron Horse collection. $950.00 – 1,200.00.

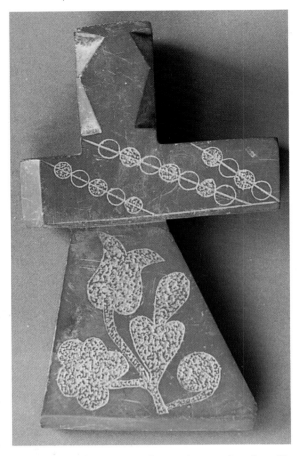

Tomahawk form pipe, historic, made of catlin-ite. With floral blade engraving, this type of pipe was made by the Menomini Indians of Upper Michigan. It measures 2⅞ x 4¾" high. Upper Michigan. Collection of and photograph by Duane Treest, Illinois. $350.00.

Pipe-tomahawk pipe, figural blade and highly deco-rated stem, ca. 1900. The bowl and blade portion are 6½" high and the stem measures 12½" long. Very ornate catlinite pipe-tomahawk pipes typically have fairly short catlinite stems. Private collection. $1,200.00 – 1,500.00.

Catlinite pipe-tomahawk pipes, all with decorative blades and ornate catlinite handle-stems, ca. 1890 – 1920. Bowl and blades are about 5¾" high while average length is 15½". Top, #FM/85, rectangular stem blocks. Middle, #GF/93, engraved stem. Bottom, #HL/154, squared stem designs. Iron Horse collection. Each, $900.00 – 1,250.00.

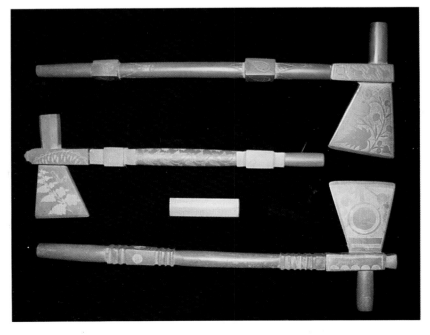

Tomahawk style pipe with buck and snake designs and stem, both in catlinite and ca. 1890 – 1910. The bowl portion is 2¾" high and the stem is 13" long. This set was collected in 1994 in an antiques store in Lincoln City, Oregon. J. Steve and Anita Shearer collection, California. $1,000.00.

Pipe-tomahawk type pipe, catlinite, with long reed stem. Ca. 1890s, the two measure 15½" long. The pipe and stem are ex-collection Dr. Joseph Hart, New York City. Dave Summers, Native American Artifacts, Victor, New York. $375.00.

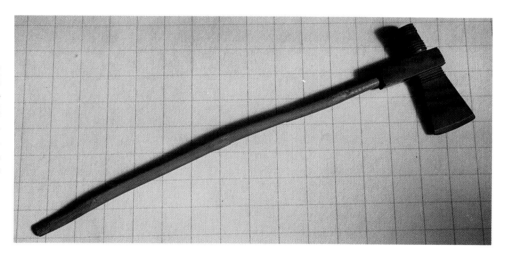

Tomahawk style pipe and fish effigy stem, the red catlinite set ca. 1890 – 1910. Nicely matched and in excellent condition, the pipe and stem were collected at an antiques shop in Fremont, California, in 1990. J. Steve and Anita Shearer collection, California. $850.00.

Catlinite pipe-tomahawk pipe, 7 x 15½" with catlinite stem. Late 1800s, both have age patina and use polish. They are professionally mounted with a sepia photo from an 1880 – 1890 glass negative, photo size 11 x 15". With cherry frames and conservation glass, this is a unique display. Larry Lantz, First Mesa, Indiana $2,500.00.

Effigy catlinite pipe, raccoon on fish, 7" long. This historic pipe is nicely detailed in medium-red material and may be early 1900s. Kentucky. Bob Johnson, Eagle Eye Gallery, Schenectady, New York. $750.00.

Bird head effigy pipe, Mississippian period, made of red catlinite. This pipe is nicely carved and well polished, measuring 2" high and 2¼" long. It came from Salina County, Missouri. Private collection, Georgia. $585.00.

Catlinite effigy pipe, late historic, very unusual and distinctive form. The fish is 1 x 2 x 7½" though the effigy is only ½" thick and the bowl is another ½". The stone is a moderate red color and the fish is quite detailed and carefully carved. This was collected near Rapid City, South Dakota. Larry Lantz, First Mesa, Indiana. $685.00.

Unusual catlinite effigy pipe with bowl inside the buffalo or bison atop the platform. This is a large piece at ¾ x 1⅞ x 8½" long, and the stone is dark mahogany red. Lines and dots decorate the platform, and the bison figure is very well done. Iron County, Wisconsin. Larry Lantz, First Mesa, Indiana. $950.00.

Great Lakes T-shape human effigy pipe, Iroquois, ca. 1700 – 1850. #GF/10/93 is made of rich deep red catlinite, with a stem 4¼" and bowl height of 3". The figure may represent a fur trader from post-contact times. Great Lakes area. Iron Horse collection. $450.00 – 750.00.

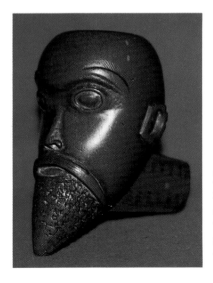

Human effigy pipe, Iroquois, ca. 1700 – 1800. This is a nicely detailed head in dark catlinite, the pipe 2" long and 2½" high. #GF-8-12-97 represents a white man with beard, an unknown personage. This is a scarce depiction, from western New York. Iron Horse collection. $500.00 – 1,000.00.

Effigy pipe, Sioux type, deep red catlinite. This is an historic piece in a bird effigy, pipe 3⅝" long. The pipe has the bowl colored deep black from long-time use. Eastern Plains. Len and Janie Weidner collection, Ohio. $650.00.

L-shaped Plains type catlinite pipe with effigy of pregnant woman. This exceptional pipe in rich maroon is 4½" high and 4" long. Ca. 1840 – 1850s this historic pipe was collected from a private source in Mansfield, Massachusetts. J. Steve and Anita Shearer collection, California. $1,800.00.

Acorn-shaped catlinite pipe bowl with catlinite stem, ca. 1890 – 1910. The bowl is 4" long and the stem is 11" long. A fine set, these were collected from a private source in San Diego, California. J. Steve and Anita Shearer collection, California. $750.00.

Fish effigy pipe, mottled catlinite, mid-twentieth century. This artistic rendition measures 12" long and was obtained at auction. Dave Summers, Native American Artifacts, Victor, New York. $875.00.

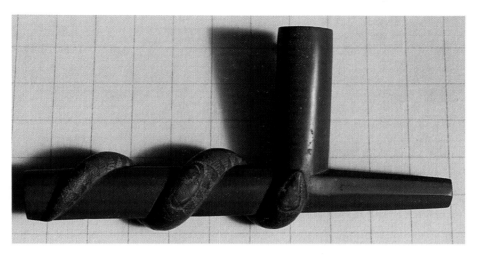

T-shape snake catlinite effigy pipe, probably mid-twentieth century. The pipe is 10¼" long and is signed "Willis Ward." The pipe is well executed and nicely polished. Plains type. Dave Summers, Native American Artifacts, Victor, New York. $700.00.

Catlinite effigy pipe, wolf(?) or other animal, very dark red patinated material. It measures 4¾" long and was joined to a wooden stem 17⅝" long. This pipe set also had a human effigy of steatite fastened to the stem and a steatite bear-head mouthpiece. Swain County, North Carolina. Bob Johnson, Eagle Eye Gallery, Schenectady, New York. Museum grade.

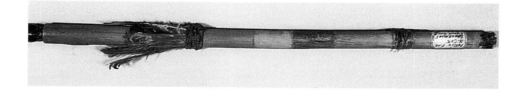

Pipe stem which goes with the catlinite effigy wolf(?) pipe 4¾" long, shown above. The stem 17⅝" in length, has painted bands and an attachment of feathers in addition to the two other steatite effigies. Swain County, North Carolina. Bob Johnson, Eagle Eye Gallery, Schenectady, New York. Museum grade.

Steatite Pipes

Steatite or soapstone is found in outcrops over much of the eastern United States, along parts of the West Coast and at isolated locations in between. Steatite is an ideal material for pipes, being fairly available, medium-hard for ease of carving, and quite attractive when the surface is smoothed and polished. A major characteristic is that steatite is highly resistant to heat, and retains heat to an uncommon degree.

Steatite derives from words meaning "tallow stone" because of some lighter-colored varieties. Many people have seen steatite only in commercial applications such as stoves, heating slabs, or counter-tops where it may be a mottled gray. Steatite, however, exists in many colors, from dull yellow through many shades of green to nearly black, plus intermixed, mottled, and flecked forms.

Color and durability of steatite were main attractions to prehistoric artisans beginning in Early Woodland times, ca. 500 BC or slightly before. Then medicine tubes (double-ended tubular pipes) were made, plus a few other forms were turned out in Middle Woodland times. The Late Woodland had many excellent steatite pipes, mostly platform varieties. And most Great Pipes were made of colorful, fine grades of steatite. Historic groups like the Cherokees produced numerous elegant steatite pipes, many in effigy forms.

Throughout the long period of use, steatite seems to have been traded as a raw material (local pipe forms made of out-of-area steatite) or as finished products (exotic pipe forms of steatite in local areas). Interestingly, once steatite was introduced as a pipe material in a certain region, Indian groups seemingly attempted to stay with it whenever possible.

Steatite was favored for very large pipes of many kinds in the southern United States. "The restricted center tube pipes represent the oldest use of steatite in large pipes. These appear in Burial Mound I period of Candy Creek Culture just following Watts Bar Culture of Tennessee. Watts Bar began declining at 800 B.C. This appears to be the earliest use of steatite for pipes in general. ... The earliest documentation of a large steatite effigy pipe occurred in association with Eastern Adena. ...Many of the massive steatite effigy pipes are associated with Hopewell

and, later in the Southern area, with Copena cultures." (Baldwin, John. "Massive Steatite Art," *Central States Archaeological Journal.* Vol. 29 No. 3. July 1987, pp 120 – 121.)

In addition to the region that is now the southeastern United States, steatite was very important in the West and West Coast regions. Steatite or soapstone was worked extensively in Wyoming, and the steatite industry was widespread in California. Major deposits and quarries were located on Santa Catalina Island, especially at Pots Valley. (Holmes, W. H. *Handbook of Aboriginal American Antiquities, Part I.* 1919, pp 238 – 239.)

The material known as steatite was long a favorite of pipe makers across the present United States, especially in the Southeast. "Steatite or talc, in its various colors, from North Carolina or the eastern borders of Tennessee, was the material generally utilized in the manufacture of fine stone pipes. No other stone was so suitable for this purpose. It is not injured by heat, and compact steatite is not easily fractured. It can be carved or drilled without very great labor, and some of the varieties have a surface nearly as brilliant as marble, when polished. Fine quarries of steatite are found near Roane Mountain, in East Tennessee." (Thruston, Gates P. *The Antiquities of Tennessee.* 1890, p 179.)

Regarding steatite, this material was a favorite for pipes on both the East and West Coasts. ("Tobacco pipes...were made, mostly no doubt from choice bits of stone carried away for the purpose, or perhaps often from fragments of the thick-walled (cooking) vessels broken in use." (Holmes, W. H. *Handbook of Aboriginal American Antiquities, Part I.* 1919, p 230.)

Not all steatite for pipe making in North America, of course, originated in what is today the United States. "Soapstone — the gray variety occurs in a ledge, Lutherworth Twp., Victoria Co." (Laidlaw, Col. G. E. "Some Archaeological Notes on Victoria County, Ontario," *The Archaeological Bulletin.* Vol. 6 No. 3. May – June 1915, p 54.)

Today's state of Tennessee may be the heartland for large effigy steatite pipes. "These finely carved stone calumets in the form of birds and animals must have been very numerous in ancient Tennessee, both in the middle and eastern sections of the state. A great number of them have been discovered; more of the large pipes, indeed, than have probably been found in any other state." (Thruston, Gates P. *The Antiquities of Tennessee.* 1890, p 206.)

Steatite was a major pipe material, and it is part of the talc group. Steatite is coarse and granular, with a greasy (soapy) feel and is medium-hard to work. This stone retains heat and exists in various dark colors. Further: "Green and black steatite quarried from the Virginia – Carolinas region was a favorite raw material of prehistoric pipe makers. All forms of pipe types were manufactured in almost all cultural periods throughout prehistoric time. As Woodland culture trade networks expanded westward quantities of both raw steatite and finished steatite products such as pipe forms, were distributed throughout the Ohio and Cumberland River drainages." (Shipley, Gregory. "The Steatite Platform Pipe Family," *Artifacts.* Vol. 13 No. 4, 1983, p 89.)

Eastern North America is a major geographic region for steatite outcroppings, which were eventually quarried for artifacts such as large cooking vessels and pipes. "Steatite is of very general distribution in eastern Canada and the Atlantic States and has been mined by the aborigines in numberless localities, especially in New England, Pennsylvania, Maryland, District of Columbia, and the Appalachian regions of the south." (Holmes, W. H. *Handbook of Aboriginal American Antiquities, Part I.* 1919, p 230.)

Called "The most exquisitely striking pipe that has been found in Kentucky," a black steatite Intrusive Mound pipe was picked up in Cumberland County. The flared bowl rim was 4½" in diameter while the bowl was 1". The stem was 2" wide and 9¼" long. The pipe was highly polished overall. (Young, Col. Bennett H. *The Prehistoric Men of Kentucky.* 1910, pp 279, 293.)

A large steatite elbow pipe came from Scott County, Illinois, picked up in a sand pit. It measured 5" long and 4¾" high. (*Central States Archaeological Journal.* Vol. 31 No. 1. January 1984, p 42.)

Smith County, Tennessee, an area where many Great Pipes have been found, was the source for a steatite bird effigy pipe. Crafted in dark green steatite, it was 3¼ x 7¼" long. (Waggoner, John Jr. "A Smith County Tennessee Bird Pipe," *The Redskin.* Vol. 10 No. 2. 1975, p 48.)

A fine alate (also called winged or fan-base, from the flared stem sides) pipe came from Russell County, Virginia. Made of gray steatite and with incising on both wings, the size was 3⅝ x 8½". These are ca. AD 550. (*Artifacts.* Vol. 7 No. 2. 1977, cover photograph.)

Large southern steatite effigy pipes are usually based on tubular designs, but a bear effigy pipe exists based on the elbow design. It was found ca. 1895 in Choctaw County, Alabama. The pipe was 4" high and 5¼" long. (Bushey, Dennis. "The Allen Bear Pipe," *Prehistoric America.* Vol. 26 No. 1. 1992, p 6.)

A fine, long steatite platform pipe, probably from Virginia, was made in Late Woodland time. Once in two pieces, the restored pipe with high bowl near the platform end measured 4 x 8". (Baldwin, John. "From the Moon," *The Redskin.* Vol. 10 No. 3. 1975, p 115.)

Made of black steatite, a highly unusual platform pipe from Mercer County, Ohio, depicts a sunflower on the platform top. The centers of three flowers apparently all had inlays, possibly mother-of-pearl. Ex-collections Dr. Bunch and Knoblock (of bannerstone book fame), the pipe measured just under 4½" long. (Knoblock, Byron. "Sun-flower Pipe," *Central States Archaeological Journal.* Vol. 1 No. 2. October 1954, p 49.)

Gray-green steatite was the material used for a bird-effigy Great Pipe which was picked up in southeast Alabama in 1975. Well carved, this pipe was over 9" long. (*Prehistoric Artifacts.* Vol. 20 No. 4. 1986, p 15.)

A large square-bowl elbow pipe made of black steatite with gold flecks came from Georgia. It measured 4¾" high and 4⅝" long. The weight was 4 pounds. (*The Redskin.* Vol. 5 No. 4 October 1970, p 118.)

Years ago a fairly scarce pipe type known as an alate (winged) pipe was recovered in a Kentucky rock shelter. Made of steatite, this acute-angle Carter County find was graceful and incised with various markings. It measures 6⅛" long. (*Central States Archaeological Journal.* Vol. 16 No. 4. October 1969, p 172.)

In old writings, one reads of this or that steatite pipe form or type being common or not scarce or some other quantitative rating that indicates pipes are fairly everyday finds. Nothing could be more misleading, for pipes of any kind tend not to be average finds. Some surface-hunters, in fact, have hunted almost a lifetime without finding a single complete pipe.

The materials used in some steatite pipes can be traced to the actual quarry source by a modern scientific technique. Chemical mixtures vary in different steatites and this diversity is capable of being pinpointed by a process termed neutron activation analysis. (Dann, Kevin T. *Traces on the Appalachians: A Natural History of Serpentine in Eastern North America.* 1988, p 129.)

An outstanding black steatite bird effigy Great Pipe was found in Lincoln County, Kentucky. Just over 6" long, it was well crafted and highly polished. (*Artifacts.* Vol. 11 No. 3. 1981, pp 80-81.)

Platform pipe, Intrusive Mound people of Late Woodland times, greenish steatite. This shows the typical ridge above the drilled stem hole; the base bottom has marks of the specialized tool used on some pipes and birdstones which left shallow, parallel lines. Size is 1¾ x 3⅞". Hocking County, Ohio. Len and Janie Weidner collection, Ohio. $1,000.00.

Platform pipe, Late Woodland period, 3⅛" long and 1⅞" high. There is an expansion in the bowl middle and the rim is flanged. Material is dark green steatite for this finely shaped and crafted pipe. Pennsylvania. Richard Savidge collection, Pennsylvania. $2,500.00.

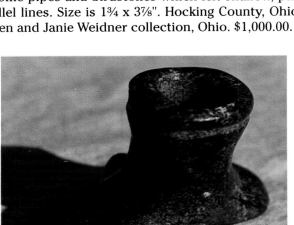

Platform pipe, Woodland period, with groove around the outside top of the bowl. It is made of steatite and measures 2½" long and the bowl is 1³⁄₁₆" high. This pipe was found in Columbiana County, Ohio. Dennis Link collection, Ohio. $800.00.

Curved-bottom platform pipe, Woodland period, gray steatite with the mouthpiece end of platform degraded, probably by weathering. This pipe evidences the parallel scrape marks of furrowing mentioned by Gordon Hart, *Hart's Prehistoric Pipe Rack,* p 148. Size, 1 x 5¾ x 1¾" high. Eastern Tennessee. Bill Mesnard collection, New Jersey. $500.00.

Platform pipe, Woodland period, highly polished in black steatite. It is drilled through the edge at top and measures 1¾ x 3⅛" high and 4⅜" long. With Davis authentication certificate, the pipe is from Smyth County, Virginia. Bill Mesnard collection, New Jersey. $2,700.00.

Platform pipe, Late Woodland period, found in 1960. Material is dark highly polished steatite with a coating of red ochre. This excellent pipe measures 1⅝ x 4½". It came from Plymouth County, Massachusetts. Bill Mesnard collection, New Jersey. $1,500.00.

Hopewell platform pipe, Middle Woodland and ca. 500 BC – AD 500, raised bowl with rim reinforcement. This pipe is #702 made of black steatite, the platform is 5" and bowl height is 1⅜". A very rare type, this pipe is from the Geneseo area, New York. Iron Horse collection. Museum grade.

Platform pipe with angled bowl, 2" high and 4" long. It has a graceful, streamlined form and is ca. AD 1000 – 1400. Done in black steatite the pipe is from Caldwell County, North Carolina. David Abbott collection, North Carolina. Unlisted.

High-bowl keeled pipe, late prehistoric (AD 1400) to early historic (AD 1750). It is made of steatite and measures 3⅝" high and 6¾" long. Canoe-shaped, this pipe is from Coosa County, Alabama. H. B. Greene II collection, Florida. $850.00.

Large double tube or medicine tube pipe, late BC centuries, half of artifact shown. It measures 3¼" x 12¼". This is a very rare pipe form, made in steatite. It is from Crittenden County, Kentucky. Private collection, Ohio. Museum grade.

Shaman's tube or medicine tube pipe, rare, biconical with raised center ring, pipe 5¾" long. This southern form is made of dark steatite and was found in Kentucky. Len and Janie Weidner collection, Ohio. $3,500.00.

4-1/2 inch Steatite
Woodland Culture
"Counsel Style" Elbow
Pipe Found in 1916

Coweta County
Georgia

Elbow pipe, Woodland period, 4½" long. Well made and nicely finished, this steatite pipe still retains most of the original polish. Picked up in 1916, this is a find from Georgia. Photo courtesy Larry Garvin, Back to Earth, Ohio; collection of Steve Cooper, Tennessee. Unlisted.

Elbow pipe, squared outline, dark gray steatite with good polish. This rectangular pipe was found exposed in a horse pasture in the 1980s. Woodland period, it is 1¾ x 3½ x 2" high. Bill Mesnard collection, New Jersey. $500.00.

Elbow pipe, rectangular configuration and squared cross-sections, gray-green steatite. The pipe measures 3½" high, 5⅝" long, and 2" wide. It is Late Woodland in time, from Green County, Tennessee. Len and Janie Weidner collection, Ohio. $900.00.

Squared elbow pipe, highly engraved and with tallied bowl rim, steatite. This sturdy yet artistic pipe measures 3 x 3½". Woodland period, it is from Edmonson County, Kentucky. Private collection, Ohio. $1,200.00.

Iroquois snake effigy pipe, gray-green steatite, ca. AD 1600 – 1750. #201 is a large and well-fashioned pipe with fine polish, 6½" long and 3" high. This museum-quality piece came from near Victor, New York. Iron Horse collection. $1,200.00 – 2,000.00.

Pre-Iroquois vase-shaped pipe, #RM/FN, ca. AD 1400 – 1500 and made from brown steatite which was burned black over the years. Bowl height is 2¼" and it is 1¾" wide. The pipe is from Livingston County, New York. Iron Horse collection. $350.00 – 450.00.

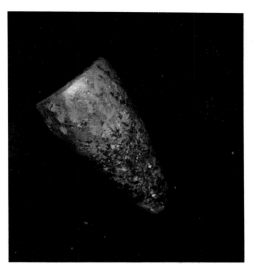

Owasco obtuse-angle tube pipe, brown and black steatite with both stem and bowl 1". An interesting small pipe, #GF-9 is from the West Rochester area, New York. Iron Horse collection. $350.00 – 475.00.

Slanted elbow pipe in greenish, gray, black, and olive steatite, 6" long. Attractive material and unusual location with old tag: "Tonkawa (Texas) stone pipe bowl, 18th Century." Larry Lantz, First Mesa, Indiana. $495.00.

Pre-Iroquoian vasiform pipe, attractive cream-colored steatite, #AK-40. Bowl height is 2½" and the bowl rim has long and angled tally marks. It is from Livingston County, New York. Iron Horse collection. $550.00 – 800.00.

Iroquois hoof-shape pipe in cream steatite, ca. AD 1500 – 1680. This pipe, #10-13/MS, is well shaped and highly polished with the stem 3¾" and bowl 2" high. Chautauqua County, New York. Iron Horse collection. $950.00 – 1,500.00.

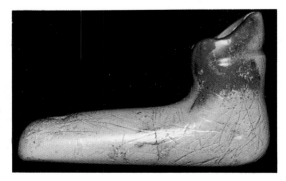

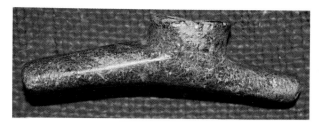

Intrusive Mound curved platform pipe, ca. AD 500 – 1100, #28-OGD/56-25FF. It is made of gray steatite and has a 3" stem with a short bowl only ½" high. Jefferson County, New York. Iron Horse collection. $450.00 – 550.00.

Owasco obtuse-angle pipe, heavily engraved, gray and black steatite, with 2" stem and bowl height 1¾". #T-353/13002 is from near Canandaigua, New York. Iron Horse collection. $1,000.00 – 1,500.00.

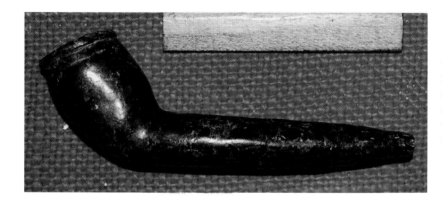

Owasco obtuse-angle pipe, #HA-1982, made of attractive black speckled steatite. Highly polished, this pipe has a stem 3¾" and bowl height is 2". Ontario County, New York. Iron Horse collection. $900.00 – 1,100.00.

Pre-Iroquois trumpet pipe with pentagonal bowl, #BC/2, ca. AD 1600 – 1700. This is a superb pipe, highly polished, made of gray speckled steatite. It has a 4" stem and bowl height is 2". The pipe was found near Chautauqua Lake, Chautauqua County, New York. Iron Horse collection. Museum grade.

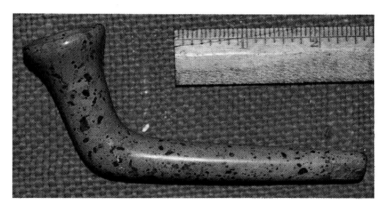

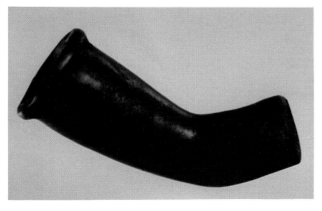

Pipe, black steatite, long bowl and short stem, bowl top with reinforcing ring. This is a well-made pipe with very thin bowl walls, late prehistoric. Kentucky. Robin Fiser collection, Ohio. $350.00.

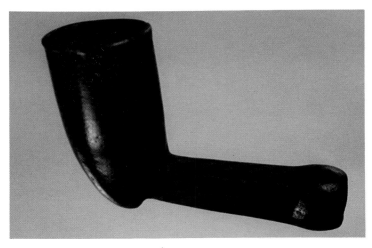

Bowl type pipe, dark steatite, 1½" high. This pipe is undoubtedly a copy of white-made kaolin mold-formed pipes and would be Indian-made. This example has thin bowl walls and is well polished. Overton County, Tennessee. Larry Garvin, Back to Earth, Ohio. $225.00.

Pipe, late prehistoric – early historic, black steatite. It is 2½" long and 1⅝" high. Made with very thin bowl walls, this pipe is from Kentucky. Robin Fiser collection, Ohio. $500.00.

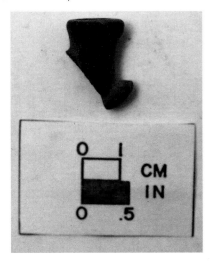

Elbow pipe, Mississippian era and ca. AD 1200 – 1600, made of gray-brown steatite. This well-shaped pipe is 1⅞" high and 6⅜" long. Stokes County, North Carolina. Jim Maus collection, North Carolina. $700.00.

Handle-bowl pipe, knob engraved, steatite. This piece is probably Cherokee and ca. 1450 – 1835. A miniature form, this pipe is from Clay County, North Carolina. Gary Henry collection, North Carolina. $100.00 – 150.00.

Historic personal pipe from the Northern Plains region, Blackfoot type, ca. 1750 – 1850. It is nicely made in black steatite and is 1½" in diameter and 3" high. Possibly from the northern Montana area, this was a 1990 acquisition in an antiques shop in Seattle, Washington. J. Steve and Anita Shearer collection, California. $350.00.

Elbow pipe, historic, ca. 1850 – 1880, made of greenish-black steatite. The pipe is possibly Iroquois or Huron in New York state and measures 2" high and 2¼" long. Smoothly shaped and polished, the pipe was collected from an antiques shop in Burbank, California. J. Steve and Anita Shearer collection, California. $400.00.

Elbow pipe, black steatite, ca. AD 1000 – 1500. Ex-collection Capehart, it is 1¼" long and 1⅝" high. This small pipe came from Granville County, North Carolina. Jim Maus collection, North Carolina. $250.00.

Elbow pipe, gray-brown steatite, 2⅛" long and 1⅜" high. It is unfinished, being pecked and shaped and with bowl drilled, but the stem is undrilled. This interesting example of a work-in-progress was found in McDowell County, North Carolina. Jim Maus collection, North Carolina. $100.00.

Elbow pipe, deeply engraved, made of near-black with gray steatite. It was probably a large elbow pipe which was broken and converted with the bowl becoming the stem hole and a new bowl made at the base of the former stem. Scarce salvage example, with size of 1½ x 1⅜ x 3" long. Virginia. Bill Mesnard collection, New Jersey. $250.00.

Elbow pipe, Monogahela focus, finely polished black steatite. The bowl and stem are octagonal and there are 27 tally marks. This well-done pipe measures 1⅜" high and 1 x 2½" long. It was found in Ashtabula County, Ohio. Bill Mesnard collection, New Jersey. $250.00.

Elbow pipe made of black steatite with inclusions, this piece with glossy polish measures 1¹³⁄₁₆ x 2⅜ x 1¾" high. It is from Pickens County, South Carolina. Bill Mesnard collection, New Jersey. $250.00.

Iroquois elbow pipe, ca. 1700 – 1800, made of black and brown steatite. #JC-117, the stem is 2" long and the bowl is 2¼" high. Syracuse area, New York. Iron Horse collection. $300.00 – 450.00.

Elbow pipe, well polished in a green steatite, size 3½ x 3¾". The bowl is unusually high and the overall piece quite attractive. This pipe, probably Woodland, came from the Moundville area of Alabama. Private collection, Georgia. $500.00.

Long-stemmed elbow pipe, repaired break in stem, thin walled and well made. This pipe is made of steatite and came from Hardin County, Tennessee. Private collection, Ohio. $950.00.

Elbow pipe, coffee bean type, ca. AD 1200 – 1500. This Mississippian era piece is made of black steatite and measures 1½" high and 2⅜" long. It was found in Caldwell County, North Carolina. This pipe is nicely made in typical material. Jim Maus collection, North Carolina. $650.00.

Pipe with coffee bean nodes or protrusions around the bowl base, ca. AD 1500 – 1600. Material is dark gray steatite and the pipe measures 1½" high and 5" long. This artifact came from Stokes County, North Carolina. Rodney M. Peck collection, North Carolina. $1,000.00.

Elbow pipe, gray steatite, 2" high. This weathered piece with a rounded configuration was found around 1910. Harrisburg area, Pennsylvania. Len and Janie Weidner collection, Ohio. $400.00.

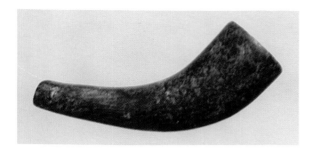

Elbow pipe, black steatite, ca. AD 1000 – 1500. This pipe measures 3½" long and 2" high. It was found in Burke County, North Carolina. Jim Maus collection, North Carolina. $250.00.

Elbow pipe, squared bowl and stem, material probably brown steatite. This pipe is 2⅜" both long and high. Woodland in time, the pipe is from eastern Kentucky. Len and Janie Weidner collection, Ohio. $400.00.

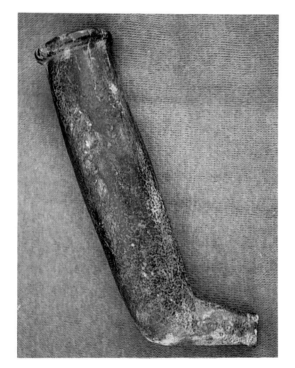

Elongated-bowl elbow pipe, Woodland period, 6⅞" high. It is made of steatite and is ex-collection Ben Thompson. This pipe is shown on page 90 of *Who's Who in Indian Relics No. 6.* Origin unknown. Dale and Betty Roberts collection, Iowa; Betty Roberts photograph. $700.00.

Elbow pipe with large bowl. Late Woodland – Mississippian period, made of mottled steatite. This pipe is 2" long and 2½" high, with bowl diameter of 1½". It is from Kenosha County, Wisconsin. Collection of and photograph by Duane Treest, Illinois. $300.00 – 400.00.

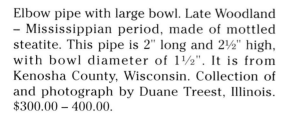

Elbow pipe, polished green steatite, ca. AD 800 – 1200. This pipe with clean, flowing lines is 4⅝" long and 2⅞" high. It is from Jackson County, Tennessee. Jim Maus collection, North Carolina. $250.00.

Tube pipe, well-patinated California steatite, high overall polish. It is 5⅜" long and tapers from ¾" to 1¼". The two connected and raised rings add to artistic appeal. San Joaquin Valley, California. Larry Lantz, First Mesa, Indiana. $850.00.

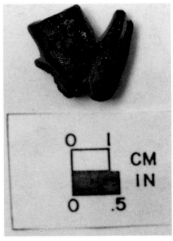

Handle-bowl pipe, snake-head effigy, steatite. This is probably a Cherokee work, ca. AD 1450 – 1835. It was picked up in Clay County, North Carolina. Gary Henry collection, North Carolina. $200.00 – 250.00.

Expanded tubular pipe, dark steatite, well polished, size 1¾ x 5". This pipe has artistic lines and the deeply incised line forms a rim around the bowl top. Tennessee. Private collection, Ohio. $1,200.00.

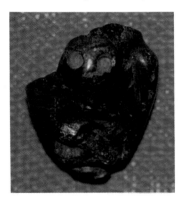

Effigy pipe, owl, Huron-Petun ca. AD 1400 – 1650, #GL-2. This pipe is made of black steatite and measures 2" high. The position here is with the owl's head near the top with eyes looking directly at the viewer. Simcoe County, Ontario, Canada. Private collection. $375.00 – 500.00.

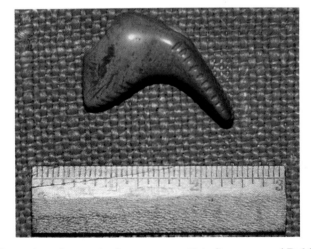

Effigy pipe, Iroquois, beaver or otter figure, ca. AD 1600 – 1700. Material is gray and green steatite for #FM/90, which is 1½" wide and 1¾" high. From near Erie, Pennsylvania. Iron Horse collection. $650.00 – 875.00.

Effigy pipe, human head with weeping eyes and face away from smoker, Ft. Ancient and late prehistoric. #GH-94 is made of cream-colored steatite and the stem is 1½", while bowl height is 1¼". Ohio. Iron Horse collection. $650.00 – 850.00.

Effigy pipe of woman giving birth, historic, probably Cherokee. This interesting pipe is made of steatite and is 3¾" high and 4¾" long. Clay County, North Carolina. Hogan Gallery Inc., Naples, Florida. $900.00.

Deer effigy pipe, late prehistoric – early historic and ca. AD 1200 – 1600. It is made of mottled steatite and measures 3" high and 8" long. This pipe is from the southeastern United States, probably the Tennessee – Georgia area. H. B. Greene II collection, Florida. Museum quality.

Eagle effigy copy of Great Pipe, probably Cherokee and ca. AD 1600 – 1800, gray steatite. The pipe measures 8½" long and 2½" high. It came from Ashe County, North Carolina. Rodney M. Peck collection, North Carolina. $2,000.00.

Killer whale effigy pipe, dark California steatite, size 3 x 3 x 5⅞" long. The stone is gray-black with some blue, plus cream-tan spotting occurs where original finish is eroded. The stem hole is in the tail and abalone inlays are at the eyes and side fins, plus one on each side of the dorsal fin. Santa Barbara County, California. Larry Lantz, First Mesa, Indiana. $3,500.00.

Monolithic axe effigy pipe, very rare, Mississippian period, in polished black steatite. In top condition, this beautiful pipe measures 6" long and bowl height is 3⅜". #A/B is from Towns County, Georgia. Iron Horse collection. Museum grade.

Eagle-talon effigy pipe, gray steatite, 2⅞" high and 6½" long. This pipe is proto-historic – very late Mississippian and was found in 1875. This is a popular motif and later examples were made from molded clay by whites. Madison County, Alabama. Larry Garvin, Back to Earth, Ohio. Museum quality.

Eagle-talon effigy pipe, bowl and foot detail, overall size 2⅞ x 6½". This well-carved pipe in gray steatite is in perfect condition. Larry Garvin, Back to Earth, Ohio. Museum quality.

Vasiform or tulip-shaped pipe, brown steatite, with engravings and tally marks. Late prehistoric, this well-done pipe measures ⅞ x 1 x 1½" high. Seneca area, New York. Bill Mesnard collection, New Jersey. $200.00.

Pre-Iroquois vasiform bowl, line engraved, ca. AD 1550 – 1580. #GY-6 is carved from black steatite and is 4" high. Erie County, New York. Iron Horse collection. $375.00 – 550.00.

Iroquois keel-type pipe, ca. 1600 – 1700, made of black steatite. #9 is well polished, 2¼" high, and was found in Franklin County, Pennsylvania. Iron Horse collection. $350.00 – 450.00.

Elongated vase-type pipe, Fort Ancient people, made of black steatite. The pipe measures 3½" high and was found in Belmont County, Ohio. Private collection. $350.00.

Barrel-shaped pipe, Sandusky people, tally marked bowl top, dark steatite. This pipe is ex-collection Dr. Meuser and is 2⅜" high. Hardin County, Ohio. Private collection. $500.00.

Pipe, dark and well-polished steatite, with an effigy (possibly a turtle) worked in above the short stem. This pipe is 1⅝" long and 1½" high. It was found in Pennsylvania. Len and Janie Weidner collection, Ohio. $300.00.

Bowl pipe on platform, gray steatite with slight polish. It measures 1⅞" long, 1¼" wide, and 2" high. The bowl was broken off and has been glued back on. This is Late Woodland, Intrusive Mound people. (See fig. 3 p. 12 in *Hart's Prehistoric Pipe Rack.*) This pipe came from Montgomery County, Ohio. Bill Mesnard collection, New Jersey. $175.00.

Obtuse-angle platform pipe, black steatite, Late Woodland and Intrusive Mound in origin. The pipe measures 3" long and 1¾" high; it has Perino authentication papers. This is a fine pipe from an expert pipe-making period in the classic material, steatite. There are tally marks around the platform sides near the base of the flared bowl. Highly polished, this is from Pike County, Ohio. Bill Mesnard collection, New Jersey; Sarah Bones, photographer. $2,700.00.

Obtuse-angle pipe, Late Woodland and ca. AD 450 – 700, made of green steatite. This fine example measures 2½" high and 7" long. It was found in Washington County, Virginia. Rodney M. Peck collection, North Carolina. $1,000.00.

Obtuse-angle pipe, late prehistoric, made of black steatite. This pipe is nicely shaped and highly polished with reinforcing rings around both the stem end and bowl top. It is 2¾" long and 1¾" high. Chattahoochie County, Georgia. Collection of Bruce Butts, Winterville, Georgia. $2,500.00.

Obtuse-angle pipe made of black steatite, late prehistoric period. It has a small repair and still retains a high polish. The pipe is ¾" wide, 1¾" high, and 3¾" long. It was recovered in Smyth County, Virginia. Bill Mesnard collection, New Jersey. $950.00.

Obtuse-angle Intrusive Mound pipe, stem tally marked, black steatite. Both stem and bowl measure 2½", and the bowl rim is lightly reinforced. #49, it is from Ontario County, New York. Iron Horse collection. $1,000.00 – 1,500.00.

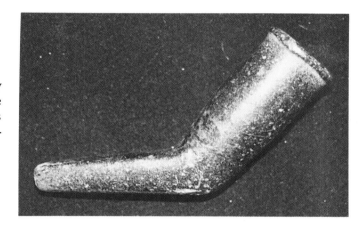

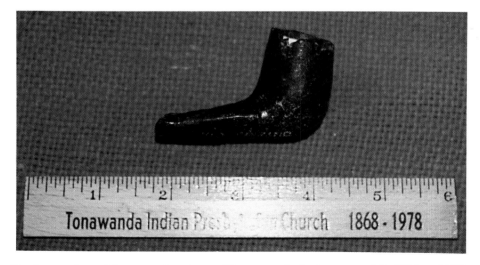

Pre-Iroquoian obtuse-angle pipe with expanded stem, ca. AD 1200 – 1300, #OHD-10. Made of gray and black steatite, the stem is 2¼" long and bowl height is 1½". Ontario County, New York. Iron Horse collection. $275.00 – 350.00.

Alate or winged pipe, Late Woodland and ca. AD 700 – 1000, engraved on the wide stem wings. Material is dark greenish-gray steatite for this rare form which is 11¾" long. It came from the Yadkin River area of Davidson County, North Carolina. Rodney M. Peck collection, North Carolina. $10,000.00.

Obtuse-angle alate (winged) pipe, AD 1000 – 1200, side view. Made of black steatite, it is 2½" high and 5½" long. Note the rimmed bowl. Caldwell County, North Carolina. Jim Maus collection, North Carolina. $4,000.00.

Obtuse-angle alate (winged) pipe, AD 1000 – 1200, bottom view. Size, 2½ x 5½"; the incised designs are fairly common on alate pipes. Caldwell County, North Carolina. Jim Maus collection, North Carolina. $4,000.00.

Alate or winged pipe, Late Woodland and ca. AD 700 – 1000, made of dark brown steatite. This beautiful pipe is 9¼" long and came from the Yadkin River area of Surry County, North Carolina. Rodney M. Peck collection, North Carolina. $2,500.00 – 3,000.00.

Obtuse-angle alate (winged) pipe, AD 1000 – 1200, side/top view. Size, 2½ x 5½". Additional incised designs can be seen to the left and right of the pipe stem hole. Caldwell County, North Carolina. Jim Maus collection, North Carolina. $4,000.00.

Pipestone Pipes

Along with catlinite and steatite, pipestone is the third great natural pipe-making material used in North America. Like steatite, pipestone was heavily employed in prehistoric times, but it was largely replaced by catlinite in historic times. Also like steatite, pipestone exists in different shades and regions. A distinction is, that while there was only one true catlinite source, there were many sources for steatite and for pipestone.

Pipestone exists in deposits over much of the eastern Midwest. In Illinois there is a fine pipestone, perhaps 90% of which is an olive-green color. Southern Ohio, above Portsmouth, has the famous Ohio pipestone in pastel shades, many of them creamy. Pennsylvania has a high-quality gray pipestone in several shades. Wisconsin even has a reddish pipestone that closely resembles catlinite.

Most pipestone was easy to quarry and worked well with the tools available to ancient pipe makers. The height of pipestone use in the Midwest was in Early and Middle Woodland times. Then, pipestone was the material of choice for Adena tubular pipes and for Hopewell platform pipes, both plain and effigy.

Oddly, pipestone use seems to have halted with Hopewell artistic creations, and largely skipped the Late Woodland period. Pipestone use resumed again with Ft. Ancient and other Indians of Mississippian times, at least in the eastern Midwest. Probably this was because such people are noted for using local material sources, which included both flint and pipestone.

Whatever the story in prehistoric times, pipestone use (along with steatite) gradually faded in historic times with the advent of metal and high-quality ceramics.

Flattened-end tubular Adena pipe, 1 x 5". This piece is smoothly finished and highly polished, with bowl end showing the large-diameter drilling. Made of Ohio pipestone, this excellent pipe is from Seneca County, Ohio. Private collection, Ohio. $1,500.00.

Adena tubular pipe, Early Woodland period, made with an oval cross-section. Material is greenish-tan pipestone; the bowl hollow is tapered for about 1½" and the remaining length is the long, narrow stem hole. Nicely polished, the pipe is 5⅜" long. Ohio. Len and Janie Weidner collection, Ohio. $900.00.

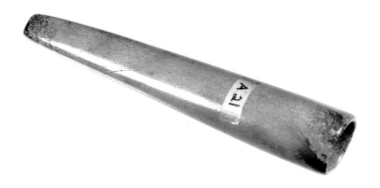

Blocked-end Adena tubular pipe, showing the small stem hole. The hole through the remainder of the pipe is much larger. This fine example measures 1 x 4¼" and is made from typical material, Ohio pipestone from the lower Scioto Valley. Carroll County, Kentucky. Private collection, Ohio. $1,600.00.

Blocked-end Adena tubular pipe, this showing the large bowl-end drilled hole. This beautiful example, 1¼ x 5¼", is made of Ohio pipestone and came from Adams County, Ohio. Private collection, Ohio. $1,600.00.

Blocked-end pipestone tubular pipe, Adena, with very unusual drilled side holes. Size, 1 x 3" long. This unique specimen was found in Fairfield County, Ohio. Private collection, Ohio. $700.00.

Hopewell platform pipe, with one end of the platform broken in prehistoric times and salvaged by grinding, smoothing, and polishing. Material is mottled brown pipestone for this example, 1¼" high and now 1½" long. It was found in the Chillicothe area, Ross County, Ohio. Ted McVey collection, Ohio. $1,000.00.

Effigy platform pipe, frog image, Hopewell and Middle Woodland period. Material is blue-gray mottled Ohio pipestone and the pipe measures 3⅛" long and 1⅜" high. This is an extremely rare artifact, both in type and condition for the specimen. Note the high degree of polish that has endured for 1,500+ years. Ohio. Len and Janie Weidner collection, Ohio. $9,000.00.

Hopewell platform pipe, broken and reworked in prehistoric times. It is made from brown Ohio pipestone that retains the typical high polish of many pipestone artifacts. It is 2¼ x 1¼ x 1½" high. The pipe was found by Herman Henke in Wisconsin in 1897. Bill Mesnard collection, New Jersey. $800.00.

Hopewell platform pipe, Middle Woodland period, 1¼ x 2⁵⁄₁₆". This pipe, made of pipestone, is ex-collection Willard Maurer. It came from Shawano County, Wisconsin. Dale and Betty Roberts collection, Iowa; Betty Roberts photograph. $1,000.00+.

Hopewell effigy platform pipe, greenish-tan Ohio pipestone, Middle Woodland. It is ex-collection Brownfield and marked "Trumbull County, Ohio / AWK #132." Despite some damage, this is a beautiful pipe and highly artistic. Size, 2¼" high and 2⅜" long. Private collection. Unlisted.

Platform pipe, very large size, 9¾" long. This artifact was reassembled after extensive damage and is intact enough to show the original superb creation. Intrusive Mound people, Late Woodland period, mottled tan Ohio pipestone. Ross County, Ohio. Len and Janie Weidner collection, Ohio. Museum grade.

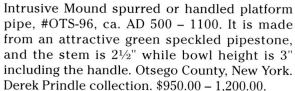

Intrusive Mound spurred or handled platform pipe, #OTS-96, ca. AD 500 – 1100. It is made from an attractive green speckled pipestone, and the stem is 2½" while bowl height is 3" including the handle. Otsego County, New York. Derek Prindle collection. $950.00 – 1,200.00.

Vase-type pipe, Fort Ancient people, Mississippian period, 1⅝" high. The pipe is made of gray Ohio pipestone and it was picked up in Ohio. Len and Janie Weidner collection, Ohio. $350.00.

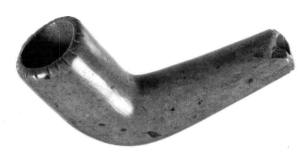

Elbow pipe, late prehistoric period, greenish pipestone. The bowl top is tally marked on this highly polished example which is 2¹⁄₁₆" long. It is probably from the Great Lakes region. Len and Janie Weidner collection, Ohio. $475.00.

Vase-type Ft. Ancient pipe, greenish pipestone, 2¹⁄₁₆" high. An "X" is incised on the bottom. Ohio. Len and Janie Weidner collection, Ohio. $300.00.

Elbow pipe, gray pipestone, probably proto-historic or early historic period, 2⅞" long. It is from Newton County, Indiana. Len and Janie Weidner collection, Ohio. $650.00.

Obtuse elbow pipe, late prehistoric, green pipestone. The pipe is 2¾" long and was made by the Whittlesey people of northeastern Ohio. Cuyahoga County, Ohio. Len and Janie Weidner collection, Ohio. $650.00.

Pipe, cream Ohio pipestone, 3" long. This Mississippian pipe is ex-collection Atkins and was found in Noble County, Ohio. Larry Garvin, Back to Earth, Ohio. $450.00.

Platform T-shaped pipe with one arm drilled as the stem. It is 2¼" high and overall 9" long, 1⅜" in diameter through the bowl. The pipe is made from a red pipestone of unknown origin. This is probably a Spiro phase piece, Mississippian period, and was a surface find south of Fort Smith, Arkansas. Private collection. Museum quality.

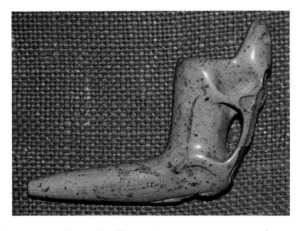

Iroquois pipe, a superb example in pipestone 4" long, with graceful contours and high polish. This outstanding example came from the northwest corner of New York state. Richard Savidge collection, Pennsylvania. $1,800.00.

Iroquois lizard effigy pipe, a very rare form with body recesses and panels for copper or shell inlays. Ca. 1600 – 1750, #1982HL is made of unusual material for the area, gray speckled Ohio pipestone. The stem is 3½" long and bowl height is 3¼". Steuben County, New York. Iron Horse collection. Museum quality.

Effigy pipe, bird figure, 4" high. Material is tan pipestone for this Mississippian piece, once in the well-known Shipley brothers collections. It may have been made by a northern group, possibly the Whittlesey people. Len and Janie Weidner collection, Ohio. $2,800.00.

Pre-Iroquois fish effigy pipe, side view, ca. 1570 – 1600. The effigy figure was done rather realistically and measures 2½" long. #NH-7, Erie County, New York. Iron Horse collection. Museum grade.

Pre-Iroquois fish effigy pipe, stem-end view, ca. 1570 – 1600. It was manufactured from light gray Ohio pipestone and measures 2½" long. This pipe once had a wooden stem. #NH-7 is from Erie County, New York. Iron Horse collection. Museum grade.

Pre-Iroquois bullet-shaped pipe, ca. 1570 – 1600, made of gray Ohio pipestone. Height is 2¼ for #NH-6 which is well polished and once had a wooden stem. Erie County, New York. Iron Horse collection. $375.00 – 600.00.

Historic-era rimmed bowl on squared platform, made of unusual material, Ohio pipestone. The pipe is 1⅞" long and 1¾" high. Scioto County, Ohio. Dennis Link collection, Ohio. $300.00.

Pipe Materials

With book chapters on catlinite (mainly historic), steatite (mainly prehistoric), and pipestone (also prehistoric) there are yet important reasons for listing additional materials used for making pipes. One reason, of course, is to obtain some broad knowledge about the huge number of stone and stone-like materials used for pipes.

Another reason is to list the kinds of pipes made from certain materials, such as Adena pipes in pipestone and sandstone or Intrusive Mound pipes in steatite. Still another is to list pipes that were once in a single important collection, as here.

The chapter information all refers to Ohio pipes once in the famous collection of Dr. Gordon Meuser of Columbus, Ohio. The sole reference for chapter materials is the artifact registration kept by Dr. Meuser; please note that this is not the auction catalog which is better known. This is "Catalogue of the Archaeological Collection Gath-ered by Dr. Gordon Frederick Meuser of Columbus, Ohio/Assisted by Dr. Dewitt C. Lavender of Mansfield, Ohio/Begun in the Year 1919," reprinted in 1970.

To make each listing as brief as possible and yet include basic facts, the pipe type (often a sub-type or unique form that defies categorization) is placed first. This is followed by key information on the material (in boldface) and terminates in pipe size.

This included information (pipes of duplicate or near-duplicate materials are not listed) gives an excellent idea of which materials were used in a single region, now the state of Ohio. A collector would do well to remember that not all pipes made of unusual materials are fake, and be on the lookout for pipes made of non-traditional materials such as those listed. To indicate the extent of use, there are no duplications of materials.

PIPE MATERIALS

Bird effigy platform pipe, **flesh and maroon colored pipestone**, ¾ x 3¼"

Platform pipe, **gray-green pipestone**, 1⅛ x 4"

Tubular pipe, **green-brown banded slate**, 2⅛"

Ovoid pipe, **tan serpentine** 1⅝ x 2⅝"

Round bowl pipe, **green slate** 1½ x 2½"

Pipe, **deer-bone**, Scioto County, no size listed

Angular pipe, **reddish pipestone**, 1 x 2"

Tube pipe, **greenish steatite**, 1¾ x 3"

Handled pipe, **tan speckled indurated claystone**, 2 x 3¼"

Tube pipe, **gray talcose slate**, 1 x 3½"

Deer-head effigy pipe, **gray sandstone**, 2¾ x 3 x 6¾"

Vase-shaped pipe, **red banded slate**, 1¼ x 3"

Egg-shaped pipe, **translucent white quartzite**, 2 x 3"

Platform pipe, **undrilled, translucent quartzite**, 1¾ x 2 x 3"

Vase-shaped pipe, **translucent tan quartzite**, 1½ x 2½"

Cylindrical pipe, **limestone fossil**, 1 x 2½"

Disc pipe, **weathered limestone**, 1¼ x 2½"

Unfinished platform pipe, **tan syenite**, 2 x 3"

Egg-shaped pipe, **"coal black stone,"** 1¾ x 3½"

Vase-shaped pipe, **yellowish crystalline limestone**, 1½ x 3"

L-shaped pipe, **brown sandstone**, 2 x 2½"

Tubular pipe, **green banded slate**, 1½ x 6½"

Cylindrical pipe, **brownish steatite**, 1½ x 2"

Crow's head effigy pipe, **gray pipestone**, 1¾" high

Tubular pipe, **dark green slate**, 1½ x 4½"

Lizard effigy pipe, **gray stone**, 1¼ x 2½"

Tubular pipe, **gray-tan syenite**, 1 x 4"

Tubular pipe, **tan-pink pipestone**, 1½ x 4¼"

Mic-mac pipe, **maroon pipestone**, 1 x 2"

Pipe, **red pipestone**, ¾ x 1½"

Bird effigy pipe, **dark green steatite**, 1½ x 2¼"

Hopewell platform pipe, **brown pipestone**, 1¼ x 2¾"

L-shaped pipe, **light green banded slate**, 1½ x 1½"

Tubular pipe, **gray banded slate**, ¾ x 7¼"

L-shaped pipe, **glossy gray siliceous banded slate**, 2½ x 2⅝"

Claw effigy pipe, **tan pipestone**, 1¼ x 2"

Mic-mac pipe, **red pipestone**, 1 x 1¾"

Tube pipe, **gray-tan pipestone**, 1⅛ x 2¼"

Tapering tube pipe, **highly banded gray slate**, ⅞ x 4⅛"

Duck effigy pipe, **tan steatite**, 3½ x 5¼"

Tubular pipe, **gray-tan mottled pipestone**, 1⅛ x 3½"

L-shaped pipe, **brown micaceous steatite**, 1¾ x 2½"

Platform pipe, **red mottled pipestone**, 2¼ x 4¼"

Spindle-shaped tube pipe, **dark gray steatite**, 1¼ x 5½"

Disc pipe, **red pipestone**, 2¼" long

Platform pipe, **yellow-red pipestone**, 1¼ x 3"

Tube pipe, **green steatite**, 1 x 1¾"

Bird effigy pipe, **dark steatite**, 1½ x 2"

Mic-mac pipe, **tan-red pipestone**, 1½ x 3"

Animal head effigy pipe, **dark blue steatite**, 2¼ x 3¼"

Pipe, t**an metallic crystalline stone**, 1¼ x 2½"

L-shaped pipe, **pottery**, 1½ x 2½"

L-shaped pipe, **maroon-tan mottled translucent calcite**, 2¼ x 3½"

Platform pipe, **gray-tan pipestone**, 1 x 2"

Platform pipe, **black steatite**, 1 x 3⅜"

Platform pipe, **translucent cream quartzite**, 2 x 3¾"

Elbow pipe, **glossy black steatite**, 1½ x 2¼"

Tubular pipe, **tan pipestone**, 1½ x 3½"

L-shaped pipe, **glossy green mottled steatite**, 1¼ x 1⅝"

Modified Mic-mac pipe, **green mottled slate**, 1 x 2⅛"

Platform pipe, **yellow pipestone**, 1½ x 2¼"

Tube pipe, **translucent amber calcite**, 1 x 2"

Tube pipe, **brown banded slate**, 1 x 3½"

Platform pipe, **brown micaceous steatite**, 1¼ x 3½"

Bird effigy pipe, **gray micaceous schist**, 3½ x 4"

Keel-shaped pipe, **translucent green mottled calcite**, 2"

L-shaped pipe, **tan indurated claystone**, 2 x 5"

Tube pipe, **banded gray slate**, 1¼ x 6¾"

Mic-mac pipe, **greenish stone**, 2¼ x 3½"

Platform pipe, **yellow-brown pipestone**, broken, 1½" high

Snake effigy pipe, **light and dark gray calcite**, 2¼ x 5"

Wolf head effigy pipe, **gray-tan pipestone**, 2¼ x 2¾"

Elbow pipe, **black banded slate**, 2½ x 5"

Vase-shaped pipe, **tan slate**, 1¼ x 2½"

Tubular pipe, Late Archaic – Early Woodland period and either Glacial Kame or Red Ochre people. This outstanding pipe was found by the Shipley brothers in 1930 and is ex-collections Shipley, Coulter, and Nelson. This was a gift to the owner from Mike Nelson in 1996. Drilled full length, the pipe is 3¾" long and 1½" in diameter at the large end. It has a tapered hole, material is rare dark green chlorite, and the polished surface of the pipe is engraved. Scioto County, Ohio. Glenda Sines collection, Ohio. Museum grade.

Archaic period tubular pipe, made of scarce multicolored chlorite. Formerly in the Dr. Meuser collection, this is one of the two best Archaic examples known and the doctor considered it to be one of his finest pipes. Franklin County, Ohio. Private collection, Ohio. $2,500.00.

Handled elbow pipe with below-bowl extension, very artistic piece with high polish. Material is also scarce, being mottled chlorite. The pipe is 1½ x 3". Cuyahoga County, Ohio. Private collection, Ohio. $1,500.00.

Hopewell platform pipe, Middle Woodland period, made of translucent fluorite. This is one of the very few authentic examples in this rare material. Size is 1½ x 2½". It is from Vanderburgh County, Indiana. Private collection, Ohio. $2,000.00.

Elbow pipe, tan stone, probably Late Woodland – Mississippian period. Nicely decorated with simple incised lines, the pipe is 2" high and 2¼" long. It came from along the Tennessee River in Tennessee. Collection of Dave Swanson, Illinois; photograph by Duane Treest, Illinois. $225.00 – 350.00.

Platform pipe with bowl at end, brown stone, probably proto-historic, nine tally marks. The pipe has a bowl 1" across and pipe length is 2½". This example is from Michigan. Collection of and photography by Duane Treest, Illinois. $100.00 – 175.00.

Hopewell platform pipe, Middle Woodland era, 1½ x 3". Not only is this a rare pipe form but it is made of quartz, only utilized by Hopewell craftspeople in several examples. This very attractive pipe in ultra-hard stone is from the Decatur area, Indiana. Private collection, Ohio. $4,000.00 – 6,000.00.

Hopewell platform pipe, 1½ x 2¾", made of mottled limestone. Unusual material for a Hopewell worker, this interesting pipe is from the Dixon area of Illinois. Private collection, Ohio. $2,500.00.

Effigy platform pipe, possibly a raccoon, ca 200 BC – AD 400. It is made of dolomite and measures 1⅜ x 4" long. Pulaski County, Illinois. Hogan Gallery Inc., Naples, Florida. $1,050.00.

Hopewell platform pipe, Middle Woodland period, 3" long. This example is made of limestone and was found in Clark County, Ohio. Len and Janie Weidner collection, Ohio. $1,000.00.

Oval pipe, 1 x 2¼", made of nicely banded glacial slate. The pipe has a highly unusual form and came from Muskingum County, Ohio. Private collection, Ohio. $550.00.

Bowl pipe on thick stem, Woodland period, made of gray pipestone or silicated shale. It is nicely finished and has symmetrical designs on the tip. Measuring 1⅜" wide, 4" long, and 2⅛" high, this pipe is from Ohio. Bill Mesnard collection, New Jersey. $250.00.

Large platform pipe, Middle Woodland, made of quartzite. It is 3½ x 7" long and is ex-collections N. E. Carter and Willard Maurer. The pipe is dated May 1, 1904, and came from Middlesex County, Ontario, Canada. Dale and Betty Roberts collection, Iowa; Betty Roberts photograph. $700.00.

Pipe, sandstone, probably Woodland, 2½" long. This pipe with generous centered bowl was found in Jefferson County, Wisconsin. Collection of and photograph by Duane Treest, Illinois. $150.00 – 200.00.

Intrusive Mound platform pipe, ca. AD 500 – 1100, polished green hardstone. It is #5622 with stem length of 2¾" and bowl height of 1¼". A nicely made and polished example, the pipe is from Seneca County, New York. Iron Horse collection. $450.00 – 550.00.

Woodland human face pipe, with the face away from smoke, #OHL. This vase-shaped pipe is made of sandstone and is 2¼" high. It was found in the Genesee River, Allegany County, New York. Iron Horse collection. $375.00 – 550.00.

Vase-shaped pipe bowl, Fort Ancient people, 2⅛" high. The material is quite unusual, probably chlorite. Found near Newtown, Clermont County, Ohio. Len and Janie Weidner collection, Ohio. $1,200.00.

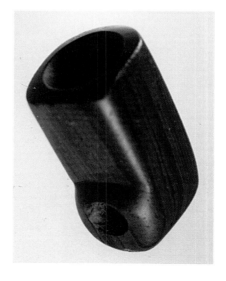

Pipe, probably Mississippian, banded green glacial slate, 1⅞" high. This pipe is ex-collection Diller and has a medium polish. Richland County, Ohio. Larry Garvin, Back to Earth, Ohio. $200.00.

Bowl-type pipe, Fort Ancient of the Mississippian period, 1⅝" high. It is made of green and tan mottled chlorite and has Xs on the sides and other lines incised. While the pipe has a simple design, material is quite rare. Len and Janie Weidner collection, Ohio. Museum grade.

Conical pipe, 2" high and with 1¼" bowl diameter. It is made of unusual material, cannel coal, and came from Tuscarawas County, Ohio. Pipe style, material, and recovery site indicate the artifact is from the Mississippian period. Collection of and photograph by Larry G. Merriam, Oklahoma. $225.00 – 300.00.

Vase-shaped pipe, Mississippi time period, black hardstone with fossil inclusions. Ex-collection Henson, this pipe made of unusual and scarce material came from Union County, Kentucky. Larry Garvin, Back to Earth, Ohio. $500.00.

Cone or pick-shaped pipe, unusual form, 1 x 4". The material is scarce and beautiful chlorite for this piece, Mississippian. Clearfield County, Pennsylvania. Private collection, Ohio. $600.00.

Elongated vase pipe, Mississippian period and probably Sandusky people. It is made of very durable and attractive material, sugar quartz. The size is 1 x 3" and the pipe came from Henry County, Ohio. Private collection, Ohio. $1,200.00.

Fort Ancient vase-type pipe, very late prehistoric with flared rim. The material is quartzite in four colors and the bowl is 2⅝" high. This is a fine specimen in a sought-after material. Indiana. Private collection. $1,250.00.

Flared-rim oval pipe, crisp lines, 1 x 2". The material is banded glacial slate for this Mississippian period artifact, and it is either from the Ft. Ancient or Sandusky people. Hancock County, Ohio. Private collection, Ohio. $450.00

Vase-type pipe, Fort Ancient people, a very highly developed form made of green translucent quartzite, with extreme rim expansion suggesting the Late Mississippian period. Made of rare and lovely material, this pipe is 2¾" high and nicely polished. Crittenden County, Kentucky. Len and Janie Weidner collection, Ohio. $1,800.00.

Flared-rim vase pipe, cream and yellow calcite, late Ft. Ancient times. This highly developed form is 1½" in diameter and 2¾" high. It was found in Highland County, Ohio. Ted McVey collection, Ohio. $1,500.00 – 2,000.00.

Vase-shaped pipe, Fort Ancient era, 2¼" high. Material is very durable and attractive yellow and cream quartzite. This pipe was found in Butler County, Ohio. Len and Janie Weidner collection, Ohio. $1,200.00.

Keeled elbow pipe, 2 x 2½", made of sandstone. Not a common form, this pipe was found in Franklin County, Ohio. Private collection, Ohio. $300.00.

Keeled ovid pipe form, 2 x 3", with incised markings. This is a very unusual type, and this example is made of sandstone. Franklin County, Ohio. Private collection, Ohio. $450.00.

Fort Ancient barrel-type pipe bowl with tally marks at the top in four groups of three. It measures 2⅝" high and material is a yellow-tan unknown stone. The pipe was probably made by northern Ohio's Whittlesey people. Summit County, Ohio. Private collection. Unlisted.

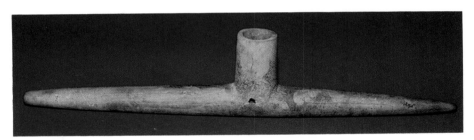

T-pipe, early Caddo period (Spiro phase), ca AD 900 – 1100. This is a stone pipe made of gray colored shale or mudstone, possibly a fine-grained siltstone. The pipe measures 18" long and has no restoration. Extremely rare, this is one of the longest pipes found in North America; ex-collections Millsap and Dr. Westbrook. Probably eastern Oklahoma. Dr. Jim Cherry collection, Arkansas. Museum grade.

Acute-angle pipe, dense white stone with polish. This pipe measures 2⅝" long and 2¼" high. Four separate drillings were made into the bottom of the bowl in order to properly contact the stem hole. This example is possibly from Ohio. Bill Mesnard collection, New Jersey; Sarah Bones, photographer. $200.00.

Stone pipe, late prehistoric, octagonal bowl and stem. Material is fine-grained tan-brown hardstone which has black pepper-like inclusions. With moderate polish the pipe is 1⅛" in diameter and 1⅝" high. Wabash County, Illinois. Bill Mesnard collection, New Jersey; Sarah Bones, photographer. $125.00.

Vase-shaped Ft. Ancient pipe, brownish gray silicated shale, dull polish on the exterior. The top and stem side and opposite side are flattened, while the remainder is rounded. This pipe measures 1¾" high and 1⅛ x 1¼". West Virginia. Bill Mesnard collection, New Jersey; Sarah Bones, photographer. $125.00.

Elbow pipe, red argillite, Huron-Petun. The pipe stem is 1¼" long and bowl height is 2". #GL-28 once had a long wooden stem, and the pipe was found in Victoria County, Ontario, Canada. Private collection. $300.00 – 350.00.

Bowl-type pipe, 1¼" high, made of dark sandstone. Ex-collection Lawyer, it has a fringed bottom and some engraving. Lancaster County, Pennsylvania. Richard Savidge collection, Pennsylvania. $225.00.

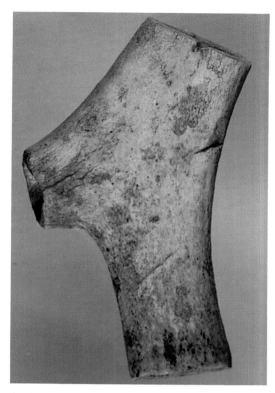

Antler pipe, highly unusual, 3¼" long. The bowl is in the upper portion and the stem hole projects to one side. This piece in rare material is from Limestone County, Alabama. Robin Fiser collection, Ohio. Unlisted.

Pre-Iroquois vase-shaped pipe, with decorative lines or elongated tally marks on the bowl side. #366 is ca. 1400 – 1550, made of black slate which carries a high polish, and 2¼" high. Cattaraugus County, New York. Iron Horse collection. $300.00 – 500.00.

Stone pipe bowl with lines around the top, hardstone, 1½" high. A rather plain and basic pipe, yet well made, #220/175 is from Erie County, New York. Iron Horse collection. $150.00 – 250.00.

Pre-Iroquois vasiform pipe, ca. 1550 – 1580, an early pipe in red and black slate. #GY-5 is 1¾" high and has the bowl rim tally marked. Erie County, New York. Iron Horse collection. $350.00 – 450.00.

Iroquois vase-shaped pipe, close-grained sandstone, ca. 1500 – 1650. It has the drilled stem hole for a wooden stem, and is 2¼" high. #1981/HL is from Livingston County, New York. Iron Horse collection. $250.00 – 350.00.

Disc pipe, yellow-tan limestone, late prehistoric – early historic. It is 1¾ x 3½ x 1½" high. The pipe was found in southwestern Ohio. Bill Mesnard collection, New Jersey.

Owasco obtuse-bowl pipe with flat stem, #E-71594, made of green speckled serpentine. Carrying a medium polish, the pipe has a 3" stem and bowl height is 2". It was found near Canandaigua Lake, Canandaigua, New York. Iron Horse collection. Museum grade.

Elongated elbow pipe made of highly unusual material, Petoskey stone. Size is 2 x 4¼" and the bowl rim in reinforced with extra material. Charlevoix, Michigan. Private collection, Ohio. $800.00.

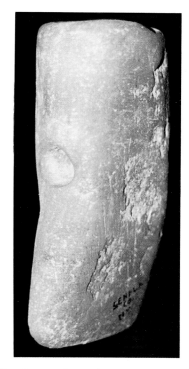

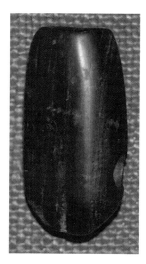

Vertical bowl pipe, dark banded slate, ca. AD 1550 – 1650. Highly polished, pipe #JP/8 is 2½" high and 1¼" wide. It is from Pennsylvania. Iron Horse collection. $350.00 – 400.00.

Pre-Iroquoian pipe-axe, dark brown slate, ca. 1450 – 1550. #438, it has engraving and is 4¼" high. Oswego County, New York. Iron Horse collection. $300.00 – 450.00.

Pre-Iroquoian pipe-axe, gray slate, ca. 1450 – 1550. This stone pipe design may well be a prototype for the later white-made pipe-toma-hawk. #E-794, the height is 4" and the example is from Seneca County, New York. Iron Horse collection. $250.00 – 350.00.

Elbow pipe in red hematite material, very rare for pipe use. This is probably Mississippian period, and length is 3½". This pipe is illustrated in *Indian Artifacts of the Midwest* – II, page 260. The pipe came from the Lexington, Kentucky, area. Zell Adams collection, California. Museum quality.

Great Lakes calumet pipe, Iroquois, ca. 1700 – 1800. The pipe is made of black steatite and is inlaid with pewter; note the brass carrying chain affixed to the pipe via hole in fin. See scale for size. The pipe, #1085, is a rare example from Ontario County, New York. Iron Horse collection. Museum grade.

Monitor or platform pipe, red sandstone material, 5⁵⁄₁₆" long. This is a well-designed and finished pipe, from the area of Marshall, Arkansas. Zell Adams collection, California. $450.00 – 700.00

Elbow pipe, single ring on bowl, #72697, made of mottled green serpentine. Ca. 1550 – 1650, this polished pipe has a stem 1¾" long and bowl height is ¾". It is from Warren County, Pennsylvania. Iron Horse collection. $250.00 – 350.00.

Late prehistoric extended-elbow or obtuse-angle pipe made of rare material, pale green chlorite. This pipe is very well made and highly polished, 3¼" long. Marshall County, West Virginia. Private collection. $1,500.00.

Effigy pipe, Ft. Ancient people and Mississippian period, greenish stone. The bird figure has a small head and eyes plus indistinct folded wings on the sides. The pipe was found by a fisherman in 1981 along the Muskingum River, and the figure is 2⅛" long and 2" high. Muskingum County, Ohio. Bill Mesnard collection, New Jersey; Sarah Bones, photographer. $400.00.

Effigy pipe, Late Mississippian period, made of unknown greenish-brown stone. The pipe is 3⅝" high and is from Ohio. Len and Janie Weidner collection, Ohio. $1,200.00.

Effigy pipe, frog, Mississippian period, 2 x 4" long. This piece is very well made in dark steatite and is highly polished. Quite naturalistic in both size and detail, this piece is from Tipton County, Tennessee. Private collection, Ohio. $2,200.00.

Effigy pipe, hawk, Mississippian period, 5 x 7½". This is a very large pipe and a rare bird example done in limestone. It is from McLean County, Illinois. Private collection, Ohio. $1,500.00.

Effigy pipe, owl, made of purple flourspar, also called fluorite. This scarce material was sometimes used by the Ft. Ancient people for ornaments, rarely for pipes. It is 2" high and the mouth forms the stem hole. It came from Crittenden County, Kentucky. Private collection, Ohio. $1,500.00.

Human effigy elbow pipe, Woodland period, made of greenish-yellow quartzite with crystal inclusions, #2105. The stem is 1¾" and bowl height is 1½". It is from near Thalls, New York. Iron Horse collection. $750.00 – 1,000.00.

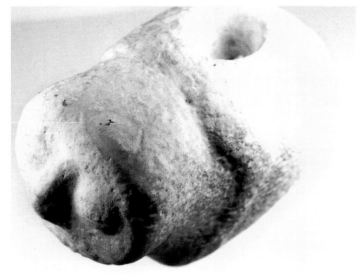

Owl effigy pipe, Mississippian period, large at 3½ x 6¾". The pipe is made of unusual material, limestone, and the design is considered a rare form. Madison County, Illinois. Private collection, Ohio. $2,500.00.

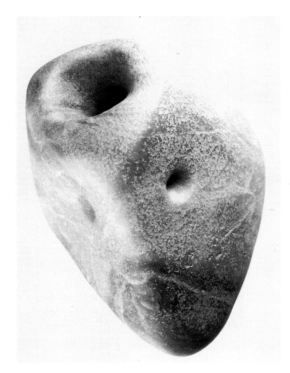

Bird effigy on a basic vase form, ca. 1400 – 1550. #E-3728 is made of dark hardstone with height of 2" and bowl width of 1¾". Note suspension or decoration hole in base; Monroe area, Michigan. Iron Horse collection. $475.00 – 600.00.

Deer head effigy pipe, 2½ x 3¼". It is made of durable and attractive quartz in several colors, with the deer's nose area being darker. Mississippian period, this is a large pipe in a scarce material. Richland County, Ohio. Private collection, Ohio. $2,000.00.

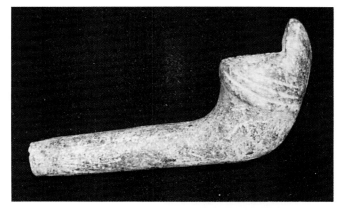

Iroquois snake effigy pipe, made of gray hardstone, ca. 1600 – 1750. #2HL has a stem 3" long and bowl 1¾" high. This solid, well-made pipe is from Allegany County, New York. Iron Horse collection. $550.00 – 750.00.

Obtuse-angle elbow pipe made of green and black stone, well polished. Probably Mississippian, the pipe measures 2½" long and 1½" high. The origin is unknown, but is eastern United States. Wilfred Dick collection, Mississippi. $550.00 – 800.00.

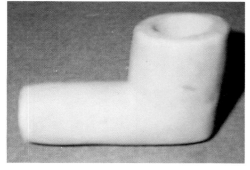

Copena (Copper-Galena people) style elbow pipe, Woodland period and ca. AD 500, well shaped in polished limestone. Size is 1½" high and 2½" long, with width of ¾". It came from the Tombigbee Basin, Mississippi. Wilfred Dick collection, Mississippi. $400.00 – 600.00.

Elbow pipe, light-colored and weathered limestone, 1¾" high. This pipe was found in Kentucky. Len and Janie Weidner collection, Ohio. $250.00.

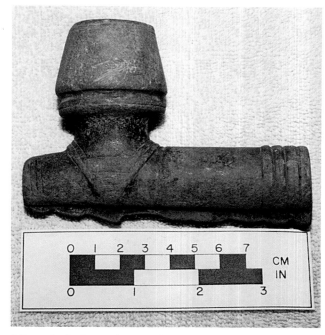

Historic L-shaped pipe, fine-grained limestone. It is 4½" long, 3¼" high, and has a bowl diameter of 1⅝". The stem section, now glued, broke during cleaning due to a frost crack. This pipe is probably Sauk or Fox because it was found near a known historic Sauk encampment. Ca. 1750, the pipe was found along the Rock River, Illinois. Doug Miller collection, Illinois. $400.00 – 600.00.

Mic-mac pipe, an extremely rare example made of wood, the only one known to exist. Such examples show the ingenuity of early craftspeople. Ca. 1650 – 1750, #2436 is 2½" high and has line designs. Allegany County, New York. Iron Horse collection. Museum grade.

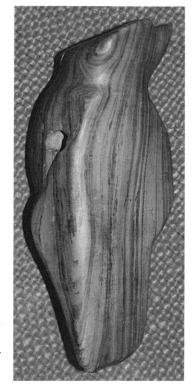

Bird effigy pipe, #77, made of green banded glacial slate. This is a large pipe at 2" wide and 4¼" high. Ca. 1600 – 1675, it is from New York state. Iron Horse collection. $900.00 – 1,200.00.

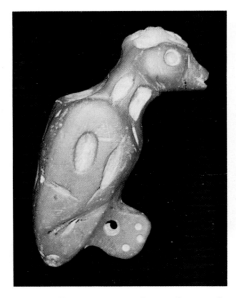

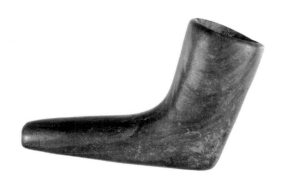

Elbow pipe, late prehistoric – early historic period, unusual brown banded glacial slate. The pipe with comparatively large bowl is 2¼" long and is from Fairfield County, Ohio. Len and Janie Weidner collection, Ohio. $400.00.

Bird effigy pipe, #10-500, carved in red stone. It is ca. 1600 – 1675 and is nicely designed and worked. Size, 1⅝" high. Niagara County, New York. Iron Horse collection. $800.00 – 1,000.00.

Bird effigy pipe, pileated woodpecker, #368, made of black slate. It is ca. 1600 – 1675 and measures 3½" high, 1¼" wide. Cazenovia area, New York. Iron Horse collection. $900.00 – 1,500.00.

Iroquois vase-shaped pipe with faceted sides, ca. 1500 – 1650, #RXB\2. Made of black slate the pipe is 3¼" high, and is from Allegany County, New York. Iron Horse collection. Unlisted.

Forged iron pipe, Iroquois, ca. 1650 – 1750. #4 is constructed of hammered iron, with 2" stem and bowl height of 1¾". Genesee River Valley, Monroe County, New York. Iron Horse collection. $300.00 – 400.00.

Sandstone elbow pipe, probably Woodland period, 1½ x 2 x 2⅝" long. It is well made with pleasing lines and in unblemished condition. Adair County, Kentucky. Larry Lantz, First Mesa, Indiana. $475.00.

Historic-era stone pipes. Top, slate, bottom flange as on many trade pipes, ca. 1750 – 1850. It is made of reddish slate, measures 1⅝ x 2⅝", Great Lakes area. $100.00.
Bottom, ca. 1800s, probably steatite, 2⅛ x 2½". Northcentral United States. Hogan Gallery Inc., Naples, Florida. $80.00.

Historic Cherokee pipe, probably mid-1800s, steatite with inlays. Additional materials are catlinite and pewter for this highly decorated and complex pipe. It is 3¾" high, from the southern Appalachians. Private collection. Museum grade.

Pottery Pipes

After pipes had been made for awhile, around 1000 BC and earlier in some regions, pottery pipes made an appearance. This of course coincided with the general introduction of pottery for bowls and pots, which replaced steatite containers of the Late Archaic. Even baked-clay cooking balls were made by the Late Archaic people at the Poverty Point site in Louisiana, perhaps because of a lack of suitable native stones.

Like pottery, clay for pipes had to be tempered with other materials so it would fire properly and not crack during firing or in use. Tempering agents included grit, sand, ground shell, crushed stone, pulverized pottery, and the like. Many kinds of pipes had at least some examples made of clay, where it was available and there were craftspeople familiar with processing it.

In some regions, like the Southwest and the Northeast, there were more pipes made of clay than stone during certain prehistoric periods. Most students of Amerind technology agree that the hardest, most durable prehistoric pottery was made in the Southwest. After all, any pottery shards that retain crisp, sharp edges through time tend to be of high initial and enduring hardness. Many pipes of the region tend to be of related quality.

Pottery had some advantages over stone. It was relatively quick and easy to mold into whatever plain or fanciful shape the maker desired, and there were usually unlimited amounts of clay for the taking and working. Due to the amount of labor involved in making most stone pipes, the loss of a clay pipe was not a major event. Over the centuries clay was used for large numbers of pipes, and in some regions it was the favored material.

Pottery pipe, probably Ft. Ancient and Mississippian, grit-tempered clay. It is 2" high and 2½" long, ex-collections Barron and Goodwin. The pipe is gracefully shaped and undamaged. Scioto County, Ohio. Private collection, Ohio. $250.00

Elbow pipe, brown pottery with incised lines around the bowl. This is a late prehistoric pipe, possibly Whittlesey people, 1¾" high. Cuyahoga County, Ohio. Robin Fiser collection, Ohio. $200.00.

Pottery elbow pipe, acute angle design, reddish fired clay. This would be late prehistoric – early historic and has a blackened bowl interior from much use. It is 2⅜" high and 3¼" long. Wayne County, Ohio. Robin Fiser collection, Ohio. $175.00.

Double-stemmed pipe, sand-tempered pottery, late prehistoric. Each side has a stem hole; most of one stem has been replaced, as seen on the right side. This platform pipe has a flat bottom and the pipe is 6¾" long. Florida. Bill Mesnard collection, New Jersey; Sarah Bones, photographer. $100.00.

Effigy pipe, Mississippian period, shell-tempered pottery. In the image of a snake, the pipe is ¾" wide and high, 2⅞" long. It is decorated with incised lines of several kinds. Clark County, Kentucky. Bill Mesnard collection, New Jersey; Sarah Bones, photographer. $275.00.

V-shaped pipe, pottery, 2½" high and 2⅜" across; bowl diameter is 1". Probably Mississippian, it is ex-collection Pickenpaugh and from the Ohio area. Collection of and photography by Larry G. Merriam, Oklahoma. $125.00 – 175.00.

Pottery pipe, large and long stemmed, 8¼". The pipe with protrusions for standing or bowl protection is ca. 700 – 1400, and came from New Mexico. Len and Janie Weidner collection, Ohio. $550.00.

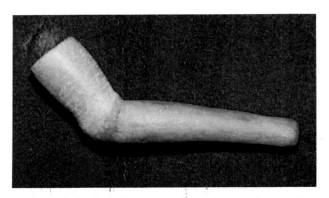

Monongahela "arm" pipe with punctate decoration, pottery, Late Woodland period. It is from Clearfield County, Pennsylvania, and has the stem restored. Gary L. Fogelman collection, Pennsylvania. $75.00.

Pottery pipe in glazed brown color, incised and punctate decorations, 3" long. This pipe is from Northumberland County, Pennsylvania. Richard Savidge collection, Pennsylvania. $500.00.

Keel-type pipe, ca. 1600 – 1700 with double-line engraving. Made of brown pottery, #B-167 is 2" high and came from Pennsylvania. Iron Horse collection. $300.00 – 375.00.

Elbow pipe, Late Woodland period, made of dark pottery. This example is 2¾" high and 3½" long. It came from Baxter County, Arkansas. Baxter Hurst collection, Arkansas. $275.00.

Elbow pipe, dark-colored pottery, probably Late Woodland period. This nicely molded example is 2⅛" high and 2⅝" long and is from Boone County, Arkansas. Baxter Hurst collection, Arkansas. $225.00.

Pottery pipe with light shell tempering, made of brown ceramic material. Found in 1986, this pipe is 2 x 3⅞" long and 2¾" high. Mississippi, County, Arkansas. Bill Mesnard collection, New Jersey. $300.00.

Flared-bowl elbow pipe, pottery, 2⅝" high and 3¾" long. This pipe is ex-collection Thompson and came from Calloway County, Missouri. Len and Janie Weidner collection, Ohio. $650.00.

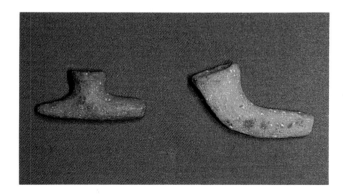

Mississippian pottery pipes, shell-tempered red clay, ca. 1300. Left, centered bowl, 3" long, Cross County, Arkansas. $75.00. Right, bent trumpet style, 3½", Green County, Arkansas. $75.00. Dave Summers, Native American Artifacts, Victor, New York.

Obtuse-angle pipe, pottery with punctate decoration. It is Late Woodland period, ca. 900 – 1000, and was found in Lycoming County, Pennsylvania. Gary L. Fogelman collection, Pennsylvania. $1,000.00 – 1,500.00.

Tubular pipe, curved, probably Mississippian period, pottery. It is 5" long and was found in New York State. Collection of Jim Bickel, Huntington, Indiana. $200.00.

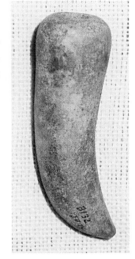

Bowl fragments, pottery, plus two complete bowls. These are in various styles and all are ca. 1550 – 1640 These make fine study pieces. The 1" to 2" specimens are Seneca, from central and western New York. Complete two bowls — each $25.00. Seven broken pieces — group $120.00. Dave Summers, Native American Artifacts, Victor, New York.

Pottery pipe, rare flat stem with engraved ring near bowl rim. The pipe is broken at the bowl-stem junction and measures 4¼" long. Ca. 1610 – 1630, it is ex-collections Hoffman and Wray. Lima, New York. Dave Summers, Native American Artifacts, Victor, New York. $400.00.

Elbow pipe, pottery, ca. 1500 – 1700. This pipe is tempered with brown sand or crushed quartz. Size is 2⅛" long and 2¼" high. It was found in Bartow County, Georgia. Jim Maus collection, North Carolina. $300.00.

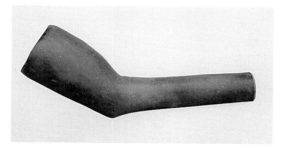

Elbow pipe, pottery, ca. 1400 – 1600. Material is a brown baked clay tempered with crushed quartz. Measuring 1½" high and 3½" long, the pipe is from Stokes County, North Carolina. Jim Maus collection, North Carolina. $300.00.

Elaborate elbow pipe, pottery, Caddo Indian, 1⅞" high. This well-developed pipe form is from Bowie County, Texas. Larry Garvin, Back to Earth, Ohio. $175.00 – 200.00.

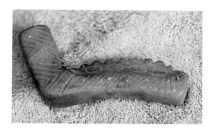

Elbow pipe, shell-tempered pottery, probably late prehistoric. Reddish brown, the pipe is covered with engraved geometric designs. Measuring ⅝ x 4½ x 2¼" high this pipe may be from the eastern Midwest. Bill Mesnard Collection, New Jersey. $200.00.

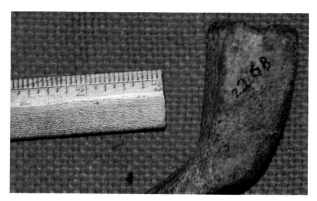

Owasco obtuse-angle squared bowl pipe, #22GB, made of grit-tempered brown pottery. This pipe is ca. 1200 – 1400 and is from western New York. Iron Horse collection. $250.00 – 300.00.

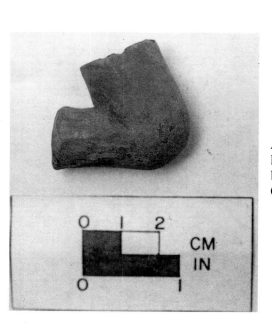

Angular pipe with short stem, pottery, probably Cherokee and ca. 1450 – 1835. There is some damage to the bowl of this specimen, from Buncombe County, North Carolina. Gary Henry collection, North Carolina. $50.00+.

Large historic clay pipe, yellow-tan color, 3" long and 3⅝" high. This example is from King George County, Virginia. Hogan Gallery Inc., Naples, Florida. $125.00.

Iroquois dark pottery pipe, 2⅜" long. It was found in 1862, near Elmira, New York. Richard Savidge collection, Pennsylvania. $300.00.

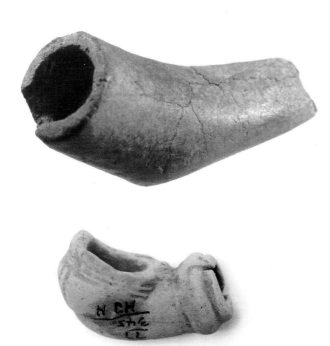

Tan pottery pipe, elbow shape, grit tempered, 2⅞" long. With some pressure cracks and damage, this Owasco tradition pipe came from an island in the Susquehanna River near Williamsport, Pennsylvania. Richard Savidge collection, Pennsylvania. $150.00.

Biconical pottery pipe, probably Creek Indian and ca. 1720 – 1830, with minor damage. This pipe is from Alabama. Gary Henry collection, North Carolina. $200.00+.

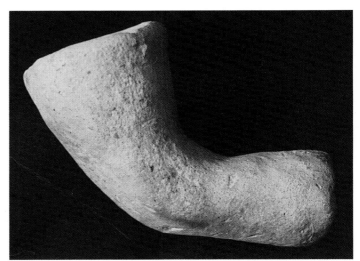

Pottery elbow pipe, gray-tan and grit tempered. This large example was found with Chesser side-notch and Levanna triangular points, suggesting a Middle Woodland through Mississippian time frame. Pipe thickness is about ¼". It came from a West Virginia rock shelter. Mike Lambert collection, West Virginia. $250.00.

Elbow pipe with expanded bowl, Caddoan culture of late prehistory, from near Clarksville, Texas. It is 1¾" long and 2" high, with bowl 1½" in diameter. Material is a light brown pottery. Collection of and photograph by, Duane Treest, Illinois. $50.00 – 75.00.

Effigy pipe, bird foot, pottery, probably Creek Indian and ca. 1720 – 1830. This pipe came from Blount County, Alabama. Gary Henry collection, North Carolina. $200.00+.

Elbow pipe on platform, Mississippian period, buff pottery with shell temper. It is 2¼" high and 3¼" long. The pipe was found on a Mississippian site in southeastern Missouri. Collection of Bob Rampani, Bridgeton, St. Louis County, Missouri. $150.00 – 200.00.

Elbow pottery pipe on platform, Mississippian period, made of buff-colored clay with shell temper. It is 2⅝" high and 3⅜" long. The pipe was found in Pike County, Arkansas. Collection of Bob Rampani, Bridgeton, St. Louis County, Missouri. $190.00 – 250.00.

Bi-conical pipe, gray pottery, 3⅝" long and 2⅝" high. This artifact was found in Mississippi County, Arkansas. Larry Garvin, Back to Earth, Ohio. $200.00.

Late prehistoric pottery elbow pipe with expanded stem and bowl openings. It is 4" long, 3" high, and 2½" wide. This pipe was found in Mississippi County, Arkansas. Wilfred Dick collection, Mississippi. $250.00 – 375.00

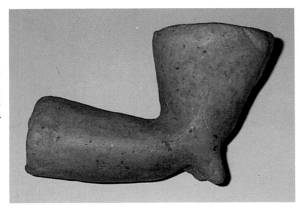

Mississippian biconical pipe, ca. 1000 – 1650, light brown pottery. #JP\10 is 1¼" long and 1¾" high. Poinsett County, Arkansas. Iron Horse collection. $250.00 – 325.00.

Pottery Mississippian-era biconical pipes, average length 3 to 3½" and average height 2 to 3". Top, #J\12; left, #JP\11; right, #MC\15. Iron Horse collection. Each $250.00 – 300.00.

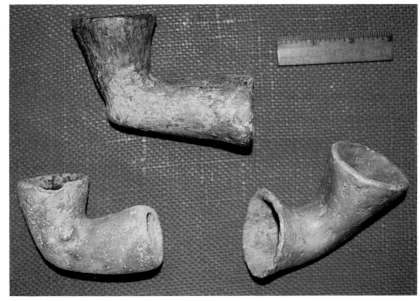

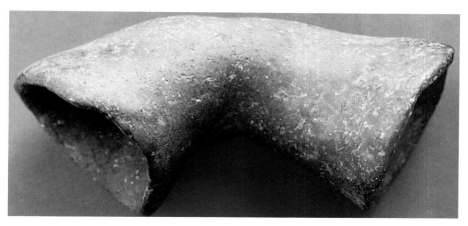

Elbow pipe, brownish pottery, Woodland – Mississippian periods. This example is 3½" high and 2½" long, and was found in Baxter County, Arkansas. Baxter Hurst collection, Arkansas. Unlisted.

Elbow pipe, expanded bowl and stem openings, with material a shell-tempered clay. Both openings are 2" in diameter and the pipe is 4½" long. Mississippian, the pipe is from southern Illinois. Collection of and photograph by Duane Treest, Illinois. $100.00 – 150.00.

Miniature Hopewell pottery platform pipe, tally marked on the platform end opposite the mouthpiece end. It is made of high-grade ceramic material and the pipe was probably broken by agricultural equipment. It is 2⅜" long and from Pike County, Ohio. Ted McVey collection, Ohio. Unlisted.

Barrel pipe, pottery, Late Woodland period, made of shell-tempered clay. The pipe measures 2⅛ x 5¼", and was found in Holt County, Missouri. Mike George collection, Missouri. $100.00.

Obtuse-angle pipe, Late Woodland – Mississippian period, made of pottery. It is 2¾" long and came from Lancaster County, Pennsylvania. Lee Hallman collection, Pennsburg, Pennsylvania. $300.00.

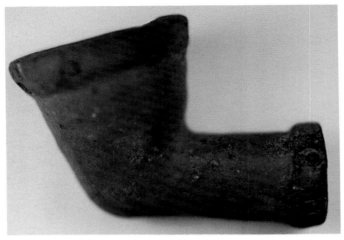

Tulip-bowl style pipe, Late Woodland period, pottery. It is 2" long and 1¼" in diameter at the center. This example came from Lancaster County, Pennsylvania. Lee Hallman collection, Pennsburg, Pennsylvania. $300.00.

Elbow pipe with flared bowl mouth, pottery, Late Woodland period. It is 2" long from stem end to the elbow and 1¾" high. This pipe came from Westmoreland County, Virginia. Lee Hallman collection, Pennsburg, Pennsylvania. $200.00.

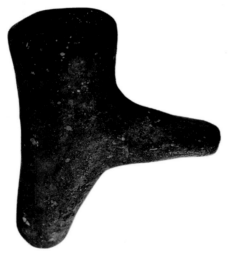

Pipe with stem and mouthpiece extension to the right, brownish-orange pottery. The pipe is 2¼" high and is Jersey focus, Late Woodland. Pike County, Indiana. Len and Janie Weidner collection, Ohio. $250.00.

Pottery elbow pipe, Woodland period, made of buff-colored clay with grit temper. It is 2" high and the bowl top is notched. It was found while surface hunting in Pike County, Missouri, in 1983. Collection of Bob Rampani, Bridgeton, St. Louis County, Missouri. $100.00 – 130.00.

Curved-platform Intrusive Mound pipe, shell-tempered pottery, #HL-106. This is an unusual form, with the stem 5½" and bowl height 1¼". Cattaraugus County, New York. Iron Horse collection. $950.00 – 1,100.00.

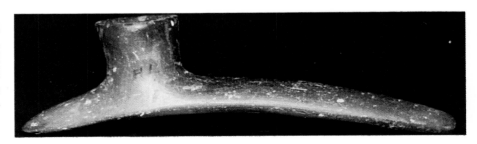

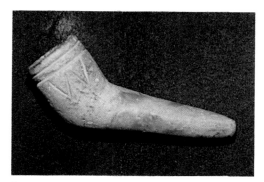

Obtuse-angle pipe, pottery, ca. 800 – 1100. It is from Luzerne County, Pennsylvania, and has a restored stem. Gary L. Fogelman collection, Pennsylvania. $50.00.

Pipe, tan pottery with maroon top, incised lines on side. This unusual pipe, from the Southwest, has two bowls and four stem holes. It measures 2" high, 1½" deep, and 2¾" wide. Larry Garvin, Back to Earth, Ohio. $250.00.

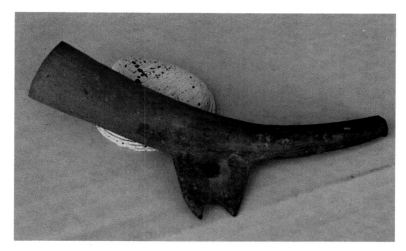

Diegueno bowl pipe, buff-colored pottery, late prehistoric to historic times. Such pipes were often suspended from the neck of the wearer. The pipe, from the San Diego area of California, is 6" long and 1" across at the bowl. Jim Cressey collection, California. Unlisted.

Double-stemmed pottery pipe, black and tan color, 6½" long. This would be a Mississippian period artifact, and it was found in Oklahoma. Robin Fiser collection, Ohio. $250.00.

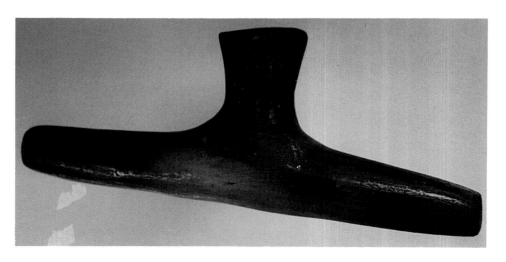

Caddo culture pottery pipe with strap bowl, 3" long and with bowl 1½" in diameter. It came from Clark County, Arkansas. Collection of and photograph by Duane Treest, Illinois. $150.00 – 200.00.

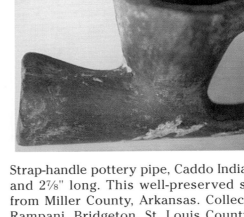

Strap-handle pottery pipe, Caddo Indian, 1¾" high and 2⅞" long. This well-preserved specimen is from Miller County, Arkansas. Collection of Bob Rampani, Bridgeton, St. Louis County, Missouri. $200.00 – 250.00.

Strap-handle pottery pipe, Caddo Indian, gray color, 2⅝" high and 3⅛" long. This piece came from Clark County, Arkansas. Collection of Bob Rampani, Bridgeton, St. Louis County, Missouri. $200.00 – 250.00.

Caddo pottery pipe, strap handle and with two stem holes, about 2" long. This pipe is prehistoric into early historic and was found in Mississippi County, Arkansas. Gary Henry collection, North Carolina. $200.00+.

Biconical pottery pipe, probably Dallas culture and ca. 1450 – 1720. This pipe has the side projections missing from just in front of the bowl base. The pipe is from Bradley County, Tennessee. Gary Henry collection, North Carolina. $200.00+.

Pottery pipe, Caddo Indian, Mississippian period. This pipe is 1½" high, 2¾" long, with a bowl diameter of 1¾". Yell County, Arkansas. Collection of and photography by Duane Treest, Illinois. $150.00 – 200.00.

Caddo pottery pipe, snake-head effigy, late prehistoric into historic time. With minor stem damage, this pipe is from Mississippi County, Arkansas. Gary Henry collection, North Carolina. $200.00+.

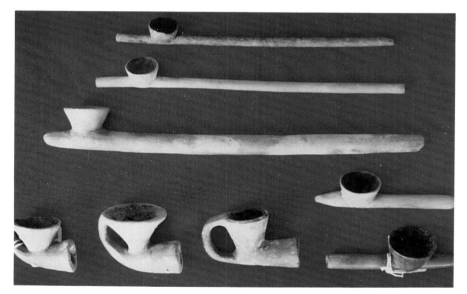

A fine display of Caddoan pottery pipes, showing three different pipe styles. Top, long-stem; bottom right, short-stem; bottom left, with strap handles. The longest stem is 11½" and the shortest is 4½". These came from various counties in Arkansas. Collection of Bob Rampani, Bridgeton, St. Louis County, Missouri. $150.00 – 600.00 each.

Caddo Indian pipe, Mississippian period, made of red to tan colored pottery. The pipe is 5" long, 1¼" high, and 1½" wide. It was found in Pike County, Arkansas. Wilfred Dick collection, Mississippi. $350.00 – 500.00.

Engraved elbow pipe, late prehistoric – early historic, made of yellow-tan pottery. Each end is about 1" square and the pipe is 3½" long. Mississippian in design inspiration, this pipe came from central Michigan. Collection of and photograph by Duane Treest, Illinois. $100.00 – 150.00.

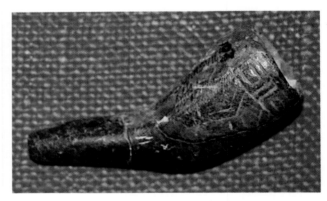

Owasco obtuse-angle pipe with fine engraving, ca. 1200 – 1400. This pipe, #BA\102, is made of dark brown pottery, has a 2" stem, and bowl height is 2". It is from the Baldwinsville area, New York. Iron Horse collection. $375.00 – 450.00.

Biconical pottery pipe with two projections for stabilization, 4½" long and 3¾" high. A nicely shaped Mississippian pipe, the bowl rim has minor restoration. The type is commonly found along the Arkansas River Valley, and this example was located by the owner west of Little Rock, along the Arkansas River. Dr. Jim Cherry collection, Arkansas. Museum grade.

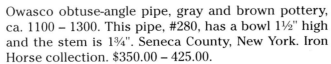

Owasco obtuse-angle pipe, gray and brown pottery, ca. 1100 – 1300. This pipe, #280, has a bowl 1½" high and the stem is 1¾". Seneca County, New York. Iron Horse collection. $350.00 – 425.00.

Owasco obtuse-angle pipe, brown and black pottery, #P-20. The form is 1200 – 1400, with stem of 4" and bowl height of 2¼". It came from near Iona, Onondaga County, New York. Iron Horse collection. $400.00 – 550.00.

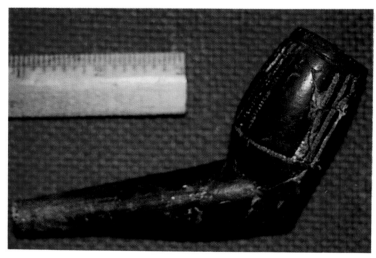

Owasco obtuse-angle pipe, with fine line designs, ca. 1200 – 1400. Material for #P-102 is a black pottery with high gloss. The stem is 3½" and the bowl is 2¼" high. Broome County, New York. Iron Horse collection. $450.00 – 650.00.

Pre-Iroquoian ring-bowl pipe with dot decorations, #K1-HL. It is made of dark brown pottery, ca. 1400 – 1500. The stem is 2¼" and bowl height is 2". From Cattaraugus County, New York. Iron Horse collection. $350.00 – 450.00.

Pre-Iroquois ring bowl with incised human stick figure, ca. 1550 – 1580, light brown pottery. #GY-7 has a 3" stem and bowl height is 1½". From, near Elma, Erie County, New York. Iron Horse collection. $350.00 – 500.00.

Pre-Iroquois effigy pipe, large open-mouth bird, ca. 1550 – 1580. #GY-8 is made of light tan pottery with black staining; it has a 3" stem and bowl height is 3½". Found near Elma, Erie County, New York. Iron Horse collection. $650.00 – 850.00.

Pre-Iroquois broken and salvaged pipes, both light brown pottery. Left, #P-21, broken bowl redrilled for wood stem, 2½" high, from near Hopewell, New York. $200.00 – 250.00. Right, #P-22, broken ring bowl redrilled for wood stem, 2" high, Livingston County, New York. $200.00 – 250.00. Iron Horse collection.

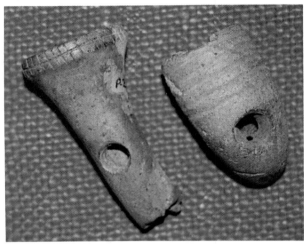

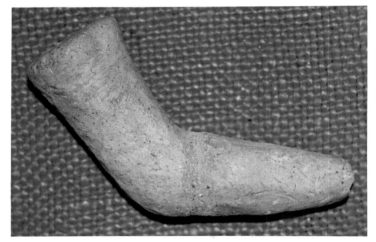

Pre-Iroquois plain trumpet pipe, ca. 1570 – 1590, #SIM-2. It is made of light brown pottery, the stem is 2½" and bowl height is 2¼". Erie County, New York. Iron Horse collection. $300.00 – 400.00.

Pre-Iroquois plain bowl pipe, #GY-11, ca. 1550 – 1580, dark brown pottery. The stem is 2½" and the bowl is 1¾" high. Erie County, New York. Iron Horse collection. $200.00 – 300.00.

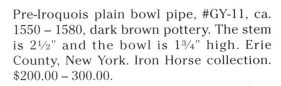

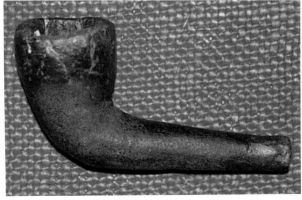

Pre-Iroquois castellated bowl pipe with dot decoration, ca. 1550 – 1580, light brown and black pottery, #GY-10 has a 6" stem and bowl height is 3". Erie County, New York. Iron Horse collection. $750.00 – 1,000.00.

Pre-Iroquois large trumpet pipe, light brown and gray pottery, ca. 1550 – 1580. The stem is 6" long and bowl height is 3". #GY-9 was picked up near Elma, Erie County, New York. Iron Horse collection. $350.00 – 450.00.

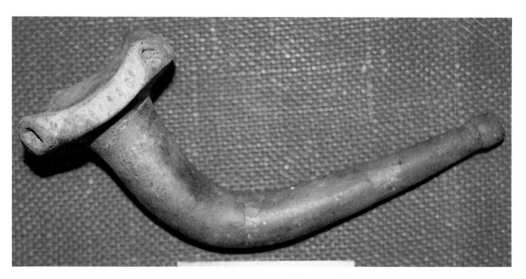

Pre-Iroquois castellated pipe with dots, ca. 1570 – 1590, brown and gray pottery. #SIM-4 has a 6" stem and bowl height is 4¾". Erie County, New York. Iron Horse collection. $750.00 – 1,000.00.

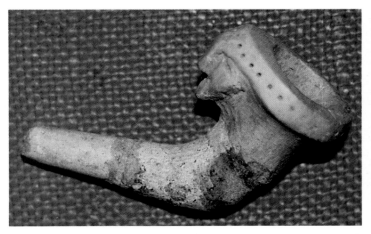

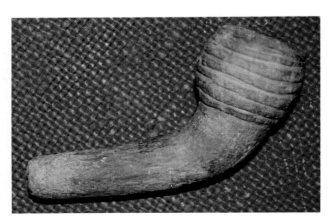

Pre-Iroquois effigy pipe, human head with dotted headband, ca. 1570 – 1600. #NH-5 is made of light brown pottery, the stem is 2½" and bowl height is 2". From near Elma, Erie County, New York. Iron Horse collection. $950.00 – 1,200.00.

Pre-Iroquois ring bowl pipe, ca. 1500 – 1620, #4177. Stem length is 3" and bowl height is 2" for this light brown pottery pipe from Seneca County, New York. Iron Horse collection. $350.00 – 400.00.

Pre-Iroquois trumpet pipe, triangle designs, ca. 1500 – 1650. #778A is made of red grit-tempered pottery, has a stem 2⅞" long and bowl height is 1¾". Cayuga County, New York. Iron Horse collection. $300.00 – 400.00.

Pre-Iroquois obtuse-angle pipe with five tally marks on one side, ca. 1500 – 1650. #2014/33 is made of red pottery and the stem is 2½", bowl height 1½". Owasco Lake area, New York. Iron Horse collection. $350.00 – 450.00.

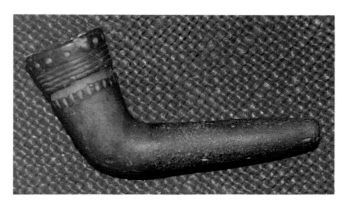

Pre-Iroquois trumpet pipe, ringed bowl with dots, ca. 1550 – 1650. Red and brown pottery, pipe #83 has a thick stem 2¾" long with bowl height 1¾". It was found near Watertown, Jefferson County, New York. Iron Horse collection. $450.00 – 500.00.

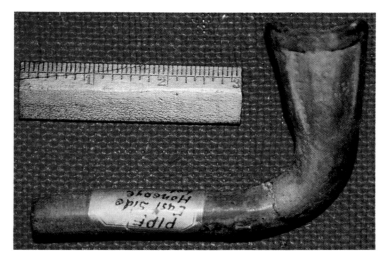

Pre-Iroquoian indented-design bowl, punctates and dots, ca. 1450 – 1500. Pipe #RL-2 is made of gray and brown pottery, with a 4" stem and bowl height of 3". It was found on the east side of Honeoye Lake, New York. Iron Horse collection. $350.00 – 425.00.

Pre-Iroquois trumpet pipe with ringed and chevron-design bowl, dark brown pottery. #AT-96 is ca. 1400 – 1500, with a stem of 4½" and bowl height of 3¼". Jefferson County, New York. Iron Horse collection. $400.00 – 500.00.

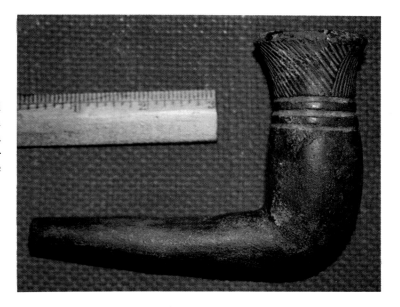

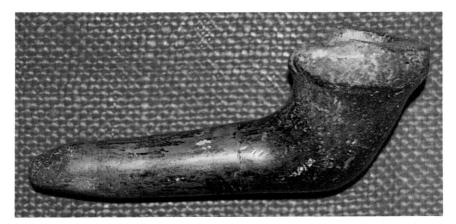

Pre-Iroquoian heavy-duty plain-bowl pipe, brown pottery, #AK-215. Ca. 1400 – 1550, the top of the bowl is battered from knocking out tobacco ashes. With a stem of 4" and bowl of 2", this pipe is from near Watertown, Jefferson County, New York. Iron Horse collection. $250.00 – 350.00.

Pre-Iroquois plain trumpet pipe, ca. 1450 – 1550. Made of reddish-brown pottery, the stem is 4½" long and bowl height is 2¾". #2R12, this pipe is from near Sandusky, Ohio. Iron Horse collection. $475.00 – 575.00.

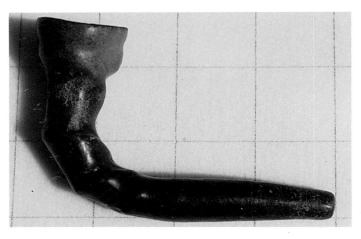

Twisted-stem pipe, pottery, ca. 1620. It measures 2¼ x 3½" and was found in southeastern Ontario, Canada. Dave Summers, Native American Artifacts, Victor, New York. $975.00.

Pre-Iroquoian (Erie) trumpet pipe, brown pottery, #EAT\DB. Ca. 1450 – 1550, the stem is 2½" long and bowl height is the same. Erie County, New York. Iron Horse collection. $275.00 – 350.00.

Pre-Iroquois trumpet-shaped ring bowl pipe, ca. 1500 – 1650, #P25\420. It was fired in brown pottery with both stem length and bowl height 1¾". Syracuse area, New York. Iron Horse collection. $300.00 – 400.00.

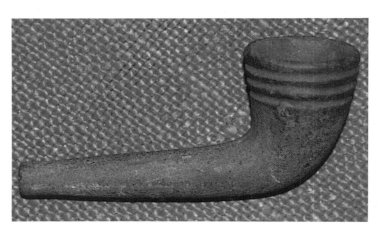

Pre-Iroquois ring bowl pipe, ca. 1500 – 1650, red grit-tempered pottery. #K2-HL has a stem 3¾" and bowl height is 1¾". Cattaraugus County, New York. Iron Horse collection. $350.00 – 450.00.

Pre-Iroquois, obtuse-angle bowl, ca. 1400 – 1500. This early pipe, #2015, is made of red and brown pottery with stem 2½" and bowl height 1½". Found near Holcomb, Ontario County, New York. Iron Horse collection. $350.00 – 450.00.

Pre-Iroquois pipe, #4\8, trumpet-shaped with flared rim, ca. 1500 – 1650. This is a well-shaped pipe in gray and brown pottery, with a 3" stem and bowl height of 2". Geneseo area, New York. Iron Horse collection. $350.00 – 450.00.

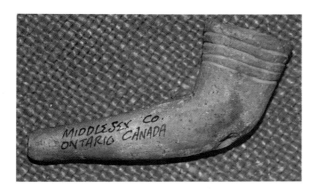

Pre-Iroquois ring bowl pipe, #P-23, ca. 1500 – 1600. It is made of tan-colored pottery; the stem is 2½" and the bowl is 1½". Middlesex County, Ontario, Canada. Private collection. $300.00 – 350.00.

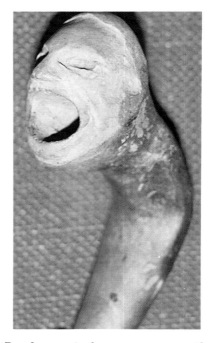

Pre-Iroquois large open-mouth human (mask) pipe, ca. 1570 – 1590, brown and black pottery. #SIM-1 has a 4" stem and bowl height is 4". This is a rare pipe, from Erie County, New York. Iron Horse collection. Museum grade.

Pre-Iroquois large castellated pipe with dots, ca. 1570 – 1590, brown pottery. The stem is 6" long and bowl height is 4¼". #SIM-5 was acquired in Erie County, New York. Iron Horse collection. $750.00 – 1,000.00.

Pre-Iroquois open-mouth human effigy pipe, ca. 1570 – 1590, light brown pottery. The stem of this pipe is 3" long and the bowl is 2" high. #SIM-3 was found in Erie County, New York. Iron Horse collection. $500.00 – 750.00.

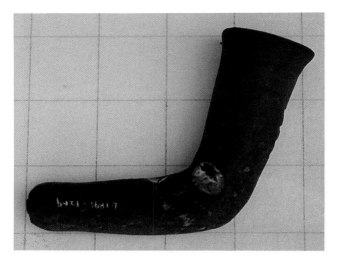

Pottery pipe, long-bowl variety, ca. 1550 – 1650. This pipe has some old minor repair and measures 3 x 4" long. Origin for this pipe style is western New York and southeastern Ontario, Canada. Dave Summers, Native American Artifacts, Victor, New York. $300.00.

Pre-Iroquois ring bowl pottery pipe, #369, ca. 1500 – 1650. The stem is 2½" and bowl height is 2" for this pipe, #369. Chautauqua County, New York. Iron Horse collection. $350.00 – 450.00.

Pre-Iroquois obtuse-angle pipe, decorated with lines, dots, and checks, ca. 1500 – 1600. #636 is made of brown pottery and is from the Canisteo area, Steuben County, New York. Iron Horse collection. $350.00 – 450.00.

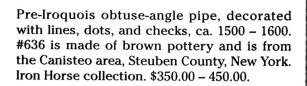

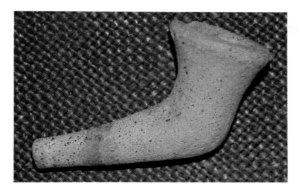

Pre-Iroquois trumpet pipe, tan grit-tempered pottery, ca. 1500 – 1650. #1995 has a 2" stem with a bowl of 1½". Jefferson County, New York. Private collection. $350.00 – 450.00.

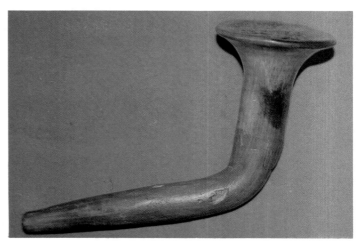

Trumpet pipe, Huron-Petun, ca. 1500 – 1650. It is made of light brown pottery, the stem is 4" long and bowl height is 3¼". #GL-5 was found in Simcoe County, Ontario, Canada. Private collection. $750.00 – 950.00.

Ring bowl with dots, Huron-Petun, ca. 1500 – 1650. #GL-32 is made of red pottery that has burned black. Stem length is 4¼" and bowl height is 2½". Simcoe County, Ontario, Canada. Private collection. $300.00 – 375.00.

Trumpet pipe, Huron-Petun, ca. 1500 – 1650. #GL-6 is light brown pottery that has burned black, and both stem length and bowl height are 3". The pipe came from Simcoe County, Ontario, Canada. Private collection. $700.00 – 800.00.

Ring bowl pipe with dots, Huron-Petun, ca. 1500 – 1650. #GL-30 is made of red pottery and came from Simcoe County, Ontario, Canada. Private collection. $300.00 – 350.00.

Ring bowl pipe with dots, Huron-Petun, ca. 1500 – 1650. This is #Gl-31 and material is red pottery which has been burned black. Stem is 3¼" long and bowl height is 2". It was found in Simcoe County, Ontario, Canada. Private collection. $300.00 – 350.00.

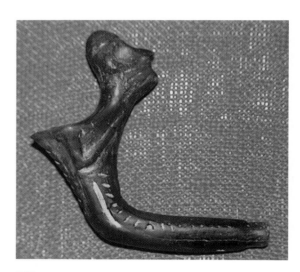

Crown pipe, Huron-Petun, ca. 1500 – 1650. It is made of red pottery and has a stem that is 3¼" long with a bowl 3" high. #GL-26 came from Simcoe County, Ontario, Canada. Private collection. $700.00 – 850.00.

Effigy pipe, pinched-face blower, Huron-Petun, ca. 1500 – 1680. This is a salvaged pipe made of black pottery, 4" high. #REA/300 came from Simcoe County, Ontario, Canada. Private collection. $350.00 – 450.00.

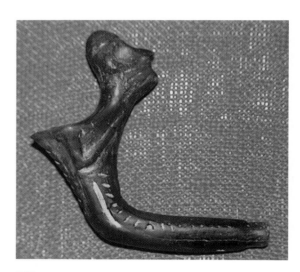

Effigy pipe, pinched-face blower, Huron-Petun, ca. 1500 – 1650. Made of dark brown pottery, #GL-16 has a stem 4¾" long and bowl height is 4½". The pipe was found in Simcoe County, Ontario, Canada. Private collection. $800.00 – 1,000.00.

Effigy pipe, pinched-face blower, Huron-Petun, ca. 1500 – 1650. This pipe, #GL-12, is made of dark brown pottery and both stem length and bowl height are 2¾". It came from Simcoe County, Ontario, Canada. Private collection. $800.00 – 1,000.00.

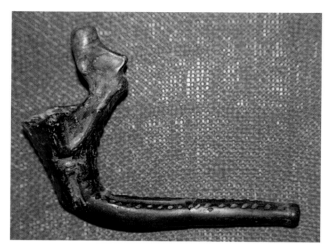

Effigy pipe, pinched face blower, Huron-Petun, ca. 1500 – 1650. It is made of brown and black pottery, and has a stitched stem. Overall pipe length is about 5½". #GL-15 came from Simcoe County, Ontario, Canada. Private collection. $800.00 – 1,000.00.

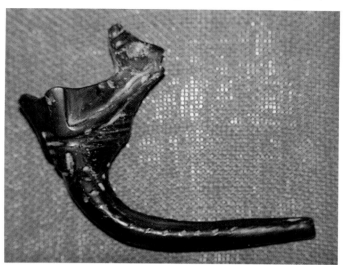

Effigy pipe, pinched-face blower, Huron-Petun, ca. 1500 – 1650. The pipe is #GL-13/B and material is black pottery. The pipe has a stem 4" long and bowl height is 4¼". Simcoe County, Ontario, Canada. Private collection. $1,000.00 – 1,500.00.

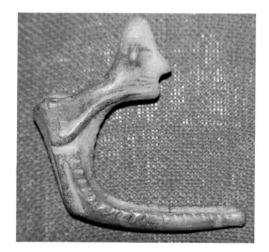

Effigy pipe, pinched-face blower, Huron-Petun, ca. 1500 – 1650. Material is light brown and red pottery for #GL-14, which has a stem 3¾" long and bowl 4½" high. Simcoe County, Ontario, Canada. Private collection. $850.00 – 1,000.00.

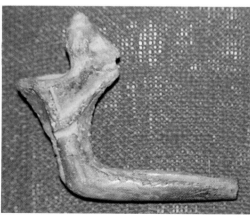

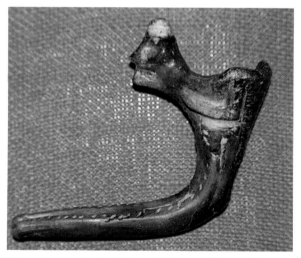

Effigy pipe, pinched-face blower, Huron-Petun, ca. 1500 – 1650. The pipe is made of yellow-brown pottery and has a 3" stem and bowl height of 3½". #GL-11 came from Simcoe County, Ontario, Canada. Private collection. $800.00 – 1,000.00.

Effigy pipe, pinched-face blower, Huron-Petun, ca. 1500 – 1600. It was originally brown pottery that has burned black. Stem length for #GL-17 is 4" and bowl height is 4¼". Simcoe County, Ontario, Canada. Private collection. $850.00 – 1,050.00.

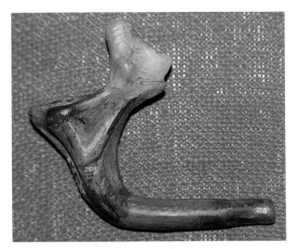

Effigy pipe, pinched-face blower, Huron-Petun, ca. 1500 – 1650. Material is red and brown pottery, the stem is 3" and bowl height is 4¾". #GL-18 came from Simcoe County, Ontario, Canada. Private collection. $800.00 – 1,000.00.

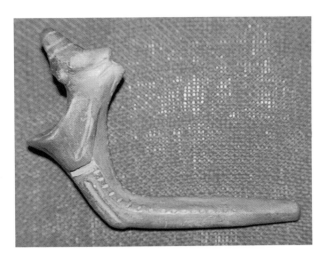

Effigy pipe, pinched-face blower, Huron-Petun, ca. 1500 – 1650. Material is red pottery, stem length is 4" and bowl height is 4¼". This scarce and fine example, #GL-10, came from Simcoe County, Ontario, Canada. Private collection. $1,500.00 – 2,500.00.

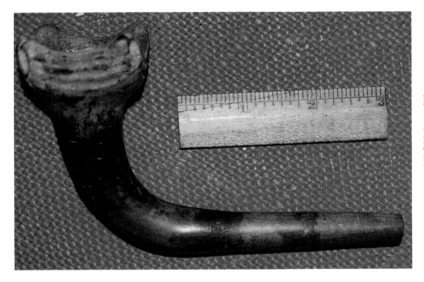

Huron crown-type pipe, #172A, ca. 1550 – 1750. This pipe is made of brown and black pottery, the stem is 4½" and bowl height is 3¼". Seneca County, New York. Private collection. $550.00 – 850.00.

Susquehanna focus tulip pipe with painted stem, ca. 1640 – 1680, light brown pottery. This piece was fired with a wrapped vine, making the black stripes on the finished pipe. Rare, this pipe has a long 6¾" stem and bowl height is 4¾". #388 is from Oneida County, New York. Private collection. $850.00 – 1,100.00.

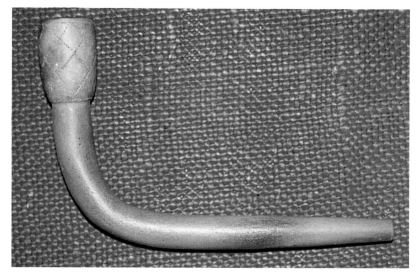

Susquehanna focus tulip pipe, ca. 1640 – 1680, light brown pottery. #P3106 has a cross-hatched bowl and long, delicate stem. Stem is 4½" and bowl height is 3¼". Lancaster County, Pennsylvania. Iron Horse collection. $750.00 – 1,000.00.

Iroquois trumpet pipe, very small, ca. 1640 – 1700. Made of gray and brown pottery, #SC-4/39 has a stem 1½" long and bowl height is 1¼". Erie County, New York. Iron Horse collection. $200.00 – 250.00.

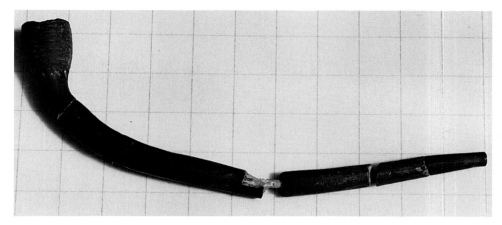

Trumpet pipe, long-stem variety with ring bowl. Made of pottery, this piece is ca. 1650 and measures 5½ x 10½". It is ex-collection Moulthrop with Susquehannock origin in southcentral New York. Dave Summers, Native American Artifacts, Victor, New York. $1,200.00.

Iroquois copy of white-manufactured kaolin pipe, this example is made of green-black steatite and originally had a wooden stem. #AK-89, the pipe is ca. 1650 – 1750. Stem length is 2½" and bowl height is 2". Ontario County, New York. Iron Horse collection. $350.00 – 450.00

Pottery pipe, angled trumpet form, with incised bowl. This pipe has a reconstructed stem and is ca. 1650. New York. Dave Summers, Native American Artifacts, Victor, New York. $125.00.

Iroquois pipe, large ringed-bowl type, gray pottery, #77CLA-740. Ca. 1600 – 1700, the stem is 4" and height is 2½". Madison County, New York. Iron Horse collection. $350.00 – 450.00

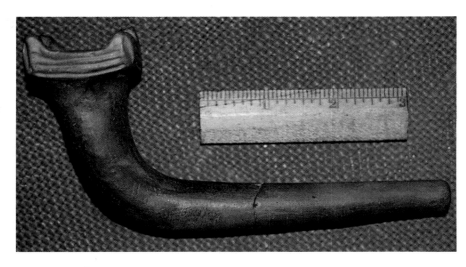

Huron crown-type pipe, reddish pottery, ca. 1550 – 1750. #6 has a stem 5" long and bowl height is 3". This pipe is from near Trenton, Ontario, Canada. Private collection. $750.00 – 1,200.00.

Iroquois pipe, small ringed-bowl type with dots, ca. 1650 – 1750. This is a fine pipe in dark brown and black pottery, with a 5" stem and bowl height of 2½". #82, it is from the East Bloomfield area, New York. Iron Horse collection. $350.00 – 450.00.

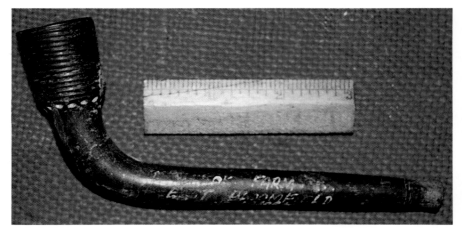

Pottery pipe, historic, obtuse-angle elbow type. It is probably Creek Indian and ca. 1720 – 1830. This pipe came from Talladega County, Alabama. Gary Henry collection, North Carolina. $300.00+.

Effigy pipe, wasp nest image, pottery decorated with rows of punctates. This interesting effigy Ft. Ancient pipe measures 1⅝ x 1½". The pipe came from northern Kentucky. Patrick Welch collection, Ohio. $400.00.

Effigy pipe, deer head, pottery with large bits of tempering, Ft. Ancient people of Mississippian times. The pipe is 1¾" high and 1½" long, and was found in northern Kentucky. Patrick Welch collection, Ohio. $125.00.

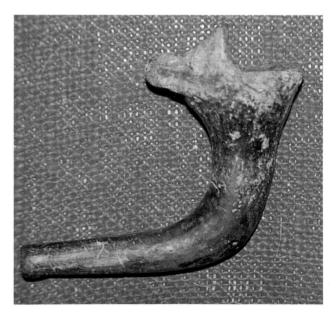

Effigy pipe, wolf image, #GL-4. Huron-Petun and ca. 1500 – 1680, the pipe is made of red pottery. The stem is 3" long and bowl height is 3⅛". Simcoe County, Ontario, Canada. Private collection. $375.00 – 450.00.

Effigy pipe, wolf with trumpet bowl, #GL-3. Huron-Petun, ca. 1550 – 1700. The pipe is made of black pottery, the stem is 2" long and bowl height is 2¼". Simcoe County, Ontario, Canada. Private collection. $375.00 – 450.00.

Effigy pipe, owl, Huron-Petun, ca. AD 1500 – 1680. #REA/700 is made of light brown pottery; the stem is 2½" long and bowl height is 2". Simcoe County, Ontario, Canada. Private collection. Museum grade.

Effigy pipe, owl, Huron-Petun ca. 1550 – 1700. #REA/800 is made of burnt-black pottery and has a 3" stem and bowl height of 3½". Simcoe County, Ontario, Canada. Private collection. $850.00 – 1,200.00.

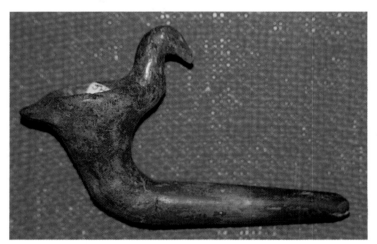

Effigy pipe, bird, Huron-Petun, #JH-6. It is ca. 1500 – 1680 and is made of red pottery. The stem is 3" long and bowl height is 2½". Simcoe County, Ontario, Canada. Private collection. $350.00 – 450.00.

Effigy pipe, bird, Huron-Petun and ca. 1500 – 1680. It is made of gray and red pottery and has a stem 3" long with bowl height 4". The pipe, #JH-5, came from Simcoe County, Ontario, Canada. Private collection. $450.00 – 550.00.

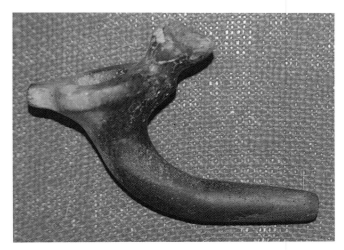

Effigy pipe, bird, Huron-Petun, ca. 1500 – 1680. It was originally made of red pottery, now burned black. Both stem length and bowl height are 3". #JH-4 is from Simcoe County, Ontario, Canada. Private collection. $375.00 – 450.00.

Iroquois bird effigy pipe, #AK-600, made of light brown pottery. Ca. 1600 – 1700, the stem is 4" long and bowl height is 4¼". This pipe is from Ontario County, New York. Iron Horse collection. $900.00 – 1,200.00.

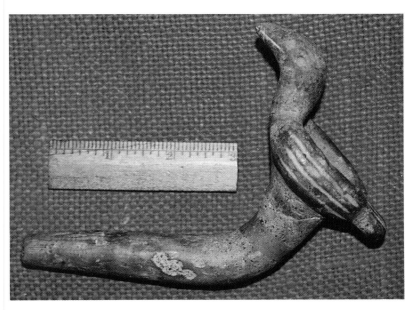

Intrusive Mound bear effigy pipe, light brown grit-tempered pottery, #6359. Ca. AD 500 – 1100, with an exterior stem length of 3⅝" and bowl height of 2", the pipe is from Livingston County, New York. Iron Horse collection. $850.00 – 1,000.00.

Pottery frog effigy pipe, Mississippian period, made of shell-tempered clay. Size is 2½ x 3". This pipe came from Floyd County, Georgia. Private collection, Georgia. $350.00.

Human effigy pottery pipe, yellow-tan color, 3¼ x 2⅛ x 3½" high. Probably Mississippian period, this example came from western Virginia. Bill Mesnard collection, New Jersey. $400.00.

Effigy face pipe, shell-tempered pottery, Mississippian period. It is 3¾" long and has two human faces, one looking toward the smoker and the other opposite, on the pipe bowl front. Lee County, Arkansas. Larry Garvin, Back to Earth, Ohio. $325.00 – 350.00.

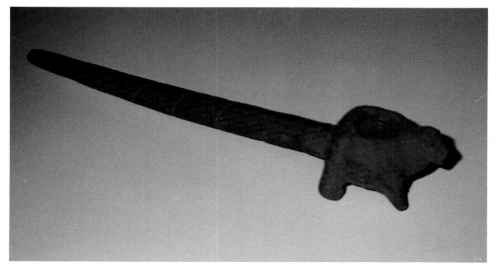

Historic-era pottery pipe with animal effigy bowl and tail forming stem. It is 7½" long and 1¼" high. Chickasaw, it is from Mississippi. Wilfred Dick collection, Mississippi. $250.00 – 375.00.

Turtle-shell effigy pipe, bottom-side view illustrating the ridged top center of the shell and the pipe stem hole. Dark steatite, 1⅜" in diameter, from Bowie County, Texas. Larry Garvin, Back to Earth, Ohio. $275.00 – 300.00.

Snapping turtle effigy pipe, gray pottery, 4" long. Probably Caddo and Mississippian period, the pipe was found in Lee County, Arkansas. Larry Garvin, Back to Earth, Ohio. $450.00.

Turtle-shell effigy pipe, top view illustrating the pipe bowl and stem hole. Only 1⅜" in diameter, this near-miniature pipe form is from Bowie County, Texas. Larry Garvin, Back to Earth, Ohio. $275.00 – 300.00.

Pelican effigy pipe, brown pottery, narrow stem and large bowl. The pipe is 2¼" high and 2¾" long. It is from northeastern Texas. Larry Garvin, Back to Earth, Ohio. $350.00.

Monolithic axe effigy pipe, probably Creek Indian and ca. 1720 – 1830. This form was likely copied from artifacts from the Mississippian period. It is made of pottery and came from Blount County, Alabama. Gary Henry collection, North Carolina. $300.00+.

Bear head effigy pipe, pottery, ca. 1670. This pipe has tooth marks on the stem and measures 2⅝ x 4¾" long. The bear's head is broken and glued. This example would be northeastern United States. Dave Summers, Native American Artifacts, Victor, New York. $1,750.00.

Bird head effigy pipe, pottery, probably Mississippian period. It measures 4" long, 3¼" high, and is 1" wide. It was found near Epps, Poverty Point, Louisiana. Wilfred Dick collection, Mississippi. $300.00 – 450.00.

Human head effigy pottery pipe, face toward smoker, ca. AD 1550. This pipe was broken in three pieces and is glued. It is 4⅛" long, Iroquoian, from western New York. Dave Summers, Native American Artifacts, Victor, New York. $950.00.

Turtle effigy pipes, tan pottery, left example 1⅜" high and 2½" long. These are Ft. Ancient in origin, Mississippian period. Both came from Brown County, Ohio. Larry Garvin, Back to Earth, Ohio. $300.00 each.

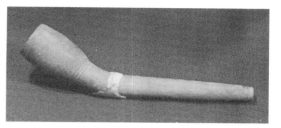

Pottery pipe, gun-sight type, early historic period. It measures 2 x 4"; the small raised knob was probably a fastening aid for securing pipe bowl to stem. Jackson County, Alabama. Private collection, Georgia. $500.00.

Pottery pipe, historic era, tulip style. Broken in two pieces, this pipe is ca. 1660 and from New York. Dave Summers, Native American Artifacts, Victor, New York. $350.00.

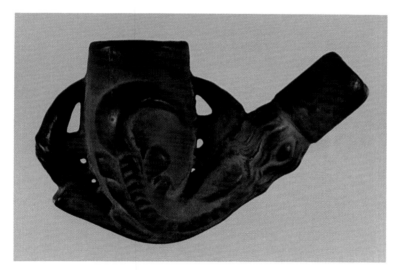

Trade-era pottery pipe, historic, dark brown color. This pipe measures 1¾" high and 2¾" long. Note polish on the talons of the bird foot from use. Keith Bosso collection, Missouri. Museum quality.

Types of Indian Pipes

There are dozens of pipe types in North America. Many of them, like the Mic-mac and disc, are well known to collectors. That is, the pipes have a distinctive style that even with minor variations can be easily recognized. This is especially true of those pipes that have a wide geographic distribution or exist in fairly large numbers.

Types and sub-types are important in that often enough study has been done to obtain at least a general idea of what the pipes were usually made of, where they were used, and how old they are.

Pipes, however, as a family artifact class have the widest number of individual styles, many of them evidently one-of-a-kind. This in fact is one reason pipe collecting is so interesting: One never quite knows what might turn up. Of all the many types of prehistoric Indian pipes in North America, and in terms of overall sheer numbers, probably half are made up of the tubular and the elbow types with variations.

One of the largest handled disc pipes found was about 9" long, with a disc about 4⅖" across. It was made of Minnesota catlinite and was found in La Crosse County, Wisconsin. (West, George A. *Tobacco, Pipes and Smoking Customs of the American Indians, Part I,* Text. 1934, p 207.)

A number of stone pipe examples from along the Atlantic Coast in tubular form with angled bowl were made quite thin, either in bowl thickness alone or in both stem and bowl. Usually made of steatite or chlorite, material thickness in such scarce examples often did not exceed 1/16".

One Mic-mac sub-variety has the usual rounded bowl and narrowed middle. The base, however, is cone-shaped and tapers to a point at the bottom. The pipe variety is sometimes called a "bottle stopper." (Beauchamp, William M. "Polished Stone Articles Used by the New York Aborigines." *New York State Museum Bulletin* Vol. 4 No. 18. November 1897, p 49 figure 116.)

While discoidals were fairly common on Mississippian sites, a pipe in the shape of a discoidal is quite unusual. Yet, one was found made of close-grained sandstone on the Feurt site (Ft. Ancient) in Scioto County, Ohio. The bowl and stem were drilled at about right angles, and the pipe was both tally marked and incised. (*Artifacts.* Vol. 6 No. 2. 1976, p 8 figure 8.)

Some Atlantic Coast pipes had long, narrow tapered stems and a raised, flared bowl at one end. Made in both pottery and stone, some examples came from shell heaps in Maryland. A fine dark red chlorite pipe from North Carolina was 11" long with a 9¼" stem. (McGuire, Joseph D. "Pipes and Smoking Customs of the American Aborigines," *Report of U. S. National Museum.* 1897, pp 609 – 612.)

Large elbow pipes in the Southeastern U. S. made of stone and having a squared cross-section may be from the Copena people. The time-period is Woodland for Alabama and Tennessee. (Thompson, Ben. "Indian Pipes," *Central States Archeological Journal.* Vol 20 No. 1. January 1973, p 13.)

Pipe form or type distribution can be broadly stated but it is also a complex subject. "It is quite likely that pipes were more generally exchanged among tribes than other artifacts. Possibly, one should except copper, but I am not even sure of that. We find Northern forms South, Eastern types West, and a general indication that aboriginal barter or trade in pipes were extensive." (Moorehead, Warren K. *The Stone Age in North America,* Vol. II. 1910, p 30.)

Ceramic pipes with tapering extensions below the bowl and short stems joining at right angles were made by the late prehistoric Jersey Bluff people of the Missouri-Illinois region. Woodland period, one example found in 1970 was about 3" high. (*Central States Archaeological Journal.* Vol. 17 No. 3. 1970, p 131.)

One early historic northeastern pottery pipe, an effigy form of the trumpet, was called the "pinch-faced" type. This was a crouching figure carrying a burden, and the human-like face was formed by pinching clay between thumb and finger. (Orr, Rowland B. *Archaeological Report/1925 – 1928.* The legislative Assembly of Ontario. 1928, pp 62 – 63.)

Some Indians along the Klamath River of northern California used tubular pipes. These had yew wood stems and steatite bowls; some were small and had a bowl with a thimble-sized interior. (Harrington, John P. (citing Thompson).

Tobacco Among the Karuk Indians of California. 1932, p 32.)

Today, disc pipes are considered to have the pipe bowl in the center of the disc and the stem hole at the end of the elongated keel or narrow base. A hundred years ago, the reverse was thought true, for several reasons. The small size of many disc holes seemed more appropriate for stem end than tobacco, while the often larger keel hole seemed suited more for tobacco than the tip of a wooden stem. And, the polished disc (often incised with designs) should face the smoker so as to be better appreciated. This was all one-sided reasoning and there are just as many common-sense observations for the other way around.

A pipe variety sometimes seen may have bowl and stem holes of similar design and even, sometimes, similar size. "Among the many types of pipes found, none are more remarkable than the biconical type, found mostly in the Central States area. The term, biconical is used because both basal and stem perforations are cone shaped, possibly from drilling with a flint drill, with the smaller ends of cones meeting at the center of the pipe at right angles to each another." (Thompson, Ben. "Indian Pipes," *Central States Archaeological Journal.* Vol. 20 No. 1. 1973, p 14.)

The Point Peninsula people to the east of Lake Ontario (New York) and Ontario (Canada) were probably related to the Intrusive Mound people since they shared some traits. One was the straight-based platform pipe with a flared bowl top; a fine example was found at the Port Maitland site, Ontario, in 1907. It was made of greenish-black steatite and had the diagnostic ridged stem hole. This well-polished example was 8$\frac{19}{32}$" long. (Ritchie, William A. *The Pre-Iroquoian Occupations of New York State.* 1944, pp 115, 169, plate 78.)

Adena modified tube pipes have a side extension, often long, that joins the tube. While in profile it would appear that the extension would be the bowl, it is actually the small-holed stem and mouthpiece. (Mayer-Oakes, William J. *Prehistory of the Upper Ohio Valley.* 1955, pp 214 – 215.)

While many collectors prefer stone pipes over pottery, some of the baked clay pipes are quite well made and attractive. "Illinois pottery pipes are among the most interesting forms of their ceramic art and some of the best modeling is found in them. ...Iroquois clay pipes in fact are the most carefully made and best modeled clay pipes made by the aborigines of North America north of Mexico." (Parker, Arthur C. *The Archeological History of New York, Part I.* 1922, pp 146, 148.)

Adena tubular pipes of the eastern Midwest exist in half a dozen different but related styles. These include cigar-shaped in stone and pottery, straight tubular with blocked end, constricted tubular with the stem end crimped, modified tubular with side protrusion, flared tubular with spread and flattened mouthpiece, and the rare tube pipe in effigy form. (Dragoo, Don W. *Mounds for the Dead.* 1963, pp 181, 183 – 184.)

The Hamilton people of Late Woodland times (ca. AD 500 – 1000) in Tennessee made long-stemmed, small-bowl pipes of stone. "The outstanding trait of the Hamilton pipes is the long stem which was not supplemented with an additional mouthpiece of wood or cane as is the case with the Mississippi pipes." (Lewis, Thomas M. N. and Madeline Kneberg. *Hiwassee Island.* 1946/1970, p 117.)

Basket Maker pipes from Arizona, while scarce, were sometimes made of pottery. Little more than bowls, they were larger than stone examples from the same cultural period, and small holes were at the base and in line with the relatively large bowl interiors. Extrapolating from other Basket Maker pipes, the hollow stems would have been made of wood or bird bone. (Kidder, Alfred V. and Samuel Guernsey. *Archeological Explorations in Northeastern Arizona.* 1919, p 188.)

Will County, Illinois, produced a very fine platform pipe, found in three pieces (broken by farming equipment) over a four-year period. The Woodland pipe, made of greenish-black steatite, had a ridge over the stem drill hole; the pipe was 1$\frac{7}{8}$" high and 5$\frac{3}{4}$" long. (Butkus, Edmund. "A Spectacular Platform Pipe Find," *Central States Archaeological Journal.* Vol. 20 No. 2. 1973, pp 84 – 85, 88.)

As an aid in generally identifying protohistoric pipes in the Southeast, one of the features was the presence of a rim atop the bowl. (King, J. C. H. *Smoking Pipes of the North American Indian.* 1977, p 14.)

On the south shore of Lake Huron, the Huron Indians in pre-French days had a variety of pipe styles. "Tobacco pipes, which were made of fired clay or stone, included both the elbow and the vase-shaped types. Among the former, trumpet-shaped bowls and other elaborate shapes were quite plentiful and represent a high degree of artistry in their manufacture. The vase-shaped types were probably more plentiful and were used with added stems of bone, reed, or wood." (Quimby, George Irving. *Indian Culture and European Trade Goods.* 1966, p 36.)

There are some southern tubular pipes in effigy forms (usually birds) that are almost a separate figure on the outside of the pipe. In real life this would appear to be a bird sitting, for example, on a log. This may well be the early form. Examples that may be later in development have the tube part as the bird's body, with the bowl at right angles and on the bird's back. It is as if in later times the pipe and bird were more unified.

Caddo stone pipes, Spiro variety, are also known as "T" pipes. The tall, straight bowls are located near the center or near one end of the long stem. Two such pipes from the Hughes Mound near Muskogee, Oklahoma, were 9½ and 20" long, respectively. (Perino, Gregory. "Some Outstanding Artifacts Acquired by the Gilcrease Institute in 1969." *Central States Archaeological Journal,* Vol. 17 No. 1. 1970, pp 30 – 31.)

Many finely crafted and finished tubular pipes have long been recognized as Adena in origin, Early Woodland in time. "The tubular tobacco pipe, and more specifically the blocked-end tubular form, is the most widespread of all traits associated with the Ohio Valley Adena culture. At least 79 have been excavated from the six largest sites while many more are reported from the smaller surface sites." (Swartz, B. K. Jr., Editor. *Adena: The Seeking of an Identity.* Ball State University. 1971, p 67.)

Sometimes pipes tend to be of one or several types from a site. Yet the Anker site along the Little Calumet River in Illinois produced many different types. The most common were disc and elbow pipes. However, also found were examples of vase-shaped, tapered-base, rectangular block, truncated cone, bear head effigy, human head effigy, and an incised pipe that was celt-shaped. (Bluhm, Elaine A., Editor. *Chicago Area Archaeology.* Illinois Archaeological Survey Bulletin No. 3. 1961, pp 91, 122 – 125.)

Monitor pipes — plain bowls nearly centered on a flattened platform — have long attracted admiration. "The monitor pipe is one upon which more care has been expended in boring its bowl and stem and in grinding and polishing the surface than upon any other type of pipe. There is no pipe more striking or better marked in its characteristics, and the delicacy of its finish, as well as its outline, is surpassed by no other." (Orr, Rowland B. *Archaeological Report/1926 – 1928.* The Legislative Assembly of Ontario. 1928, pp 57-61.)

Pipe style in some cases may have come from other examples. "There are unique types of pipes found in various parts of the country, particularly in Georgia and the Carolinas, some of which appear to have followed copper originals and some to have been influenced by European models." (Hodge, Frederick Webb. *Handbook of American Indians North of Mexico, Part 2.* BAE Bulletin 30. 1912, p 260.)

The Largo phase of the Anasazi culture in north-central New Mexico had elbow pipes with an unusual feature. The pipe bowls had two small projections which served as feet when the pipes were set down. (Wormington, H. M. *Prehistoric Indians of the Southwest.* The Denver Museum of Natural History. 1947/73, pp 102, 104.)

Intrusive Mound people of Late Woodland times are well known for their fine platform pipes, many of steatite materials. "The classic pipes of the Intrusive Mound culture from the east coast area to what is now western Indiana, and from North Carolina north into Canada, were made of the darker hues of steatite. One exception of the foregoing statement is, those made of Ohio pipestone in the central area. I myself, feel we can postulate the Intrusive Mound culture pipecrafters felt an akinship for dark steatite as the Hopewellian pipemakers did for Ohio pipestone." (Hart, Gordon L. "Kenneth O. Palmer Pipe No. 1," *The Redskin.* Vol. 10 No. 1. 1975, p 3.)

Fisher culture people of the eastern Upper Midwest made pipes in the period AD 1300 – 1400. "Tobacco pipes were made of stone and had separate stems of wood or bone. Some pipes were vase shaped. Others were small, equal-armed elbow types." (Quimby, George Irving. *Indian Life in the Upper Great Lakes.* 1960, pp 99, 102.)

Among the better made stone pipes are those turned out by the post-Hopewell and Late Woodland Indians known as the Intrusive Mound. "The 'Intrusive Mound' people modified the 'monitor' style of Hopewell pipe by creating an elbow style with a short frontal projection, thin walled highly developed spool shaped bowl and a flat base stem. Almost exclusively, the 'Intrusive' people preferred the use of blackish green steatite, a material ignored by Hopewell." (Berner, John F. "The Art of Pipe Collecting and Preservation – Part II," *Prehistoric Artifacts.* Vol. 22 No. 4. 1988, pp 27-28.)

Medium-long and thin-stemmed pottery pipes are fairly typical of the Caddo people. Examples found in Howard County, Arkansas, are called Haley pipes. (*Central States Archaeological Journal.* Vol. 33 No. 3. 1986, p 149.)

In the northeastern United States, Iroquois pipes have long been found, and some types were certainly made in historic times. "The typical Iroquoian pipe has a graceful curve in the stem and bowl resembling that of the hunting horn, and is from three to ten inches long. The bowls are usually decorated with human effigies, birds, or reptiles, all facing the smoker. They are most frequently made of hard burned clay without tempering, although sometimes the material is stone." (Lilly, Eli. *Prehistoric Antiquities of Indiana.* 1937, p 196.)

The Adena people of the eastern Midwest are well known for their tubular pipes made in pastel shades of Ohio pipestone. However another people of about the same time and a bit to the west of the Adena homeland, the Red Ochre people, also made pipes. These tubular pipes were large, gently tapered and with thin walls, though usually made of close-grained sandstone instead of pipestone.

The Flint River site in Wheeler Basin, Alabama, was an Archaic Shell Mound site with some later cultural objects. Late Archaic pipes were found. "Stone tubular pipes were made of sandstone, ground to conical form and reamed with a conical reamer at the distal end. The proximal end had a small cylindrical hole drilled into the conical bowl." (Webb, William S. and David L. DeJarnette. *The Flint River Site.* Geological Survey of Alabama. 1948, pp 49 – 50.)

Over a century ago Hupa Reservation tubular pipes were made of hardwood, stone, or a combination of wood and stone. Known examples ranged from 3 to 13" long. Some of these items may have been made purposefully for the tourist trade. (McGuire, Joseph D. "Pipes and Smoking Customs of the American Aborigines," *Report of U. S. National Museum.* 1897, pp 391 – 396.)

Some comparisons of pipes in the Northeast United States have been made, though information available since the original observations may lessen the validity of the comparisons. "Both clay and stone pipes are rare in New Jersey, and these are inferior to those of New York, where so many of the finest examples of both are found." Beauchamp, William M. *Polished Stone Articles Used by the New York Aborigines.* New York State Museum Bulletin. Vol. 4 No. 18. 1897, p 44.)

At the pueblo of Pecos, San Miguel County, New Mexico, many pipe forms were found. While 27 partial, whole, or unfinished tubular stone pipes were recovered, nearly 700 pottery pipes were counted, a ratio of 1:26. The stone pipes were made from green chloritic schist and were from 1¾ to 3¾" long. Unfinished examples show the pipes were drilled from each end, and the interior hole and exterior surface were smoothed. (Kidder, Alfred Vincent. *The Artifacts of Pecos.* Phillips Academy and Carnegie Institution. 1932, pp 1, 83 – 85, figures 59 – 61.)

The Hudson Bay pipe is a specialized form with a tall, narrow funnel-shaped bowl which expands toward the bowl top. It is centered on a thin, rectangular base which has a drilled decoration hole. This historic northern pipe was sometimes made of slate. (West, George A. *Tobacco, Pipes and Smoking Customs of the American Indians, Part II*, Plates. 1934, p 586, plate 53 figures 1 & 2.)

Some double-stemmed pipes are called "bridegroom" or "wedding" pipes, because some persons thought they were used in such a ceremony. However there is little evidence to support this suggestion.

Some 15 long, double-stemmed stone (shale) pipes came from the Spiro Mound, Le Flore County, Oklahoma. (Other reports suggest more pipes were found but not recorded.) The pipes had tall cylindrical bowls and straight stems; about half a dozen pipes also had double in-line bowls, and these were drilled from each stem end. The pipes measured from 15 to 31" in length. (Hamilton, Henry L. "The Spiro Mound," *The Missouri Archaeologist.* Vol. 14. 1952/1981, pp 38, 144 – 145, plates 20 – 21.)

Late prehistoric stone pipes are well represented in the South in some areas. "A number of excellent massive stone effigy pipes have been unearthed in Mississippi. They face away from the smoker, have flat bases, and for the most part have conical or conoidal openings." (Brown, Calvin S. *Archeology of Mississippi.* Mississippi State Geological Survey. 1926, p 249.)

Caddoan (Mississippian period) ceramic pipes from southwestern Arkansas include three types, all with conical bowls. There is a long-stemmed, a short-stemmed, and a strap-handle type with an upcurved extension of the base beyond the bowl. The strap is secured to the bowl rim. (*Central States Archaeological Journal.* Vol. 36 No. 2. 1989, p 116.)

Historic times saw a number of pipe types in use in areas such as today's Missouri. "Pipes occur in fair numbers in the Post-Contact Coalescent sites. ...The commonest form was a prowed or calumet pipe with a projection of the stem extending in front of the bowl. Bowls were either barrel-shaped or truncated cones. Elbow pipes occur with some frequency, and tubular pipes are present but rare." (Lehmer, Donald J. *Introduction to Middle Missouri Archeology.* NPS/USDL. 1971, p 150.)

At the famous Late Archaic Poverty Point site in Louisiana, a few tubular pipes were represented, mainly in the form of fragments. Two stone pipe pieces were made of brown, polished stone while another pipe section was steatite. A sandstone tube was complete. Nine broken pieces of pottery tubular pipes were also recovered. (Ford, James A., and Clarence H. Webb. *Poverty Point/A Late Archaic Site in Louisiana.* Anthropological Papers of the American Museum of Natural History, Vol. 46 Part 1. 1956, pp 103 – 104, figure 36.)

The Southeast had many pipe varieties including the Coffee Bean type, a slightly bent elbow pipe with small raised areas that resemble coffee beans. Such pipes, usually made of pottery but occasionally of steatite, often had rimmed bowls. Late in prehistoric times, the pipes date ca. 1400 – 1750. (Maus, Jim. "The Coffee Bean Pipe," *Central States Archaeological Journal.* Vol. 41 No. 4. 1994, p 185.)

One of the most unusual pipe forms in all North America was made in the Great Basin area. From the side the long bent tube is V-shaped or somewhat like a boomerang with nearly equal arms. One arm is a stem while the other is an elongated bowl. Two known examples measure, respectively, 18½" and 22¼" in total length. (Strong, Emery. *Stone Age in the Great Basin.* 1969, p 167, figure 103.)

Northern Plateau Indians used two pipe types, one of which resembled the large Plains pipes. Another had a short wooden stem and a small stone bowl. ("Guide to the Museum/First Floor," *Indian Notes and Monographs*. Museum of the American Indian, Heye Foundation. 1922, p 116.)

The late prehistoric Hagen site in Montana produced fragments of stone pipes. Pipes were of the tubular-conical type and materials used were limestone, shale, or steatite. (Mulloy, William. *The Hagen Site — A Prehistoric Village on the Lower Yellowstone*. The Work Projects Administration, The University of Montana, No. 1. 1942, pp 62 – 63, figure 31.)

Of all particular pipe types, Great Pipes had a long period of popularity. "One exception to all other forms of pipes relating to periods and cultures is the so-called 'Great Pipe' which extends from the end of early Woodland, of approximately 500 B.C. through middle Woodland almost to historic time, or approximately A.D. 1350. Within this time frame we find the same Great Pipes in affiliation with the Mississippian period people with their varied cultures from early Cahokia of A.D. 800 to Late Etowah and Spiro of A.D. 1200." (Hart, Gordon. *Hart's Prehistoric Pipe Rack*. 1978, p 15.)

Lake Winnebago people of northeastern Wisconsin ca. AD 1000 made stone pipes of the disc or disk type. "Tobacco pipes were made of polished stone, usually of catlinite, but occasionally of soapstone and sandstone. All of these pipes were of the disk-shaped variety." (Quimby, George Irving. *Indian Life in the Upper Great Lakes*. 1960, p 103.)

Tubular pipes, some of which are referred to as "cloud-blowers," may have sometimes been more than pipes. "Besides pipes, the Indians used tubes for tobacco holders; though the latter also served for other purposes, especially for bleeding or cauterizing in treatment of diseases. By setting one end over a puncture in the skin and sucking vigorously at the other end blood could be drawn safely; while by similarly placing the tube and filling it with hot water or live coals blisters could be induced." (Fowke, Gerard. "Pipes and Tubes," *Prehistoric Objects Classified and Described*. Bulletin 1, Missouri Historical Society, Department of Archaeology. 1913, p 15.)

Not much detailed information is readily available about pottery pipes in the Southwest. Kidder's collection of 668 pipes from New Mexico, however, provides much factual data. Simple tubular pipes (227) were classed as round slim, flattened slim, and heavy fat types. Elaborate tubular pipes (323) had round or oval cross-sections. There were a few (8) elbow pipes, with the remainder unclassified or fragmentary. (Kidder, Alfred Vincent. *The Artifacts of Pecos*. Phillips Academy and Carnegie Institution. 1932, p 157.)

A fine Illinois platform pipe was found in 1973 with attributes of Terminal Hopewell. The pipe description by the finder: "It is made of fossil coral and is 2⅜" long. The bowl is in the effigy of the head of a raptorial bird. The interesting thing about the pipe is that it is a transitional Hopewell pipe made when the type begins to change. The platform is straight and the stem hole is in the rear section rather than in the end facing the smoker." (Perino, Gregory. "A Platform Pipe and a Group of Cache Blades From the Knight Site, Calhoun County, Ill," *Artifacts*. Vol. 5 No. 4. 1975, p 13.)

Plains-like pipe bowls made of catlinite are quite scarce, and some have animal effigies between the tall expanded bowl and the stem end. These historic pipes at first glance resemble some Cherokee pipes, but they are distinct type and often from Canada. (West, George A. *Tobacco, Pipes and Smoking Customs of the Americian Indians*, Part II, Plates. 1934, p 756, plate 138.)

Cherokee pipes of historic times, done in steatite and with an effigy figure atop the stem between the bowl and mouthpiece, were very popular. They were exported from their homelands in the southern Appalachian Mountains. "(Illustrated are) several pipes from various sites in southern New England, which were undoubtedly made by the Cherokee Indians, and which found their way north through trade, probably in the eighteenth or latter part of the seventeenth centuries." (Willoughby, Charles C. *Antiquities of the New England Indians*. 1935, pp 184 – 186.)

A most unusual disc pipe was once acquired by the noted collector, Albert L. Addis. It was made of catlinite and the front or prow was in the effigy of a duck head, with the keel extending back under the disc and forming the duck's neck and the pipe's stem. Pipe length was about 5⅖", and the pipe was from Kentucky. (West, George A. *Tobacco, Pipes and Smoking Customs of the American Indians*, Part II, Plates. 1934, p 774, plate 147.)

A characteristic of some cultural pipe forms is the direction in which an effigy faces when set on the pipe. Effigies almost all faced the smoker for such pipes as the Hopewell platforms and the Iroquois pipes. Mississippian large platform pipes usually faced away from the smoker.

One of the few animal effigy pipes to come from Wisconsin was a turtle form in brownish-gray steatite. With the bowl set in the center of the turtle's back, the pipe was 2¼" wide and 3¼" long. (West, George A. "The Aboriginal Pipes of Wisconsin," *The Wisconsin Archaeologist*, Vol. 4 Nos. 3 – 4. 1905, pp 101 – 102.)

Effigy Mound people of Late Woodland times in southern Wisconsin made some smoking instruments. "Tobacco pipes of elbow type were made of fired clay and decorated with simple geometric designs." (Quimby, George Irving. *Indian Life in the Upper Great Lakes.* 1960, pp 84, 88.)

The Iroquois tribes dominated northeastern North America in early historic times, so their pipes are of great interest. "The smoking pipes made recently by the Iroquois consist of a stone head of moderate size, sometimes carved in the form of an animal, and used with a rather small separate stem of wood. In ancient times pottery pipes were made, often beautifully decorated with animal or human forms modeled in the round or with incised designs — a form of pipe having a short stem all of one piece with the bowl." ("Guide to the Museum/First Floor," *Indian Notes and Monographs.* Museum of the American Indian, Heye Foundation. 1922, p 24.)

Adena (Early Woodland) tubular pipes, especially those done in pipestone, have long been admired as highly artistic creations. "There were several forms of Adena tube pipes. One had a constricted or beveled mouthpiece, another a flattened flared mouthpiece with a small punctured opening. A similar tube with a small elbow projection about two-thirds of the way down the length of the hollowed tube was crafted during the Late Adena period." (Gehlbach, D. R. "Adena Artisans and Their Blocked End Tubular Pipes," *Artifacts.* Vol. 13 No. 2. 1983, p 36.)

There were a number of Late Woodland peoples who made very lovely pipes, most of them long, straight-based platform pipes with tall bowls at or near one end. The people include Intrusive Mound of the eastern Midwest, the Point Peninsula of the Northeast, and the Hamilton of the Southeast. They were also quite selective in materials used, choosing high-grade steatite and, occasionally, chlorite.

In the Upper Mississippi Valley, a group of historic tribes had pipe types related to the Plains people. The L-shaped and T-shaped pipes were smaller, with stems a little over a foot long. Big pipes were also used, with long stems. Some old pipes had very long, round stems. ("Guide to the Museum/First Floor," *Indian Notes and Monographs.* Museum of the American Indian, Heye Foundation. 1922, p 51.)

Round, flat-based pipes with a series of in-line holes around the circumference near the base have various names. They seem to have been made in late prehistoric times into historic times, some in pottery and some in steatite. "This type of pipe with more than two stems appears to be a trait found only below the Ohio River, thus becoming a true southern culture feature. The multi-stemmed pipe, circular peace pipe, chief's pipe, or council pipe are descriptive and factual names given this type." (Hart, Gordon. "The Council Pipe," *The Redskin.* Vol. 6 No. 3. 1971, p 89.)

Mic-mac pipes usually carry the name wherever they are found, but in Maine the type was sometimes called the Abnaki pipe. "This general type was and is widely used among the northern Algonquians, from the Blackfoot of the Northwest to the Nascapee of the Northeast." (Willoughby, Charles C. *Antiquities of the New England Indians.* 1935, pp 187, 190.)

Hupa pipes in northern California were of the tapered-tubular kind, with an average length of about 4½". The pipes might be all wood, all stone, or wooden stem with a carefully inset bowl of stone. These pipes were shaped with sandstone and polished with horsetail rush. (Harrington, John P. (citing Goddard) *Tobacco Among the Karuk Indians of California.* 1932, pp 28 – 29.)

Disc or disk pipes are easily recognized due to the unusual shape, and no extensive pipe grouping is complete without an example or two. "The disk pipe is a form highly sought after by collectors. The form is fairly late, occuring from around 800 AD up to the contact period. It varies greatly in quality of workmanship from very crude, unsymmetrical specimens to highly developed, beautiful examples. Many exhibit some form of decoration such as tally marks or engraving." (Wagers, Charles. "Disk Pipes," *Prehistoric Artifacts.* Vol. 23 No. 4 1989, p 14.)

The Huron Indians of the Upper Great Lakes, ca. 1600 – 1650 had a wide range of pipes for smoking. "Tobacco pipes made of fired clay or polished stone were in common use. Shapes were variable and included elbow pipes, trumpet shapes, and vase-shaped pipes. Less common were effigy forms representing humans, birds, and animals." (Quimby, George Irving. *Indian Life in the Upper Great Lakes.* 1960, pp 113, 118.)

Nodes or small, fairly regular protrusions on some late prehistoric pipes, especially in the southern United States, appear to have their counterparts on some types of pottery vessels. This may be a cultural decorating trait in both cases. Or, it may be a practical design, providing a better non-slip surface for both relatively fragile vessels and pipes. Even further, these protrusions increased surface area and helped dissipate interior heat, a matter that may or may not have been known by the makers.

Pipe use in the Midwest began more than 3000 years ago. "In the Late Archaic period the tube pipe was introduced, used through the Glacial Kame on into the Early Woodland period, and later was created in straight and modified forms by the Adena culture. Few of the earliest of this type were of art interest except to those ancient people who drilled or formed an expanded opening into a four-to-nine inch tube which was a formidable accomplishment." (Hart, Gordon. "Pondering of Prehistoric Art," *The Redskin.* Vol. 14 No. 3. 1979, p 10.)

The South originated a late prehistoric effigy type pipe of unusual form. "In several of the Southern states is found a type of image pipe which consists of a human being holding in outstretched hands a bowl or pot, which vessel constitutes the bowl of the pipe. Several of these have been described from Georgia and Tennessee." (Brown, Calvin S. *Archeology of Mississippi*. Mississippi State Geological Survey. 1926, p 264.)

The northern Pacific coastal region produced a number of unusual and distinctive pipe forms. "The pipes found along the northwest coast of America are most interesting in style, and made of a great variety of materials such as stone, ivory, bone, antler, and of these materials in combination with metal. Among the most remarkable carvers are the Haida Indians, who have been known for their artistic productions for centuries." (West, George A. "The Aboriginal Pipes of Wisconsin," *The Wisconsin Archeologist*. Vol. 4 Nos. 3 – 4, 1905, pp 110 – 111.)

Late prehistoric and early historic stone pipes with an elongated bowl as an effigy body are found from around the Great Lakes to the north and east. "The stone owl pipe and the lizard pipe...are found in the early Iroquois sites in New York and undoubtedly sites in the same period throughout the entire Iroquois area. The Province of Ontario has yielded many, numbers of them have been found in New York, still others have been found through Maryland, Virginia, and the Carolinas." (Parker, Arthur C. *The Archeological History of New York, Part* I. 1922, pp 145 – 146.)

A rare Adena modified tubular pipe was once in the Dr. Meuser collection in Ohio. Found sometime before 1939, it was made of tan sandstone. The modification to the 7¾" tube pipe was an offset projecting stem which was 3¾" long. The pipe came from Warren County, Ohio. (*Prehistoric Artifacts*. Vol. 22 No. 4. 1988, p 21, cover.)

One type of disc pipe is called a medicine bundle pipe, with triangular-shaped extensions that connect with the disc and are secured to the stem end. (Fuller, Steve. "Historic Period Pipe Bowls," *Prehistoric America*. Vol. 24 No. 2. 1990, p 9.)

Pipe style progression in North America is a complex topic, but the Far West is briefly described here: "In chronology it is impossible to draw conclusions because fashion or style developed some quite fancy forms early in the use of pipes and many straight tubes remained into historic times. But in area a definite broad conclusion can be reached, in the course of its development the pipe grew into the elbow forms with all their many variations. A few elbow types are found in northeastern California, brought by contact through Nevada and Wyoming and similarly a few on the Columbia River. ...But the Western pipes are almost exclusively either tubes or bowls with the stem hole in the bottom." (Miles, Charles. "Evolution of Pipes," *Central States Archaeological Journal*. Vol. 19 No. 2. 1972, p 84.)

Caddo pipes of pottery have long interested collectors and amateur archaeologists; there are several varieties. Coles Creek pipes have 6 – 8" stems and should date AD 700 – 800. Some Gibson Aspect pipes have much longer stems and tiny bowls, and date to AD 900 – 1000. Haley pipes (Haley focus, Gibson aspect) are more heavily constructed and well made, and are ca. AD 1000 – 1300. Additionally, there is a large platform pipe which is approximately AD 900 – 1200. (Kizzia, Glen, and Roy Hathcock. "About Certain Caddo Pipes," *Prehistoric Artifacts*. Vol. 23 No. 4. 1989, p 30.)

Mic-mac (or Micmac) early historic pipes generally had a plain bowl, narrowed bowl base, and a short platform stem area in many shapes. They were highly transportable and a favorite pipe over much of the eastern United States, especially northern parts. "Nearly twenty Micmacs were found at Fort Michelmakinac which indicates that some Micmacs may be of white manufacture. Another Micmac was found at Grosse Pointe, Michigan, that had the date 1697 carved into it." (Koup, Bill. "Micmac Pipes," *Prehistoric Artifacts*. Vol. 23 No. 4. 1989, p 16.)

George A. West, early authority on Indian pipes, lists three varieties of disc pipes. These are the handled disc pipe with disc extension, the handleless disc pipe with such a short stem that the disc covers it, and, the high-bowled (or long-stemmed) type with a relatively small disc. (West, George A. "The Aboriginal Pipes of Wisconsin," *The Wisconsin Archeologist*. Vol. 4 Nos. 3 – 4. 1905, 134 – 140.)

The South has provided a few examples of an unusual effigy pipe, this being the image of a left hand, with the pipe bowl in the hand and the stem formed by the wrist. An example from western Tennessee was made of near-black chlorite, 3" high and 6" long. Another example, from Mississippi County, Arkansas, was made of near-black pottery with shell temper. It was 3" long. (McGuire, Joseph D. "Pipes and Smoking Customs of the American Aborigines," *Report of U. S. National Museum*. 1897, p 441 figure 69, p 540 figure 162.)

A perhaps unique late prehistoric effigy form might be called a pipe-on-a-pipe. The sandstone image, 5⅖" high, depicts a seated human holding a large elbow pipe with rounded stem and rim. The pipe here is the actual smoking pipe, and the effigy came from southwestern Mississippi. (Brown, Calvin S. *Archeology of Mississippi*. Mississippi State Geological Survey. 1926, p 264, figure 227.)

Northern Maidu pipes were always tubular, generally short, and usually wooden. Stone pipes were made as well, often of steatite. When a pipe from earlier times was picked up by later Indians, the pipe was considered mysterious and treated with care. (Harrington, John P. (citing Dixon) *Tobacco Among the Karuk Indian of California.* 1932, pp 29 – 30.)

The head and neck portion of the famous Blind Wolf Pipe are echoed in an effigy tubular pipe from Williams Island, Tennessee. The sculpting is similar and no eyes are indicated for this pipe, which measures 2¾ x 9" long. (McGuire, Joseph D. "Pipes and Smoking Customs of the American Aborigines," *Report of U. S. National Museum.* 1897, p 400 figure 41.)

Hopewell Indians, makers of the classic effigy platform pipes of the Ohio and Illinois regions, actually extended several states further westward. Animal and bird effigy pipes have been found in these locations and about 100 mounds were noted years ago. (Shetrone, Henry Clyde. *The Mound Builders.* 1930, pp 330 – 331.)

Referring to tube pipes of Early Woodland period, Quimby remarks on their scarcity in the Upper Great Lakes. "Stone tubes similar to those identified as smoking pipes in adjacent regions have been found in at least one of the excavated Early Woodland sites of the Upper Great Lakes region. Moreover, occasional surface finds of tubular pipes have been made in the region. But tubular pipes are rare in the Upper Great Lakes and probably are an expression of the introduction of smoking from other regions lying south or east." (Quimby, George Irving. *Indian Life in the Upper Great Lakes.* 1960, p 70.)

At the late prehistoric Reeve site in northern Ohio, four kinds of stone pipes made up 57% of the village finds. These were vase-shaped, bird effigy, ovoid, and keel-shaped. (Ahlstrom, Richard M. *Prehistoric Pipes — A Study of Reeve Village Site, Lake County, Ohio.* 1979, p 50.)

Tubular pipes enjoyed widespread use across North America, including in the Southwest. One example, ca. AD 1300, originated in central Arizona. Made of steatite and with a small stem hole, it was 2" thick and 5" long. (Wesolowski, A. J. "Southwestern Tobacco Pipes," *Prehistoric Artifacts.* Vol. 23 No. 3. 1989, p 7.)

Eskimo pipes were made up of various materials, often with the stems wrapped with seal-skin or sinew thongs which shrank tightly after being put on wet. Some bowls were made of iron, slate, or walrus ivory, with a copper lining. Stems might be made of wood (birch or willow), split into two longitudinal sections, and lashed tightly together. Pipes could easily be taken apart for cleaning. (McGuire, Joseph D. "Pipes and Smoking Customs of the American Aborigines," *Report of U. S. National Museum.* 1897, pp 590 – 592.)

Certain roughly made stone pipes are sometimes still called pebble pipes today. "Pebble Pipes…are simply nodules of rock containing a deeply eroded depression, used as a bowl, the stem hole being supplied by man." (West, George A. *Tobacco, Pipes and Smoking Customs of the American Indians, Part I*, Text. 1934, p 129.)

Tube or cylinder-like pipes are one of the basic pipe configurations in prehistoric times across the country. "Authors of articles on tubular pipes agree that these pipes are the earliest and most commonly occurring pipes throughout North America. They extend from prehistoric to historic times. …These pipes are usually plain with raised rings in some area, mostly at the center, but several have decorations in animal forms, also. The materials used in tubular pipes include bone, wood, sandstone, steatite, catlinite, and combinations of wood, stone, and metal." (King, Rose. "Smoke Signals of Yesteryear," *Central States Archaeological Journal.* Vol. 17 No. 2. 1970, pp 54 – 55.)

A large biconical tubular pipe of steatite, probably from the Southeast, had an unusual extension at one end. The pipe was about 10½" long, and the projection of several inches was in the form of a snake head. (Brown, Allen. *Indian Relics and Their Values.* 1942, p 75 figure 118.)

Certain elbow pipes were once referred to as double conoidal because of the two wide and tapered cone-shaped holes. "In these pipes the bowl and stem holes consist of conoidal excavations, made at right angles and meeting at their apexes. Their shape varies more widely than that of any other pipe, some being nothing more than approximately square blocks, unadorned, while others are fine effigies." (Lilly, Eli. *Prehistoric Antiquities of Indiana.* 1937, p 196.)

Two kinds of stone pipes in the eastern Midwest were almost always made with great artistic skill. One was the lifelike Hopewell effigy platform pipe, highly developed and realistically detailed. The other was the straight-based Intrusive Mound platform pipe in dark steatite, with flowing lines and elegant proportion.

An unusual vase-shaped human-face effigy pipe from Wisconsin, gray limestone and 2½" high, had a unique locking stem: "(It was) fitted with an old bone stem 3½" long, and so made that a half turn is necessary before it can be withdrawn from the stem hole." (West, George A. "The Aboriginal Pipes of Wisconsin," *The Wisconsin Archeologist.* Vol. 4 Nos. 3 – 4. 1905, pp 100 – 101.)

Kaskaskia Village, an historic Indian site in southern Illinois, produced a number of pipes of different kinds. Of special note were the many Mic-mac pipes, whole and fragmentary. (Grimm, R. E. *Prehistoric Art.* The Greater St. Louis Archaeological Society. 1953, pp 80 – 81.)

The early historic Indians of what is now the area of Indiana, Illinois, Michigan, and Wisconsin had Woodland lifeways and pipe types from further west. "The smoking pipes used by the tribes of this group bear close resemblance to those of the Plains, consisting of a massive T-shape or L-shape bowl of red or black stone, with a long, usually flat, wooden stem, often highly embellished with carving, quillwork, and beadwork." ("Guide to the Museum/First Floor," *Indian Notes and Monographs*. Museum of the American Indian, Heye Foundation. 1922, pp 31, 36.)

A very good time-line of southern Ohio's Mississippian-era pipes has been worked out, based partly on Prufer and Shane's *Blain Village* book. It is as follows: Early Ft. Ancient (AD 950 – 1250), elbow pipes of the equal-arm, elongated stem, and keel-like stem types; Middle Ft. Ancient (AD 1250 – 1400), elbow pipes of the egg-shaped and equal-arm types, plus flat-based platform and effigy types; Late Ft. Ancient (AD 1450 – 1750), more decorated and elaborate types. (Gehlbach, D. R. "Pipe Chronology Within the Ohio Fort Ancient Tradition," *Artifacts*. Vol. 9 No. 1. 1979, p 5.)

Vase- or urn-shaped stone pipe bowls are commonly found in the eastern United States, as far north as the St. Lawrence River and south shores of Lakes Erie and Ontario, and as far south as North Carolina and Virginia. (McGuire, Joseph D. "Pipes and Smoking Customs of the American Aborigines," *Report of U. S. National Museum*. 1897, p 428.)

Mic-macs have a high bowl narrowed at the top, a thin waist or middle, and an angular base or keel that contains the stem hole. They, like the disc, are late prehistoric in origin but went on into historic times. Widely distributed from the Atlantic to the Rockies, north beyond the Great Lakes and south almost to the Gulf, older forms may have a rounded base that is not perforated with a carrying or securi-

ty or decorative hole. (West, George A. *Tobacco, Pipes and Smoking Customs of the American Indians, Part I,* Text. 1934, pp 228 – 229.)

The greatest recovery of Hopewell platform pipes occurred in 1846 during the excavations by Squier and Davis in the Scioto Valley of Ohio. At Mound City Group (now Hopewell Culture National Monument) just north of Chillicothe the unimposing Mound of the Pipes (Mound No. 8) produced "...upwards of two hundred stone tobacco pipes," many of effigy forms. These included animals, birds, and human heads. (Shetrone, Henry Clyde. *The Mound Builders*. 1930, p 213.)

The first tubular pipes in the eastern Midwest were from the Late Archaic period, ca. 1500 BC. "The archaic form typically is tapered with a larger bowl section. Highly developed versions resemble a baseball bat. The form is widespread in the eastern United States, with two classic cultural associations. These archaic cultures are the Glacial Kame people of the Ohio, Indiana, Michigan area, and the Kentucky Cave people of south central Kentucky, north central Tennessee. Scattered finds of this pipe type can happen most anywhere however." (Wagers, Charles. "Tube Pipes," *Prehistoric Artifacts*. Vol. 23 No. 4. 1989, p 7.)

A type of late historic effigy pipe was made by the Malecite Indians in New Brunswick, Canada. One example, made of blue-black slate, had a rounded bowl with two animal effigies. The smallest was above the stubbed stem, while the larger was fastened to the back of the bowl. This pipe was just over 1¾" high and had a removable wooden stem 8⅝" long. (Laidlaw, Col. George E. "Ontario Effigy Pipes in Stone," *Twenty-Seventh Annual Archaeological Report/1915*. The Legislative Assembly of Ontario. 1915, pp 58 – 59.)

Miniature Hopewell platform pipe, dark green Ohio pipestone, 1⅝" long and 1⅛" high. It is highly polished and delicately carved and finished. Ohio. Len and Janie Weidner collection, Ohio. $700.00.

L-shaped effigy pipe, maroon catlinite with lighter speckles and short stem. Historic, the human figure embraces the front of the tall bowl. At 2½" high, this pipe is ex-collections Phillips and Wagers. Marquette County, Wisconsin. Len and Janie Weidner collection, Ohio. $1,200.00.

L-shaped pipe, dark steatite, 3" long. This is a highly developed pipe with under-bowl extension, drilled crest, squared stem, and incised stem sides and bowl top. Historic, it is possibly a Great Lakes example. Len and Janie Weidner collection, Ohio. $600.00.

Double-stem pipe, rounded bowl, ca. 1500 – 1600. This early pipe in black steatite is nicely polished, 2" long and 2½" high. #GW-372 is from Franklin County, Pennsylvania. Iron Horse collection. $400.00 – 500.00.

Council pipe, reddish-gray pottery, 4¼" in diameter. Also called a "stump" pipe, this late prehistoric–historic pipe is from Hardin County, Tennessee. Len and Janie Weidner collection, Ohio. $750.00.

Catlinite artifacts, 1800s, as follow with figurine 4⅜" high: Top left and top right, T-shape pipes. Bottom left, unusual and expressive, perhaps a child's toy. $395.00. Bottom right, steatite fish pipe, unknown age, Tennessee. $695.00. Pipe values $450.00 – 1,250.00. Larry Lantz, First Mesa, Indiana.

L-shaped or elbow pipe in unusual material, dense Canadian slate, 2⅞" high. The bowl is the long section with expansion and the bowl top is ringed. This highly polished black example is from Ohio. Len and Janie Weidner collection, Ohio. $450.00.

Catlinite elbow pipe and wooden stem with brass trade tacks for decoration, this set is ca. 1890 – 1910. The set was obtained by the owner from a Santa Barbara, California, collector/dealer in 1991. J. Steve and Anita Shearer collection, California. $750.00.

Double-tube or medicine-tube pipe, very carefully made of steatite and highly polished. Size is 1½ x 5½". Made in the late BC centuries, this excellent example is from Colbert County, Alabama. Private collection, Ohio. Museum grade.

Ovate pipe with drilled decoration holes, reed stem, ca. 1450 – 1550. It is made of olive-green pipestone and measures 2½" high. Pipe #CYG-89 is from Cayuga County, New York. Derek Prindle collection. $750.00 – 900.00.

Effigy Pipes

Effigy pipes are those that depict a small-scale (usually, but not always) living object or creature. Pipes with effigies began fairly early, for there are a few tubular pipes from the Late Archaic that had lizard-like animals carved on their surfaces.

The Adena people of the eastern United States made a very few effigy tubular pipes. The Adena pipe of Ross County, Ohio, possibly depicting a deformed human male, is certainly the most famous prehistoric pipe in all North America. Some of the other Adena tubular pipes portray birds or some kind of interaction between birds and humans

Effigy pipes reached an artistic peak with the platform pipes of the Middle Woodland Hopewell Indians. This peak was only approached by Great Pipes, a few Late Woodland examples, and many large and small pipes in the Mississippian time-frame. Others forms were made by late prehistoric peoples of the Northeast and the Northwest.

Hopewell pipes were usually made of Ohio pipestone, though deposits in Pennsylvania and Illinois were also worked. Hopewell artisans usually depicted birds and animals known to them, and many are miniature true-to-life forms. The scarce and lovely examples are so valued that even broken pipes can bring surprising sums today.

Great Pipes were effigy in form and the usual subject was birds of some kind. Birds of prey were favorites and many seem to be hawks, eagles, and owls, which neatly relates to day and night. Great Pipes were apparently made for several thousand years and seem to be the effigy pipes with the greatest time span.

Late Woodland peoples, perhaps designing on the earlier Hopewell pipes, made some effigy platform pipes. Usually these had a long, flat stem with the bowl at one end set at about a right angle or greater in relation to the stem. Whereas pipestone dominated the Middle Woodland, steatite came to be favored in Late Woodland times.

Mississippian people over much of the central and southern United States produced countless effigy pipes. Their subject matter was endless and included humans, birds, and animals plus objects like deer hooves and monolithic axes. Much of the Mississippian pipe art depicted heads alone, though creatures like frogs were easily portrayed whole.

Cherokee pipes are noted for effigies set atop the stem, between the mouthpiece and bowl. Humans and animals were favored subjects, both created in direct and life-like poses. Iroquois pipes were often of birds or animals, in fact any figures that fitted the trumpet style of pipe. Many other Indian groups made at least a few effigy pipes, and all are admired and heavily collected today.

Certainly at least indirectly related to effigy pipes are those that are otherwise plain except that they have incised or raised figures on them. Almost any pipe surface could serve as a blank canvas for the artisan, who worked the design with a pointed flint or chert tool. Some are engravings of almost any living thing, even abstract and meandering and unknown lines. All add to the appeal and value of pipes.

Oval bowl-type pipe with snake effigy worked on the exterior surface. The pipe is 1½ x 2" and is made of fine-grained sandstone. This is a Ft. Ancient pipe, from Pike County, Ohio. Private collection, Ohio. $900.00.

Effigy pipe, curled snake form, gray-green Ohio pipestone. This pipe is 2⅝" long, with the bowl just in front of the snake's head. The pipe has been in several well-known collections, including Dr. Young and Payne. Clay County, Indiana. Len and Janie Weidner collection, Ohio. $1,250.00.

Effigy pipe, fox image, platform 2⅜" long. This is Hopewell, Middle Woodland, and the pipe is made of red Ohio pipestone. Ross County, Ohio. Robin Fiser collection, Ohio. Unlisted.

Hopewell effigy platform pipe with turtle image around the bowl top, pipe 3" long. It is made of amber-brown pipestone and is in perfect condition. The only thing more rare than Hopewell platform pipes are Hopewell effigy platform pipes, of which this is a top example. This specimen was found in 1909 in Fulton County, Illinois. Len and Janie Weidner collection, Ohio. $10,000+.

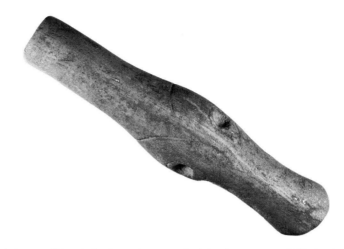

Bird effigy pipe, Hopewell, with image and pipe salvaged by reworking both ends. Made of close-grained brown stone, this pipe measures 2¾" long and is one of the few authentic Hopewell effigy pipes in private collections. Eastern Midwest. Len and Janie Weidner collection, Ohio. $3,800.00.

Adena effigy tubular pipe, probably the spoon-bill duck, carved from yellowish sandstone. This pipe measures 7½" long and is carefully finished in all respects. There are only half a dozen or so Adena effigy tube pipes in undamaged condition, of which this is one of the better examples. Ohio. Len and Janie Weidner collection, Ohio. Museum grade.

Bottom view of the Hendricks County, Indiana, pipe. Note the number of collector identification marks on this piece, put on since discovery in 1954. Such information is helpful, adding greatly to provenance. Larry Garvin, Back to Earth, Ohio. $900.00.

Effigy elbow pipe, 2⅞" high and 3⅞" long, made of dark stone. It has facial features on the lower front and a flat base. This fine pipe may be Woodland and was found in Hendricks County, Indiana, in 1954. Larry Garvin, Back to Earth, Ohio. $900.00.

Frog effigy pipe made of fine-grained dark brown sandstone with some polish, with bowl emerging above the frog's head. Size is 1½ x 3" long and 2" high. Probably Woodland period, this artifact is from central Tennessee. Bill Mesnard collection, New Jersey. $500.00.

Bear (?) effigy pipe, brown hard-stone, 2⅛" high and 4⅛" long. This may be a Mississippian period pipe, ex-collection Wagers and Hilliard. Numbered 5374 and VH-200, it came from McCracken County, Kentucky. Larry Garvin, Back to Earth, Ohio. $1,550.00.

Effigy pipe, bear figure, Fort Ancient people. This massive example is 5¼" long and 4" high, made of tan granite-like hardstone. It was found sometime between 1900 and the 1920s and came from Lincoln County, Kentucky. Len and Janie Weidner collection, Ohio. $4,500.00.

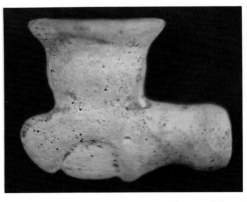

Elbow pipe, bear effigy face, probably Woodland period. It measures 1⅞ x 3¼", is made of sandstone, and came from Cheatham County, Tennessee. Dale and Betty Roberts collection, Iowa; Betty Roberts photograph. $450.00.

Effigy pipe, monolithic axe form, Mississippian period. It is made of light colored pottery and measures 2¼" long and 1⅞" high. Murray County, Georgia. Collection of Bruce Butts, Winterville, Georgia. $1,000.00.

Axe effigy pipe, probably Mississippian period, with bowl formed by celt head and pipe formerly with wooden stem. #A\C is made of light brown pottery and the stem is 2½" long, bowl height being 2¼". Bartow County, Georgia. Iron Horse collection. $750.00 – 850.00.

Human head effigy pipe, late prehistoric/early historic and ca. 1550. This interesting form is 4" high and was found in Michigan. Collection of Jim Bickel, Huntington, Indiana. $200.00.

Human head effigy pipe, side view, Mississippian period. Though the stem is missing, the head/pipe bowl itself is a small work of art. It is 2" in diameter and 2½" high. This pottery piece came from Ohio. Collection of and photograph by Duane Treest, Illinois. $50.00 – 75.00.

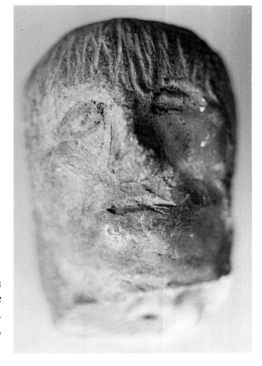

Human head effigy pipe, front view, Mississippian period, in pottery made of untempered clay. The stem is missing from this pipe which is 2½" high. Ohio. Collection of and photograph by Duane Treest, Illinois. $50.00 – 75.00.

Human head effigy, dark steatite, 2¼" high. This piece is probably Mississippian in origin and was found in Tennessee. Larry Garvin, Back to Earth, Ohio. $400.00.

Human head effigy pipe, black steatite, 2 x 2½". It has well-developed facial detailing and some use-polish. When smoked the stem was inserted into the open mouth. Johnson County, Tennessee. Larry Lantz, First Mesa, Indiana. $750.00.

Human head effigy elbow pipe, Woodland period, made of brown sandstone. With rounded head and squared stem, this unusual pipe measures 5½" long, 3½" high, and is 2" wide. Origin unknown, but certainly Mississippi watershed region. Wilfred Dick collection, Mississippi. $700.00 – 1,000.00.

Human head pipe, face with raised features, squared cross-section. This interesting pipe is made of brown sandstone and is 2⅛" x 3½" high. This Mississippian pipe was found in 1995, in Licking County, Ohio. Larry Garvin, Back to Earth, Ohio. $550.00.

Human head effigy pipe bowl, historic, 2 x 2¼ x 1⅝". Done in black steatite, the stone has four lead or pewter inlays at the side, back, and top of head. Face is well detailed with forelock and paint or tattoo lines and teeth. This was collected near Hibbing, Minnesota. Larry Lantz, First Mesa, Indiana. $875.00.

Effigy head pipe, may be protohistoric, light tan stone with measurement of 3 x 3¼ x 4¾" high. This is a well-detailed pipe with facial features and hair, shell eyes, and weeping eye motif. A large pipe, this is better made than most of the type. Neshoba County, Mississippi. Larry Lantz, First Mesa, Indiana. $2,500.00.

Head effigy vase pipe, highly refined facial details, sandstone. It is 1¼ x 2½" and is from the Mississippian era, Ft. Ancient people. Clinton County, Ohio. Private collection, Ohio. $1,500.00.

Effigy pipe, human head with weeping eye motif, a rare portrait of a person in Fort Ancient times. Material is gray-green Ohio pipestone for this unusual and beautifully crafted pipe, found in Kentucky. Len and Janie Weidner collection, Ohio. $3,500.00.

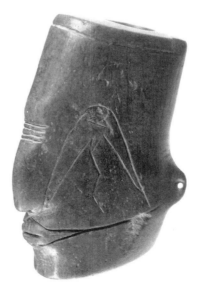

Effigy pipe, deer figure, tan pipestone. This Fort Ancient pipe measures 4¹⁄₁₆" long and was found in Fayette County, Ohio. Len and Janie Weidner collection, Ohio. $1,400.00.

Effigy pipe, wolf image, 2⅝" high, protohistoric, black polished stone. The portion shown is actually a salvaged part of the pipe; the bowl was broken away and was located at the end of the neck. The stem was also split and the stem hole now exists as a groove along the back of the neck and head. Though the pipe is damaged the effigy portion is intact, which make this a valuable specimen. Preble County, Ohio. Bill Mesnard collection, New Jersey. $1,500.00.

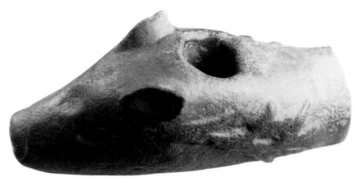

Effigy pipe, deer head, found in the year 1883. This pipe is Mississippian period and ex-collection Dr. Lasick. Made of hardstone, the pipe is 5¼" long, in top condition, and a rare type. Private collection. $7,500.00.

Effigy pipe, fish, tan and white pipestone. It has much engraving and there is a face on the surface beneath the bowl which is at top center. This small pipe is only 1½" long and 1" high. Ohio. Bill Mesnard collection, New Jersey; Sarah Bones, photographer. $175.00.

Effigy pipe, standing squirrel, 2¼" high. This Mississippian-period figure is made of gray-green pipestone and has the stem hole in lower center of the front. The pipe was found in a major area of Ft. Ancient activity, Hamilton County, Ohio. Len and Janie Weidner collection, Ohio. $2,500.00.

Effigy pipe, turtle head, Mississippian period, 1¾" high and 2" long. Material is a brown stone for this unusual example from Etowah County, Georgia. Frederick DeWitt Ufford collection, Georgia. $425.00.

Effigy pipe, frog, in dark brown stone that may be sandstone, 1¾ x 2½". This is a Mississippian pipe that is nicely carved and in top condition. Madison County, Illinois. Larry Lantz, First Mesa, Indiana. $1,500.00.

Raccoon effigy pipe, probably Fort Ancient, made of unusual material, hematite or natural iron ore. It measures 3" high and 4¼" long. This interesting piece was found in a plowed field, Delaware County, Ohio, in the year 1901. H. B. Greene II collection, Florida. $1,500.00.

Effigy pipe, highly unusual depiction of an animal vertebra, Mississippian period. It is made of brown pottery and is 2½" long. Eastern Midwest. Len and Janie Weidner collection, Ohio. $650.00.

Frog effigy pipe, Mississippian period, made of tan close-grained sandstone. This pipe is 1½ x 2⅞ x 3" long and was found in Juniata County, Pennsylvania. Bill Mesnard collection, New Jersey. $600.00.

Effigy pipe, claw or talon, Mississippian period, 2⅜" high. The material is probably quartzite for this unusual example. The Fort Ancient pipe is from Brown County, Ohio. Len and Janie Weidner collection, Ohio. $750.00.

Lizard effigy pipe, moderately fine-grained sandstone in reddish tan color, probably Late Archaic period. This pipe measures 1¾ x 1⅝ x 3¾" high. Clark County, Indiana. Bill Mesnard collection, New Jersey. $175.00.

Animal effigy pipe, pottery, image of wolf with nose, ears, teeth, and open mouth. There are no eyes, so this Woodland period artifact may portray the "Blind Wolf" motif that is occasionally seen on pipes. It is 3⅛ x 1½ x 2⅛" high. From Fulton County, Kentucky. Bill Mesnard collection, New Jersey. $1,200.00.

Elbow pipe with effigy animal, probably Mississippian, 2½" high and 3½" long. It is made of dark chocolate brown hardstone. Ex-collection Warner, it is from Hardin County, Tennessee. Larry Garvin, Back to Earth, Ohio. $425.00.

Beaver effigy pipe, Middle Woodland period, 3" long, 1" high, and 1¾" wide. Made of greenstone, this is a Tennessee example. Wilfred Dick collection, Mississippi. Unlisted.

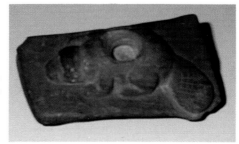

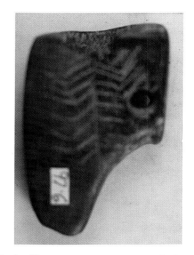

Bird effigy steatite pipe, with bowl opening at top just beneath the small ruler and bill pointing downward to the right. This example is late prehistoric and from Wyoming County, Pennsylvania. The eye-like opening is a suspension hole for the bowl. Lee Hallman collection, Pennsburg, Pennsylvania. $500.00 – 700.00.

Effigy pipe, rabbit, 4 x 5½". Material is sandstone which has been ground and polished giving a smooth exterior to one of the most attractive of the Midwestern effigy pipes. Mississippian and Ft. Ancient, from Pickaway County, Ohio. Private collection, Ohio. $2,000.00.

Human effigy pipe, cracked above stem hole, tan sandstone. It is Ft. Ancient, Mississippi period, ex-collection Yerian. This pipe is 2" wide, 3⅜" high, and 5" long. Close-grained sandstone was often used for Ft. Ancient pipes, especially those of a larger size. Larry Garvin, Back to Earth, Ohio. $500.00.

Bird effigy pipe, probably a pigeon, light gray steatite. Since the common pigeon (rock dove) came in relatively recently, this may be a passenger pigeon. The base is flat and size is 1⅝ x 2¾ x 5¾" long. Macon County, North Carolina. Bill Mesnard collection, New Jersey. $1,000.00.

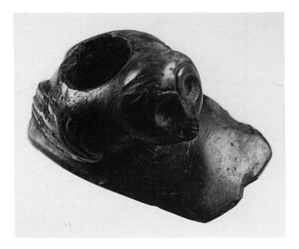

Owl effigy pipe, dark brown pipestone, Hopewell and Middle Woodland. It is 1⅞" high and 2¼" long. With some damage over the years, this is an Ohio pipe. Larry Garvin, Back to Earth, Ohio. $800.00.

Very large turtle effigy pipe, Mississippian people, made of limestone. Quite true-to-life, this big pipe measures 5¼ x 6" and is quite heavy. It came from Polk County, Missouri. Private collection, Ohio. Museum quality.

Effigy pipe, claw holding cup or bowl motif, 4" long. This is a late prehistoric pipe in pottery, from Mississippi County, Arkansas. Len and Janie Weidner collection, Ohio. $350.00.

Effigy pipe, unusual upside-down image of bird head and neck, gray Ohio pipestone. It measures 2¼" high and has the eyes and beak or bill visible. Late prehistoric, New York. Len and Janie Weidner collection, Ohio. $450.00.

Pipe in effigy form of a frog or fish, brown stone. It is Mississippian period, 2" high. The pipe was found in Kentucky; many Mississippian pipes have come from near the Ohio River in that region. Collection of and photograph by Duane Treest, Illinois. $150.00 – 200.00.

Animal effigy pipe, pottery, Mississippian period and later, 7¾" long. This is a large and well done example, from Baxter County, Arkansas. Baxter Hurst collection, Arkansas. $450.00.

Effigy pipe of the lower carapace of a turtle, ca. 1500 – 1600. This unusual pipe measures 2⅞" high and is 1¾" in diameter. Made of brown sandstone, it is from Davidson County, North Carolina. Jim Maus collection, North Carolina. $300.00.

Effigy pipe, dark pottery, probable bird form, 2⅞" long. This pipe is late prehistoric, being Dallas culture, and ca. AD 1000. Northern Florida. Len and Janie Weidner collection, Ohio. $500.00.

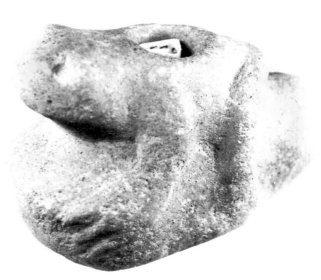

Effigy pipe, bird image, tan and yellow pipestone. This is a nicely shaped late prehistoric pipe, likely Ft. Ancient, that was found in Belmont County, Ohio. Len and Janie Weidner collection, Ohio. $800.00.

Animal effigy pipe, Mississippian, a rare stylization measuring 3 x 3¾". This sandstone figurine is called "frog on a log," and came from Clermont County, Ohio. Private collection, Ohio. $1,200.00.

Animal effigy pipe, probably a frog, 2½ x 5¼". Frogs were favorite design forms of the Mississippian people, possibly relating to rain for agriculture. It is made of sandstone and came from Pike County, Ohio. Private collection, Ohio. $1,100.00.

Human effigy pipe of kneeling person looking to the left, 3¼ x 4¼". It is made from iron-impregnated sandstone. From Mississippian times, this came from Pike County, Illinois. Private collection, Ohio. Museum grade.

Effigy pipe, Mississippian period, image of opossum or other animal. The pipe measures 2" high and eyes (original?) are set with black polished stone glued with pitch. Lawrence County, Ohio. Len and Janie Weidner collection, Ohio. $900.00.

Animal effigy pipe, probably an opossum and a scarce effigy form. This pipe is made of sandstone and measures 1¾ x 3½" high. It was found in Scioto County, Ohio. Private collection, Ohio. $800.00.

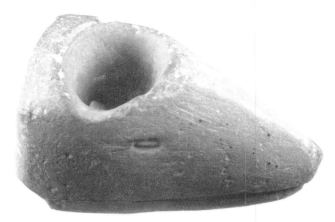

Animal effigy pipe, unknown animal, brown fine-grained sandstone. It retains peck marks and there is only a little polish. This is a Mississippian piece (Ft. Ancient) and measures 1⅞ x 3⅝ x 2¼" high. Fayette County, Ohio. Bill Mesnard collection, New Jersey. $600.00.

Effigy pipe, head of unknown animal, gray-tan sandstone. The large carefully made pipe, 5¼" long, is Ft. Ancient in origin. Big effigy pipes are always scarce and have been in demand by collectors for over a century. Ohio. Len and Janie Weidner collection, Ohio. $3,000.00.

Effigy pipe, turtle image, Mississippian period and Fort Ancient people. Material is tan pipestone for this very nicely designed and crafted example, 2⅜" long. Kentucky. Len and Janie Weidner collection, Ohio. $2,200.00.

Effigy pipe, deer head, made of brownish pipestone. Mississippian in origin, this is one of the better late prehistoric images, 3¼" high. The pipe bowl is between the ears. Ohio. Len and Janie Weidner collection, Ohio. $1,800.00.

Animal effigy pipe, possibly bear's head, dark fine-grained sandstone. This fully drilled Fort Ancient (Mississippian period) pipe is 2¼" wide and 3½" long, 2" high. Ex-collection Clay, the pipe is from Warren County, Ohio. Larry Garvin, Back to Earth, Ohio. $600.00.

Effigy platform pipe, block-shaped with human head having deeply worked features, 5½" long. This Fort Ancient pipe is made of sandstone and was found in Ohio. Len and Janie Weidner collection, Ohio. $1,400.00.

Animal effigy pipe, tan sandstone, Ft. Ancient and Mississippian period. This large pipe measures 2⅛" high, 3½" wide, and 5½" long. Larry Garvin, Back to Earth, Ohio. $450.00.

Snake head effigy pipe, tan sandstone, 5½" long. This large pipe is from the Mississippian period (Ft. Ancient) and was found along Wills Creek in 1984. Coshocton County, Ohio. Larry Garvin, Back to Earth, Ohio. $500.00.

Crow effigy pipe, late prehistoric – early historic, ca. 1200 – 1600. This pipe is 3" high and 13¼" long. It has a human head effigy held by the bird's feet. Ballard County, Kentucky. H. B. Greene II collection, Florida. Museum quality.

Detail of crow effigy pipe from Kentucky, showing the human head held between the feet. H. B. Greene II collection, Florida. Museum quality.

Human head effigy pipe, black steatite, late prehistoric – early historic and ca. 1200 – 1600. Size is 2⅝" long and 3" high. This pipe was found by Dr. Ismay in Bartow County, Georgia, in 1902. Hogan Gallery Inc., Naples, Florida. $1,200.00.

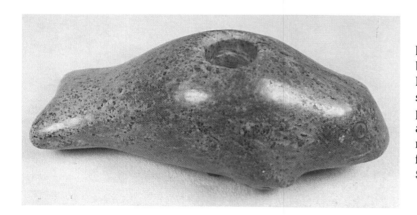

Effigy pipe in the form of a baby seal, probably historic, 2" wide, 1¾" high, and 4½" long. Material is a gray and black California steatite and it is well patinated and nicely polished. Facial features are lightly indicated and the eyes are abalone shell insets. Well-made, unusual. Santa Barbara County, California. Larry Lantz, First Mesa, Indiana. $1,500.00.

Effigy pipe, killer whale, done in mottled steatite. The stem hole is in the tail and pipe bowl is in front of the dorsal fine. Size 2 x 2⅝ x 5". This unusual piece may be late prehistoric – historic and is representative West Coast Amerind art. Santa Barbara, California. Larry Lantz, First Mesa, Indiana. $1,850.00.

Effigy pipe, killer whale image, black steatite. This is a Chumash pipe, ca. 1600s and measures 4⅜" long, 1¼" wide, and 2¼" high. It has a portion of the original bone stem, glued in with asphaltum which also secures the shell-bead eyes and side designs. With Davis authentication paper, this pipe is from California. Bill Mesnard collection, New Jersey; Sarah Bones, photographer. $2,000.00.

Bird effigy pipe, Early Caddo and ca. 900 – 1100. This big Mississippian platform pipe is made of light-colored stone and measures 8" long. A number of the large Mississippian pipes feature humans, animals, or birds. This fine example came from Miller County, Arkansas. Dr. Jim Cherry collection, Arkansas. Museum grade.

Frog effigy pipe, Late Mississippian, pottery, 4¼" long and 2¼" high. This fine large pipe had both front legs broken in ancient times and has been restored. The pipe was found by Rex Cherry in 1985 at a site in Arkansas. Rex Cherry collection, Arkansas. Museum grade.

Human effigy pipe, Mississippian period, this is a fine example of the "bound captive" or "bound prisoner" type. Made of sandstone, it is 4 x 4½". Macoupin County, Illinois. Private collection, Ohio. Museum quality.

Human effigy pipe, pale limestone, Mississippian period. It is 3½ x 5½" and is unusual in having two stem openings for the pipe bowl on the figure's back. Rutherford County, Tennessee. Private collection, Ohio. Museum quality.

Frog effigy pipe, Mississippian period, 4 x 5" long. It is ex-collection Floyd Ritter and came from Christian County, Kentucky. Dale and Betty Roberts collection, Iowa; Betty Roberts photograph. $600.00.

Mississippian human figure pipe with bowl in pack basket. This pipe is 4¼" deep, front to back, and 5⅛" high. Made of pottery with traces of white paint, this interesting piece is from near Cairo, Illinois. Larry Garvin, Back to Earth, Ohio. $700.00.

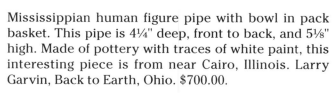

Human effigy pipe, once full figure but with head broken off, made from tan sandstone. Probably Mississippian, this large pipe measures 2" wide, 3" high, and is 6½" long. It came from St. Clair County, Illinois. Bill Mesnard collection, New Jersey. $1,200.00.

Human effigy pipe, kneeling woman figure, Early Mississippian period. The image in dark pottery is 3½" tall and came from Mississippi County, Missouri. Len and Janie Weidner collection, Ohio. $1,500.00.

Effigy figure, Fort Ancient of the Mississippian period, possibly a stylized human. The figure is made of sandstone and is 4⅜" long. It was found near the Ohio River in southern Indiana. Private collection. $1,000.00.

Effigy pipe, bird holding a human head, 7" long. Material is a chalky white to buff stone, and the scene depicted has unknown meaning. Another of the fine Early Caddo effigy forms, this pipe suggests that prehistoric Mississippian craftspeople had few limitations to subject matter. Found in Arkansas. Dr. Jim Cherry collection, Arkansas. Museum grade.

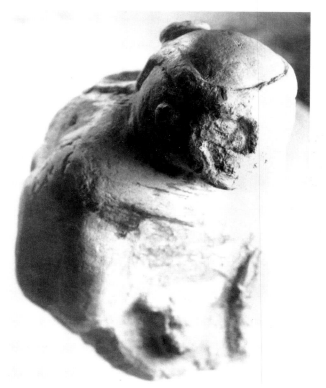

Effigy pipe detail, animal head (cat-like) positioned between the legs of the squatting human. Kentucky. Len and Janie Weidner collection, Ohio. Museum grade.

Limestone effigy pipe, overall view, human and animal, pipe 6¼" high. This solid and heavy pipe was found close to the Falls of the Ohio near Louisville, Kentucky. This large and rare Mississippian platform pipe was picked up by John Otto sometime between the years 1910 and 1920. Len and Janie Weidner collection, Ohio. Museum grade.

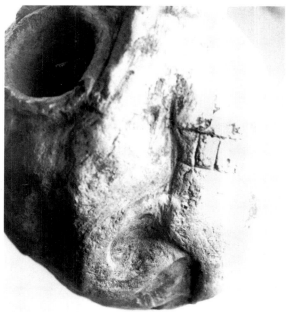

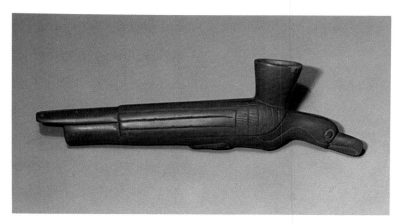

Effigy pipe, bird with forked-eye design, 7½" long. Early Caddo and ca. AD 900 – 1100, this pipe is made of a fine-grained light-colored lime-like sandstone. In addition to careful sculpting the figure has incised lines on the folded wings and elsewhere. A superb prehistoric creation, the pipe is from Arkansas. Dr. Jim Cherry collection, Arkansas. Museum grade.

Effigy pipe detail, curled animal tail emerging from behind right arm of the human figure. The animal may represent a cougar. Note the decorative arm-band above the tail. Len and Janie Weidner collection, Ohio. Museum grade.

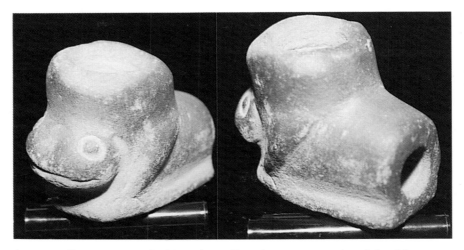

Animal effigy pipe, probably a frog, Fort Ancient people of the Mississippian period. Information on the pipe bottom refers to this as the "Robinette Pipe," and indicates it came from Point Pleasant, West Virginia. Larry Garvin, Back to Earth, Ohio. $550.00.

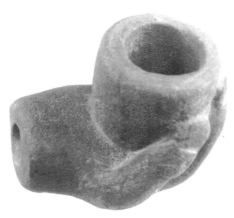

Effigy pipe, human foot, light-colored limestone. Size is 1½ x ⅞" and part of the bowl of this Ft. Ancient pipe is restored. Northern Kentucky. Patrick Welch collection, Ohio. $50.00.

Effigy pipe, human foot form, close-grained sandstone. This is a Fort Ancient pipe, 1¾" long, and the unusual artifact is from Clermont County, Ohio. Len and Janie Weidner collection, Ohio. $275.00.

Human hand effigy with bowl being cradled in palm and fingers. This is an unusual form, done in fine-grained sandstone. Size 2 x 2" for this Mississippian piece. Milwaukee County, Wisconsin. Private collection, Ohio. $800.00.

Iroquois foot-effigy pipe, #P-9, ca. 1600 – 1750. Material is gray and black grit-tempered pottery, and both stem and bowl measure 2". This interesting example is from near West Bloomfield, Ontario County, New York. Iron Horse collection. $750.00 – 1,000.00.

Side view of effigy pipe, deer-hoof and lower leg, Ft. Ancient and Mississippian period, maroon Ohio pipestone. It was found in Clinton County, Pennsylvania. It has some slight restoration which lowers value by more than half. Gary L. Fogelman collection, Pennsylvania. $200.00 – 300.00.

Stem hole view of effigy pipe, deer-hoof and lower leg. $200.00 – 300.00.

Fort Ancient effigy pipe, deer foot and hoof, 2¼" high. Material is tan-colored stone for this unusual design, found in Ohio. Len and Janie Weidner collection, Ohio. $375.00.

Right side view of bird effigy pipe, Monogahela – Late Woodland, made of brown stone. The pipe is from Lycoming County, Pennsylvania, and has slight restoration. Gary L. Fogelman collection, Pennsylvania. $200.00 – 300.00.

Left side view of bird effigy pipe.

Effigy pipe, catlinite, late prehistoric period. In dark red material, the bird form is 3⅜" high, with the bowl above the bent neck. This is a very well-done figure, found in the Lake Erie region of northern Ohio. Len and Janie Weidner collection, Ohio. $2,500.00.

Effigy pipe, long stem with turtle bowl, pipe 7¹⁄₁₆" long. Late prehistoric, this black pottery pipe came from Tennessee. Robin Fiser collection, Ohio. $350.00.

Effigy pipe, bird, late prehistoric period. This fine and large example is 4" high and is made of an unknown brown hardstone. Ohio. Robin Fiser collection, Ohio. Museum grade.

Iroquois snake effigy pipe, ca. 1600 – 1750, made of brown and black pottery. #P-17 has a stem 5½" long and the bowl is 3½" high. New York. Iron Horse collection. $650.00 – 850.00.

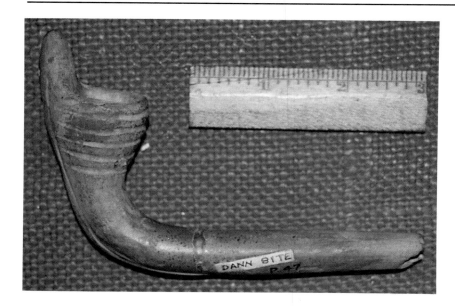

Iroquois snake effigy pipe, light brown pottery, ca. 1600 – 1750. Listed as #P-47, the stem is 4¼" and the bowl is 3" high. Genesee River Valley, Monroe County, New York. Iron Horse collection. $650.00 – 850.00.

Iroquois snake effigy pipe, ca. 1600 – 1750, light brown pottery. At 4½" long and 3" high, #2013 is from Livingston County, New York. Iron Horse collection. $750.00 – 850.00.

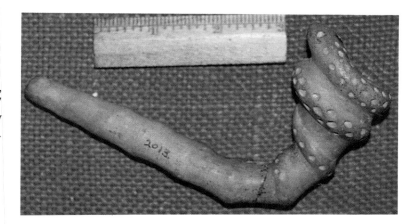

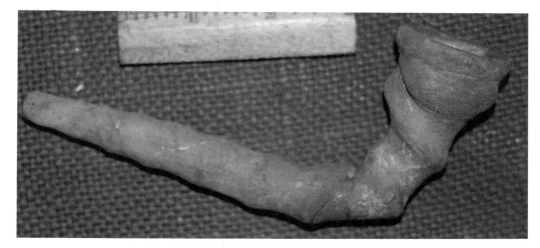

Iroquois snake effigy pipe, light brown pottery, ca. 1600 – 1750. #183 has a 5" stem and bowl height is 2½". Livingston County, New York. Iron Horse collection. $650.00 – 850.00.

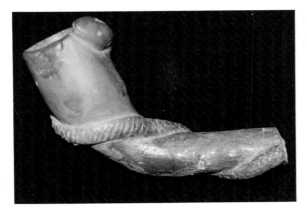

Iroquois snake effigy pipe, ca. 1600 – 1750, red and black pottery. The snake wraps around the stem and bowl of #5505/D, and is quite lifelike. The stem is 2½" long and bowl height is 2". Livingston County, New York. Iron Horse collection. $500.00 – 700.00.

Iroquois effigy pipe, duck, ca. 1650 – 1700. #CAL-64 is pottery, light brown to burned black, with 2" stem and bowl height of 2¾". This is a large and fine effigy figure from Erie County, New York. Iron Horse collection. $900.00 – 1,200.00.

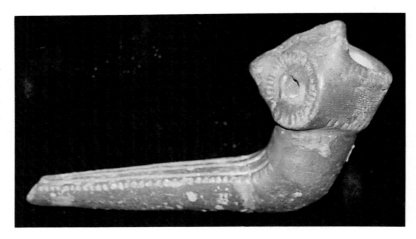

Iroquois owl effigy pipe, brownish-red pottery, #451. The stem is 4" long and bowl height is 2½". This pipe is ca. 1650 – 1700, and is from Jefferson County, New York. Iron Horse collection. $750.00 – 950.00.

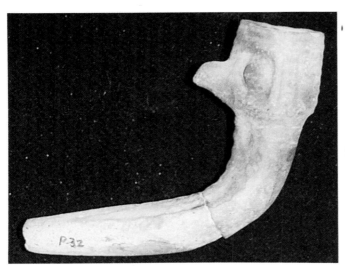

Iroquois owl effigy pipe with stitched stem, gray shell-tempered pottery. Ca. 1650 – 1700, the stem is 3½" and bowl height is 3". #P-32, this pipe is from the Victor area, New York. Iron Horse collection. $950.00 – 1,200.00.

Iroquois owl effigy pipe, gray-brown pottery, #672. The pipe is ca. 1650 – 1700, with a stem of 3½" and height of 2½". Monroe County, New York. Iron Horse collection. $950.00 – 1,200.00.

Effigy pipe, bird or human(?), gray speckled steatite, #1-22-97. Ca. 1600 – 1675 the pipe is well polished, and 4" high. Rather a mystery figure, it is from Niagara County, New York. Iron Horse collection. $900.00 – 1,200.00.

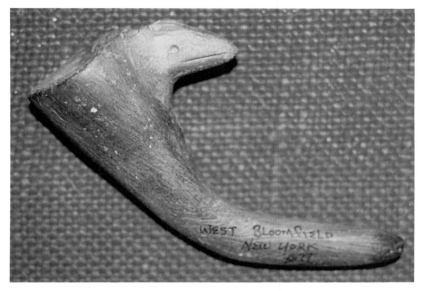

Iroquois bird effigy pipe, gray shell-tempered pottery, ca. 1600 – 1700. The stem on this pipe, #P-77, is 2" long and the bowl is 3" high. It is from near West Bloomfield, Ontario County, New York. Iron Horse collection. $900.00 – 1,000.00.

Owl effigy pipe, Mississippian period, made of sandstone. It measures 1 x 3" and is a rare effigy form. Gallia County, Ohio. Private collection, Ohio. $750.00.

Owl effigy pipe, probably Mississippian period, made of brownish-green fine-grained sandstone. The well-executed figure measures 2 x 1³⁄₁₆ x 3¼" high. It is from Lewis County, Kentucky. Bill Mesnard collection, New Jersey. $600.00.

Bird effigy pipe, fine-grained brown stone, with moderate polish. The pipe is 1¼ x 1⅞" high and 3½" long. It was found in Alabama. Bill Mesnard collection, New Jersey. $700.00.

Bird effigy pipe, stone, with hole at rear to accept a wood or reed stem. It is ca. AD 1000 – 1300 and ex-collection W. H. Lewis; it was once in the Heye Foundation museum. New York. Dave Summers, Native American Artifacts, Victor, New York. $2,000.00.

Effigy pipe, hawk(?), gray-brown pottery. The figure is 3" long, 2⅜" high, and is Havanna Hopewell in time. It was found near Cuba, Missouri. Len and Janie Weidner collection, Ohio. $1,200.00.

Effigy pipe, probably a vulture, a rare pipe form in top condition. It measures 1½ x 3" and is made of Ohio pipestone. This is a Mississippian piece, Ft. Ancient people. Greenup County, Kentucky. Private collection, Ohio. $2,200.00.

Effigy pipe, late prehistoric times, made of dark green serpentine. It is 1⅞" high and the base or keel is in the form of a stylized bird head. The eye is visible and beak is to the left. New York. Richard Savidge collection, Pennsylvania. $200.00.

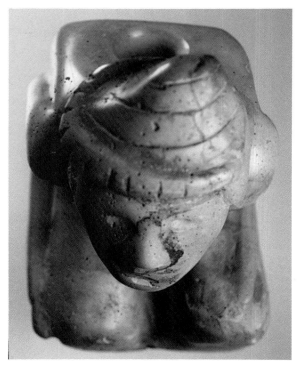

Effigy platform pipe, woodland buffalo(?), possibly late prehistoric. It is made of fine-grained sandstone and is 3" high and 3¾" long. The pipe is from the North Carolina – Georgia area. Hogan Gallery Inc., Naples, Florida. $1,675.00.

Mississippian period effigy pipe, cream colored Ohio pipestone. It is 5⅛" high and 4" long. This unusual piece was found in 1959 during posthole digging. Highland County, Ohio. Robin Fiser collection. Museum grade.

Human effigy pipe combining L-shaped and T-shaped design, historic. It measures 2⅞" high and 4½" long. This unusual pipe is made of brown stone and is ex-collection Warner. It is from Tennessee. Larry Garvin, Back to Earth, Ohio. $600.00.

Effigy pipe, leaning or seated human figure, long stem and pipe bowl on figure's upper back. Made of dark steatite, this historic pipe measures 8½" long. It is from Cherokee County, North Carolina. Bob Johnson, Eagle Eye Gallery, Schenectady, New York. $1,250.00.

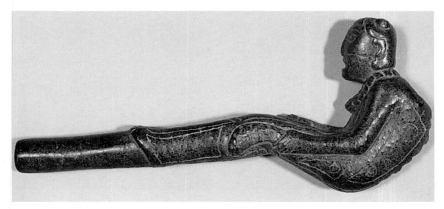

Canoe effigy pipe, historic, made of steatite. Formerly in the Watson Museum, this pipe measures 3¼" long. Minnesota. Dale and Betty Roberts collection, Iowa; Betty Roberts photograph. $350.00.

Effigy human head pipe, steatite, 2¼ x 2¼ x 2¾". Historic, this pipe is very detailed from paint or tattoo lines on cheeks to flowing hair at rear. High points have heavy use polish. Unusual and well done, from northern Georgia. Larry Lantz, First Mesa, Indiana. $1,500.00.

Bird effigy pipe, may be a hawk or falcon, 1⅜ x 3¾". The basic material is steatite and lead or pewter inlays are set for eyes, wings, and tail sections. Stem opening is the protrusion at the lower back and the foot area has another inlay. This is a highly unusual pipe, extremely well done in all aspects. May be early historic; Cook County, Illinois. Larry Lantz, First Mesa, Indiana. $985.00.

Historic pipes, pottery, an Indian-made bent tube and an European (white) trade pipe. These are ca. 1750 – 1800. The bent tube measures 1¼ x 2¾". These were found together at Great Heron Pond, Plymouth County, Massachusetts, in 1938. H. B. Greene II collection, Florida. Unlisted.

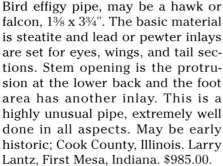

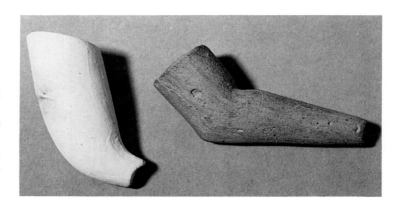

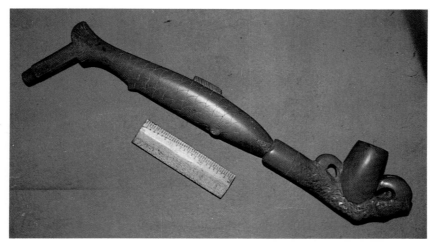

Catlinite Plains type pipe, fish effigy stem and eagle-claw bowl, ca. 1870 – 1910. (For more information see *Plains Indian Sculpture*, Smithsonian Press, 1986.) #AS-7 is a superb set with 10" stem and bowl height of 2". Yankton Sioux. Iron Horse collection. $1,200.00 – 1,800.00.

Great Pipes

Undoubtedly the easiest of all Indian pipes to recognize, southern Great Pipes were made for an extended number of centuries. It is believed their time span is from ca. 500 BC through the Woodland era and into early Mississippian times, ca. AD 1400 or so. This indicates a prehistoric popularity, time wise, unrivaled by any other single pipe type.

Great pipes are massively constructed from a single large block of stone; known examples range from 6 to 7" to well over a foot in length, with many individual pipes in the 9 to 12" range. Weights are from just under 5 pounds to nearly 10 pounds or more. Carved almost always in the form of birds, ducks, swans, hawks, and owls are depicted. The body itself makes up the bulk of the pipe.

The mouth-piece or stem end is to the rear and the large bowl is generally positioned somewhere on the back, usually much closer to the head than to the tail. Wings and tail-feathers are sometimes indicated and the head is usually quite detailed. Most Great Pipes received a high polish when completed.

Classic material for Great Pipes is steatite, befitting the southern birthplace. Some experts can establish the material origin, focusing on certain sections of a state in the region; occasionally the specific ancient quarry can be identified. One interesting thing about Great Pipes is that they were often exported in prehistoric times, ending up in states several times removed from the site from which the stone was quarried.

Of all Indian pipes, a fine example of a Great Pipe in top condition can be extremely valuable, and the best of the best can command very high figures. Truly old and authentic Great Pipes are so scarce that many pipe collections do not have a single example.

The Payne Duck Great Pipe, cataloged T-9 in the Hart collection, was found in Meigs County, Ohio. Picked up in the spring of 1853, this beautiful pipe is 9¼" long and made of dark green steatite. Early Woodland in time, the pipe has been in many famous early collections, including Braeckline, Payne, Vietzen, Young, and Shipley. Pictured in a dozen books and magazines, this pipe is very well made and highly polished. Few Great Pipes have better provenance. Gordon Hart collection, Indiana. Unlisted.

Effigy pipe, Great Pipe in bird form, material a dark steatite, Woodland through Mississippian period. The pipe is 8¼" long and 2⅜" high. This is a superb pipe which was picked up in 1985, and is one of the better examples found in the last twenty years. The elongated pipe with high polish came from Mason County, Illinois. Len and Janie Weidner collection, Ohio. Museum grade.

Southern Great Pipe, dark green steatite, 6¼" long. The head was salvaged in ancient times and the pipe is Woodland period. This artifact came from Pickens County, South Carolina, and holds G.I.R.S. (Genuine Indian Relic Society) authentication certificate number COL-95-2. Collection of Jim Bickel, Huntington, Indiana. $2,100.00.

Southern Great Pipe, bird effigy form, greenish steatite. This pipe is Woodland and ca. AD 600, picked up on Big "A" Mountain in Buchannan County, Virginia. The pipe is 6" long and has G.I.R.S. authentication certificate number E33. Collection of Jim Bickel, Huntington, Indiana. $4,700.00.

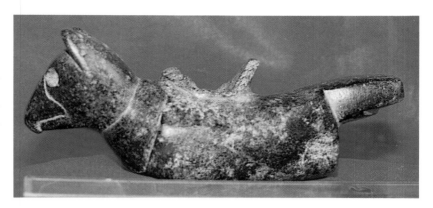

Southern Great Pipe, done in the image of a great horned owl. Material is a grayish-green steatite for this Woodland artifact, which measures 3⅛ x 7¾". This highly polished pipe was found in Morgan County, Alabama. Collection of Tim Guyse, Decatur, Alabama. Museum quality.

Effigy pipe, Great Pipe form, Woodland through Mississippian period, dark steatite. This animal or bird image has eyes and incised lines on the head and for the mouth. It is 6½" long and was found in Scioto County, Ohio. Len and Janie Weidner collection, Ohio. $3,200.00.

Effigy Great Pipe, turtle form, 5⅞" long, ca. AD 500 – 700. This example was found by the owner in April of 1950 when he was 11 years old. It is a turtle effigy in black steatite, well polished. The pipe was picked up near Boonville, Indiana. Dave Lutz collection, Indiana. Unlisted.

Right side of the Kenner Great Pipe which is 10½" long. Polish on the green steatite shows nicely in this photograph. Tentative identification of the effigy as that of a great horned owl is based on photograph #S-500 of a pipe in the Gordon Hart collection, personal correspondence, Gordon Hart, 3/18/97. Mark Kenner collection, Kentucky. Museum grade.

Rear view of the Kenner Great Pipe, which was a personal find of the owner. The pipe has slight brown staining near the stem hole due to long contact with the soil. This pipe has a more artistic treatment than some other Great Pipes. The rear body is 3³⁄₁₆" across. This extraordinary pipe was found in 1996 in Kentucky.

Top view of the Kenner Great Pipe, with owl's beak touching (and joined with) the bowl outside top. Exterior diameter of the bowl is 2⁹⁄₁₆". At one time the owl's eyes probably had shell disc inserts for a lifelike appearance.

The Kenner Great Pipe, left side view, with the pipe measuring 3¾" high. As can be seen, there is slight scraping damage caused by the construction equipment which un-earthed the pipe in Kentucky for Mr. Kenner to rescue. This superb pipe is one of the finest found in recent years.

Owl Great Pipe, found by Don Champion in 1964 and designated number S-500 in the Hart collection. (Owls may have been revered by Indians because their eyes are in the front of the head, like humans.) Size is 4½ x 8" and material is dark green steatite containing gold flecks. With shell eyes, this superb pipe has no damage and is one of the finest ever found. Two C-14 dates place it ca. 112 BC and 192 BC. The Hart collection, begun prior to 1934, has many top pipe examples. Gordon Hart collection, Indiana. Unlisted.

Small Great Pipe, wood duck effigy, Woodland period. It is made of dark green steatite and measures 3½" high and 5⅜" long. It was recovered by Dr. King of Kentucky and is from Knox County, Tennessee. Rodney M. Peck collection, North Carolina. $7,000.00 – 10,000.00.

Plains Indian Pipes

In 1844, the painter-explorer George Catlin published his book *Letters and Notes on the Manners, Customs and Conditions of the North American Indians*. And by that year, when Catlin reported his visit to the pipestone quarries at Coteau des Prairies, Minnesota, the red pipestone had already been in use for hundreds of years. Though other whites may have seen the quarries before Catlin, his publication helped name the site after the author.

Though at the time of Catlin's visit the pipestone quarries were said to be under the control of the Sioux Indians, much pipestone had already been quarried and traded. The red substance went west to the Rockies and east beyond the Great Lakes, north through Canada, and south into Arkansas and Oklahoma.

Most pipes of the Plains Indians were made of red catlinite, though some were also done in black pipestone, in steatite, and a few other materials. Stylewise, Plains pipes can instantly be recognized, even without the typical long, narrow wooden stem or calumet.

Plains pipes are usually large and slender, with elongated stem sections and high bowls. Designs favor a bold simplicity in one of two configurations, though some variations tend to merge the types. The L-shape has the bowl set on the base near the end opposite the mouthpiece. And the T-shape positions the bowl at or near the center of the base.

In cross-section both the bowl and base are usually round or at least rounded, though some examples have the surface faceted so that the outline is squared or angled. While many of these pipes are plain, with little or no embellishment, others are quite ornate.

Some pipes are of the effigy form, and the simpler type has the effigy carved atop the stem between the bowl and the mouthpiece. More elaborate effigies have the entire stone carved, with favored images often involving the head or body of the horse. Occasionally the bowl alone, or the stem portion alone, form the effigy.

Another decoration is inlaying, done either with lead or pewter, the last a combination of lead and tin. The pipe is carved with shallow surface cuts which are then mold treated and filled with the soft, molten metal. It is usually difficult to identify the metal, but lead was often more available than pewter because it was used for bullet making.

For at least partial identification, lead often patinates heavily and the surface is colored in various degrees of gray. Pewter retains a brighter lustre and looks more like dull silver. It also polishes to a brighter sheen than does lead. About inlay, a few scarce Plains pipe examples may also have bits of stone included, such as more catlinite, steatite, or even turquoise in a few cases.

Plains pipes — that is, large pipes made of catlinite in typical forms — also exist in other forms, such as fish and birds or pipe-tomahawks. These tend to be made at a later date, in the 1880s to 1920s or so, and some collectors refer to such pieces as trade or tourist items because many were made for sale as curios. At times even the stems were made of catlinite, sometimes also in effigy forms.

For all such examples, care must be taken that the stems and pipes should match in proportion, fitting, color, and style. As a final note, catlinite is attractive and durable, but long stems of this material are quite fragile. When placed in frames or showcases they should not receive too much pressure from the glass, for some pipe stems can break with startling ease.

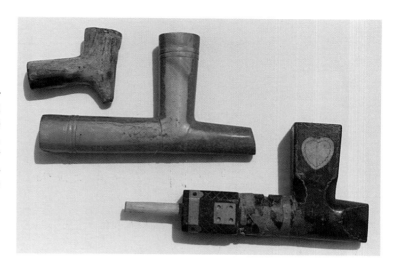

American Indian pipe selection: Top left, pre-historic, pottery, 3½", American Southwest region. $90.00. Middle, T-shape catlinite in two shades, ca. 1895, 4 x 7". $325.00. Bottom right, black pipestone, 6" long, inlaid with lead or pewter playing card pips. $795.00. Dave Summers, Native American Artifacts, Victor, New York.

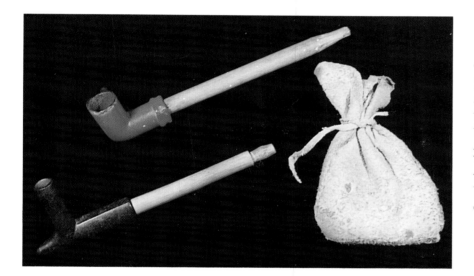

Top, woman's Plains pipe, catlinite, 1½ x 2½". It has an early carved wooden stem and there are reinforcing rings around the stem opening. The bowl is unusually thin. Pierre, South Dakota. $895.00. Accompanying tobacco bag. $295.00. Woman's steatite pipe bowl, 2½ x 3½", with original 5" wooden stem. $825.00. Unusual size, from Sawyer County, Wisconsin. Larry Lantz, First Mesa, Indiana.

L-shaped Plains type pipe, lightly speckled catlinite, 2¼" long. This pipe has high polish and is in top condition. North Dakota. Larry Garvin, Back to Earth, Ohio. $400.00.

L-shaped Plains catlinite pipe, historic and 1800s, from the Central Plains region. The bowl is 2½" high and the pipe is 3⅜" long, 1⅛" in diameter. Ex-collection Kinker, St. Louis. Collection of and photograph by Larry G. Merriam, Oklahoma. $225.00 – 275.00.

L-shape Plains pipe bowl, catlinite, 1½ x 2½" long. Color is an orange-red and the pipe has good polish and patina. The frontal projection just beyond the bowl base is present on many pipes. Sioux Falls, South Dakota. Larry Lantz, First Mesa, Indiana. $425.00.

L-shape pipe, black pipestone, historic era and ca. 1750 – 1850. Size is 2¾" high and 4¼" long. This Plains pipe is Sioux. H. B. Greene II collection, Florida. $450.00.

L-shape pipe, red Catlinite with orange speckles, ca. 1750 – 1850. Nicely polished, this pipe is a Plains piece and measures 2⅞" long and 2¼" high. Hogan Gallery Inc., Naples, Florida. $475.00.

L-shape pipe in greenish steatite, probably historic and ca. 1800s. It is decorated with incised rings around the bowl top and incised lines around the squared platform stem. The pipe is 3" long and bowl height from platform base is 2". This example came from central Wisconsin. Collection of and photography by Duane Treest, Illinois. $225.00 – 300.00.

L-shaped catlinite pipe, Sioux, historic and ca. 1890s. This pipe is 2¾" high and 3¼" long, ex-collection Tom Davis. Jim Frederick collection, Utah. $200.00.

L-shaped Plains type pipe, red catlinite with cream speckles, shown with 2" scale. Nicely shaped and polished, this recently made example is initialed "FE." Lee Hallman collection, Pennsburg, Pennsylvania. $100.00.

L-shape pipe, historic, catlinite. This pipe, with broken and repaired stem, measures 2¾" high and 3¾" long. It came from Michigan, and is decorated with incised lines. Collection of and photograph by Duane Treest, Illinois. $75.00 – 150.00.

L-shape pipes, both ca. 1900. Top, black steatite, 3 x 5½", origin unknown. $375.00. Bottom, catlinite with patination, faceted surface, 2 x 4½", Plains region. $275.00. Dave Summers, Native American Artifacts, Victor, New York.

L-shape Plains pipe bowl, catlinite, 2½ x 3½", early historic. The pipe in cross-section is oval and there are two cut lines at the bowl top and a line around the below-bowl projection. Very graceful contours for this pipe, which has a deep and dark patina. Larry Lantz, First Mesa, Indiana. $595.00.

L-shape Plains pipe, 3 x 3½", in solid red catlinite. Probably mid-1800s, this pipe has good polish and high patina. Larry Lantz, First Mesa, Indiana. $585.00.

L-shaped Plains pipe, historic period, made of orange-red catlinite. Sioux Indian, the pipe is 4¾" long and would be from the Plains area. Len and Janie Weidner collection, Ohio. $500.00.

L-shaped Plains type pipe, deep red catlinite, 2⅝" long. It came from Green County, Wisconsin. Len and Janie Weidner collection, Ohio. $400.00.

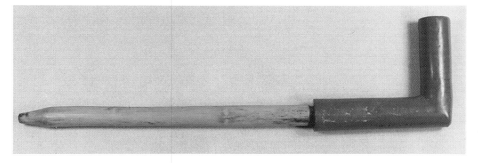

L-shape catlinite pipe, bowl size 3 x 3½". This pipe has the original 9" hand-carved ash stem. With good use polish on the bowl sides, the pipe is from Mercer County, North Dakota. Larry Lantz, First Mesa, Indiana. $950.00.

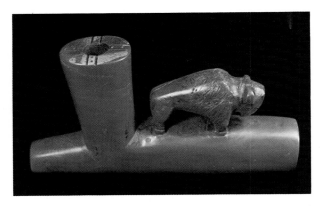

L-shape Plains pipe, catlinite, with below-bowl extension and buffalo (bison) effigy at crest position. Color and polish are exceptional, with overall deep red with pink inclusions. Size, 3¼ x 6". Beaver Dam area, Wisconsin. Larry Lantz, First Mesa, Indiana. $875.00.

T-shaped Plains type pipe with block stem end, repaired with lead plugs after splitting along the center stem and bowl holes. Size 3⅜ x 6⅝". Collected in Ohio. Private collection. $700.00.

T-shape small-size catlinite pipe bowl, 1¾ x 3¼", orange-red stone. Probably mid-1800s for this pipe with good overall polish. Cass Lake, Minnesota. Larry Lantz, First Mesa, Indiana. $495.00.

T-shaped Plains type pipe with extra-high bowl. The catlinite is rather unusual in being deep red with lighter red speckles and inclusions. It is 3¾ x 4¼" and there is use polish present. Pierre area, South Dakota. Larry Lantz, First Mesa, Indiana. $375.00.

T-shaped Plains type catlinite pipe of historic times, ca. late 1800s. Decorated with raised rings, this pipe is much better than average and nicely polished. It is 4⅛" high and 7¾" long. Richardson County, Nebraska. Mike George collection, Missouri. $650.00.

T-shaped Plains style pipe, red and yellow speckled catlinite, 3⅛" high and 6¾" long. From Holt County, Missouri, this pipe still has a broken flint drill in the stem hole. The example is carefully finished and highly polished. Mike George collection, Missouri. $550.00.

T-shaped historic pipe made of unusual material, green banded glacial slate. This is the general Plains style, which also was used eastward into the Great Lakes region. Marked "Ohio," the pipe is 4⅜" long. Len and Janie Weidner collection, Ohio. $500.00.

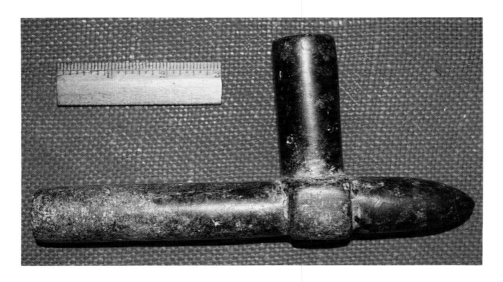

T-shape Plains type calumet pipe, this example done in unusual material for type, black steatite. #M(2)/M is carefully shaped and highly polished, ca. 1700 – 1800. The stem is 7¾" and bowl height is 3¾". Iron Horse collection. $600.00 – 800.00.

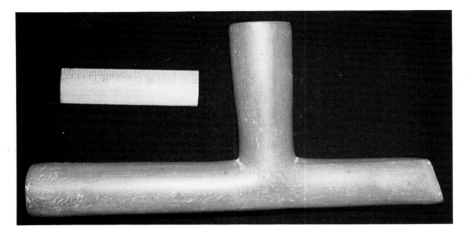

T-shape Plains type calumet pipe, medium-red catlinite, with old tag indicating Sioux origin. Ca. 1880 – 1900, see 3" scale for size for this piece, #AK-100. Iron Horse collection. $450.00 – 675.00.

T-shape large Plains calumet pipe, faceted stem end, ca. 1840 – 1900. #MT/78 has an old tag indicating this is a Sioux piece; see 3" scale for size. Iron Horse collection. $500.00 – 700.00.

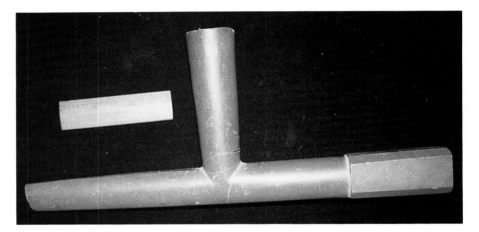

T-shape Plains type pipe, ca. 1900, catlinite. This fine pipe is made with raised ring sets and has good over-all polish. This is a Crow Indian pipe, 4" high and 8" long. Plains region. E. Woods collection, California. $500.00.

T-shaped red catlinite Plains type pipe, decorated rings at bowl top, 2" scale indicating size. It is recently made and initialed "BW." Lee Hallman collection, Pennsburg, Pennsylvania. $75.00.

T-shape pipe, historic, black steatite. The pipe is nicely made, well polished, and 5¹⁵⁄₁₆" long. Great Lakes area. Robin Fiser collection, Ohio. $500.00.

T-shaped historic Plains style pipe, two-color speckled catlinite, 4¾" long. Darkening of the bowl top suggests this pipe had long use. Upper Midwest. Len and Janie Weidner collection, Ohio. $500.00.

T-shape Plains pipe, catlinite, 3 x 5", late historic. It is nicely inset with lead or pewter which spirals around the stem and bowl, and both bowl and stem are capped with the same metal. There is warm, dark patina on this pipe from the Pierre area, South Dakota. Larry Lantz, First Mesa, Indiana. $550.00.

T-shaped historic Plains style pipe in atypical material, black Canadian slate. The pipe is 4" long and 2¼" high, and highly polished. Canada. Len and Janie Weidner collection, Ohio. $550.00.

T-shape catlinite pipe bowl, 3 x 8½" and stem area nicely inset with lead or pewter. Multicolored stone adds to visual impact of this piece, which came from the Redwing area of Minnesota. Larry Lantz, First Mesa, Indiana. $650.00.

T-shape Plains type pipe, 3¼ x 6". Material is speckled charcoal gray and black stone, steatite, with inlays of lead or pewter. Probably late 1800s for this fine example from northern Minnesota. Larry Lantz, First Mesa, Indiana. $875.00.

T-shape catlinite pipe, late 1800s, 3½ x 7½", with lead or pewter inlays joined by metal atop the stem. Dark stone with good use polish with bowl that flares from bottom to top. Sioux Falls, South Dakota. Larry Lantz, First Mesa, Indiana. $695.00.

T-shape pipe, historic and ca. 1750 – 1850. Material is catlinite inlaid with lead, and the pipe is 4" high and 6⅞" long. The inlay is unusually intricate for this pipe. Sioux, Northern Plains. Hogan Gallery Inc., Naples, Florida. $850.00.

T-shaped pipe, eastern Sioux, with pewter or lead inlay. It is historic, ca. 1890 – 1910, and made of deep red catlinite. This is a large pipe, measuring 4¼" high and 9¼" long. Robert F. Manchester collection, New York. $650.00.

T-shaped pipe, historic, with unusual double inlays. It has the typical lead inset bands plus blocks of steatite set near the stem hole. Ex-collection Paul Cline and Watson Museum, the pipe measures 2⅜ x 4½". Wright County, Minnesota. Dale and Betty Roberts collection, Iowa; Betty Roberts photograph. $850.00.

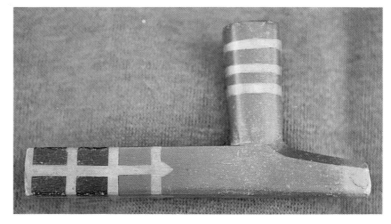

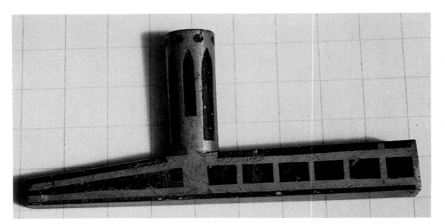

T-shape pipe in rare black pipe-stone, inlaid with lead. This pipe is historic and ca. 1880. The large example measures 4 x 8¾" and is valued both because of material and the amount of inlay. Dave Summers, Native American Artifacts, Victor, New York. $1,500.00.

Plains type pipe with double effigy, horse on the stem end and human head forming the pipe bowl. A lead inset is between the bowl and stem end. This is an ornate and finely finished example, 4⅛" long and ca. 1870s. Private collection. $800.00.

Prairie pipe, historic, red catlinite carved bear effigy facing the stem. This interesting and well-done example is 2" high and 2½" long, Mesquakie, and collected at Tama, Iowa. Richard E. Bachman collection, Washington. $1,800.00.

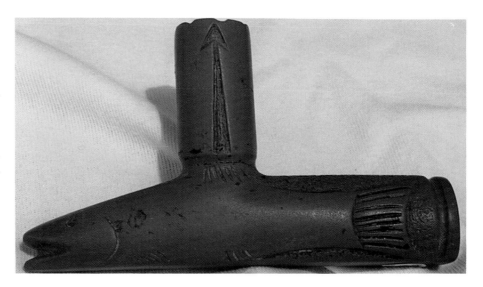

T-shaped fish effigy pipe, catlinite, with nicely carved fish base and bowl decorated with arrows. This Sioux pipe is ca. 1860s and measures 5" long and 3" high. Ex-collection John F. Neil. Jim Frederick collection, Utah. $500.00.

Effigy Plains type pipe, flying horse, unusual two-bowl shape. It is historic and probably late 1800s, 9" long. This rare pipe is Sioux, from South Dakota. E. Woods collection, California. $3,000.00.

Effigy T-shaped pipe, ornate, 8¹⁄₁₆" long. It depicts a coyote with a rabbit in its mouth and the bowl top has lead or pewter inlay. This particular pipe was once displayed in one of the great Eastern United States museums and is ex-collection Grant. Probably early 1800s this is one of the important Plains catlinite pipes. Great Plains area. Len and Janie Weidner collection, Ohio. $1,200.00.

Horse effigy pipe, historic, made of catlinite. This pipe is 2¾ x 3¹⁄₁₆" long and is ex-collection Steinbarger. This pipe is pictured on page 194 of *Who's Who in Indian Relics No. 5*. This is a Michigan pipe. Dale and Betty Roberts collection, Iowa; Betty Roberts photograph. Museum quality.

T-shaped Plains catlinite pipe in elegant high-bowl style. The wooden stem is decorated with quillwork, white ribbons, and horsehair. A fine Plains set, increasingly difficult to collect in artistic form and pristine condition. Ben Thompson collection, Missouri. Unlisted.

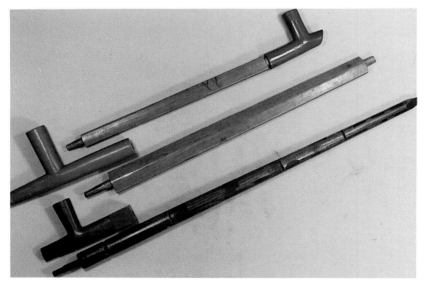

Three Plains pipes, with top two stems pictured to show the upper and lower surfaces and all bowls, catlinite. 1800s. Top, bowl 2¾ x 4", original wooden stem 14½" with incised tipi figures. $2,250.00. Middle, large bowl at 4 x 8½", two-tone stone. Beautiful and original 20¼" ash stem. Use patina is extensive for this superb set. $2,650.00. Bottom, bowl 3 x 6", original round and tapered wooden stem file-branded with rings. Stem is 25¾" long. This is a fine, old matched set of the sort that is rarely encountered outside museums. Larry Lantz, First Mesa, Indiana. $2,250.00.

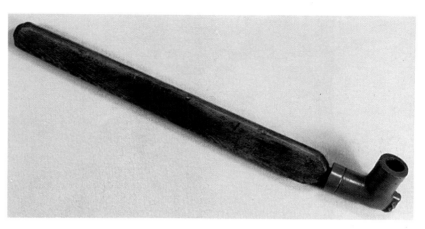

L-shaped Plains pipe, bowl 2¼ x 2½", medium-red catlinite. The old stem is 13" long and handmade of wood. This may be fairly early, mid-1800s, and is simply a very nice set. Mandan area, North Dakota. Larry Lantz, First Mesa, Indiana. $985.00.

L-shape catlinite pipe bowl with original stem turned to show top and bottom. The bowl measures 2 x 2½" and the stem is 12½" long. Late historic, the pipe set is from northern Michigan. Larry Lantz, First Mesa, Indiana. $950.00.

L-shaped catlinite pipe bowl, 3 x 3¼", colored a rich orange-red and with medium polish. The accompanying stem is ash and measures 17" long. Probably mid to late 1800s, this is a well made and outstanding bowl and stem set. South Dakota. Larry Lantz, First Mesa, Indiana. $1,850.00.

T-shaped Plains pipe, catlinite, and wooden stem, detail of pipe shown elsewhere. The fine lines of the polished bowl are obvious, and the quillwork and brass tacks on the stem indicate the maker was a skilled craftsperson. Ben Thompson collection, Missouri. Unlisted.

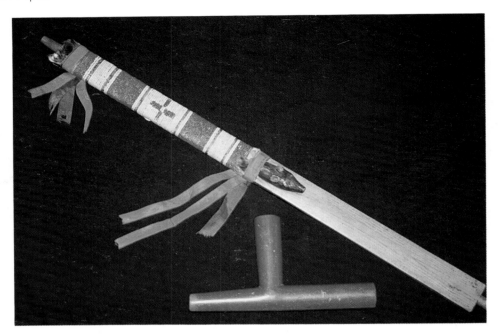

T-shaped Plains pipe, catlinite, well polished. The stem is quite attractive, having quillwork in red, white, and purple, red and blue ribbons, and a carved effigy animal head. A beautiful set. Ben Thompson collection, Missouri. Unlisted.

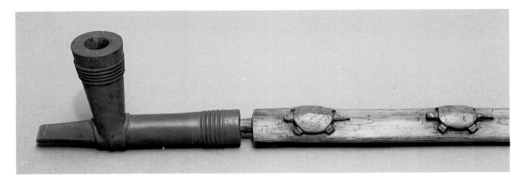

T-shape pipe, Catlinite, with raised-ring decoration. The hickory stem with two turtles is 23" long while the pipe measures 4⅜ x 7". Ca. 1750 – 1850, the set is from Winnebago County, Wisconsin. H. B. Greene II collection, Florida. Museum quality.

T-shaped historic catlinite pipe with lead or pewter inlay, 3½" high and 6¾" long. It has a long matching wooden stem. Plains states. Len and Janie Weidner collection, Ohio. $3,000.00.

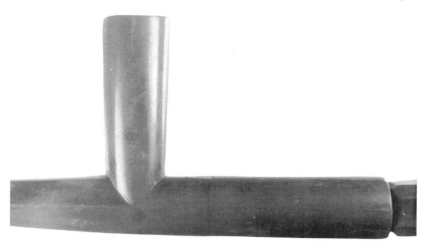

T-shaped historic catlinite pipe, nicely shaped and highly polished, 8½" long. This pipe also has a long, fitted wooden stem, probably made of ash. Plains states. Len and Janie Weidner collection, Ohio. $2,500.00.

L-shaped pipe, dark steatite, 2¾" high and 3¼" long. The bowl is joined with an original stem. Probably Plains region. Len and Janie Weidner collection, Ohio. $1,600.00.

T-shape pipe, Plains area, historic period and ca. 1800s. The pipe in catlinite has a plain ash stem with file marks. Pipe and stem together measure 22" long; the set is ex-collection Dr. Joseph Hart, New York City. Dave Summers, Native American Artifacts, Victor, New York. Unlisted.

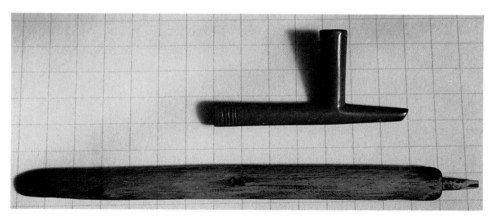

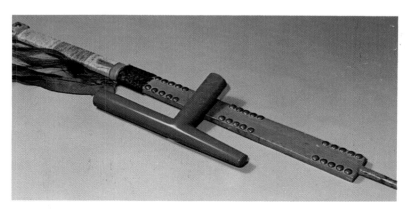

Catlinite ceremonial type pipe with tacked and quilled wooden stem, ca. 1890 – 1910. The bowl of the T-shaped pipe is 4¼" high and 8½" long, while the stem is 24" long. This set was collected in Industry, California, at an antiques show. J. Steve and Anita Shearer collection, California. $1,800.00.

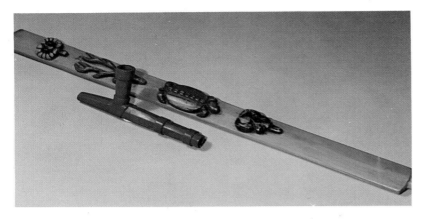

Catlinite bowl with stem carved in buffalo, turtle, elk, and bighorn sheep effigies. Ca. 1880 – 1900, the bowl is 2¾" high and 7" long while the stem is 27". This exceptional set was collected in 1996 from a private dealer in Piedmont, South Dakota. J. Steve and Anita Shearer collection, California. $2,200.00.

T-shaped pipe, catlinite, ca. 1890 – 1910. The bowl is 4⁹⁄₁₆" high and 9½" long. The wooden stem is plaited with quillwork and is 1½" wide and 24⅝" long. This exquisite set is Sioux in origin. Sam Merriman collection, Oregon. $2,000.00.

Catlinite T-shaped pipe bowl and wooden stem, ca. 1880. The ring-enhanced bowl is 4¼" high and 8⁵⁄₁₆" long. The stem has plaited quillwork, horsehair, mallard feathers, and ribbon decorations. This well-made Sioux set is among the better Plains pipes. Sam Merriman collection, Oregon. $3,500.00.

Superb historic Plains Indian pipe, ca. 1860 – 1870. This set has a red catlinite bowl and carved hardwood stem with red ochre paint. Overall length is 22¾", with stem at 16" and bowl length 6¾". From the Southern Plains, this is Kiowa or Comanche, and collected at Cache Creek, Oklahoma. The set is shown with a Southern Plains strike-a-light (flint and steel) pouch, ca. 1870. Richard E. Bachman collection, Washington. Pipe and stem $2,800.00.

Plains type Sioux catlinite pipe bowl and stem, probably late 1800s. This is an excellent old set, with T-shaped bowl and turned stem with raised decorative rings. The pipe and stem are 26" long. Jim Cressey collection, California. $1,900.00.

T-shaped pipe and stem set, historic and ca. 1890s, Arapahoe. Material is unusual, being black steatite. The pipe measures 3 x 5¼" while the stem is 18¼". The assembled pipe set is 24" long. This set was originally in an Oklahoma museum and is ex-collections John F. Neil and Ben Thompson. Jim Frederick collection, Utah. $1,250.00.

L-shaped Plains type pipe, historic and catlinite head measures 3¼" long and 2¾" high. It has the original wooden stem, which nearly triples the value of the head alone. Len and Janie Weidner collection, Ohio. $1,200.00.

Bottom. L-shape Sioux pipe, catlinite bowl 2 x 2½", with ash stem 12½" long. The bowl has fine old patina. Top, miniature pipe bag, 9½" long plus 10" fringe. Native tanned and beaded on both sides with checkerboard design. Possibly Cree and mid to early 1800s. Larry Lantz, First Mesa, Indiana. Pair, $2,500.00.

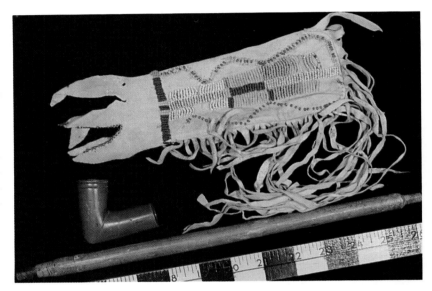

Catlinite T-shaped pipe with ornate stem, ca. 1890 – 1910. The head is inlaid with lead and measures 3¾"high and 7¾" long. The stem is decorated with horsehair and mallard feathers and is 2" wide and 20⅛" long. Of Sioux origin, this set is highly artistic both in pipe and stem. Sam Merriman collection, Oregon. $6,000.00.

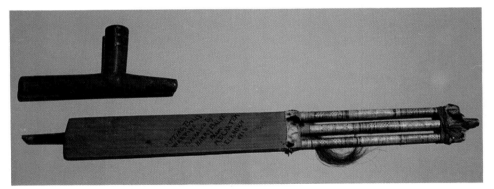

T-shaped pipe, catlinite head and stem, ca. 1890 – 1910. Quite ornate and in perfect condition, the large bowl is 10⁵⁄₁₆" long and 5½" high. The matching stem is 1½" wide and 16³⁄₁₆" long. This fine pipe set is eastern Sioux. Sam Merriman collection, Oregon. $2,000.00.

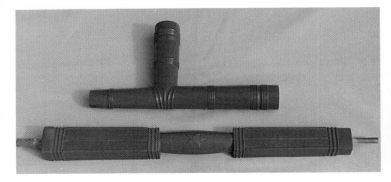

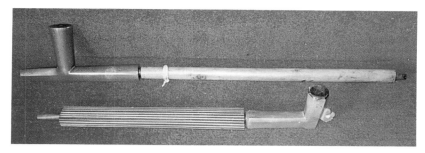

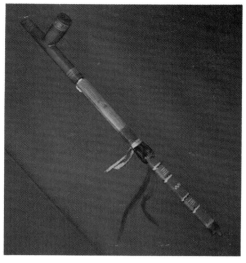

T-shaped catlinite Plains pipe, top, with polished wooden stem. L-shaped catlinite Plains pipe, bottom, with heavy fluted stem, and narrow extended mouthpiece. Ben Thompson collection, Missouri. Both unlisted.

T-shaped Plains style pipe with ornate wooden stem. The pipe itself is catlinite, decorated with incised circles. The stem or handle has quilled wrapping dyed in four colors. This is an exceptional Plains set with ribbon and horsehair. Ben Thompson collection, Missouri. Unlisted.

Catlinite pipe bowl with painted and tacked wooden stem, ca. 1860 – 1870. The octagon bowl is an age-mellowed deep, dull red. The bowl is 4" high and 7¾" long while the stem measures 18". The set was collected in 1996 at an antiques show in Hillsborough, California. J. Steve and Anita Shearer collection, California. $2,500.00.

Plains style pipe and stem, red catlinite bowl and wooden stem. It is ca. 1890 – 1900; the bowl is 4¼" high and 9½" long while the stem is 22" long. The set was collected originally from an estate sale in Arkansas and the pipe was dated then at 1927. The owner finally obtained the set at a Santa Monica antiques shop in California. J. Steve and Anita Shearer collection, California. $1,200.00.

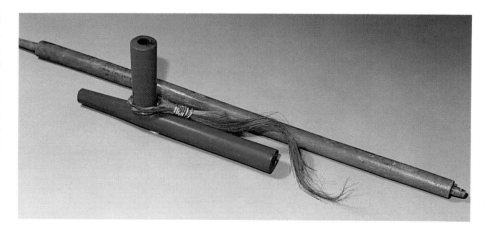

Plains type pipe with before-bowl extension, catlinite, ca. late 1800s. This fine pipe with original wooden stem is 3¾" high and 25" long. It came from the Wounded Knee area of South Dakota and is probably Sioux. Richard Krueger collection, Iowa; Sandra Krueger photograph. $1,000.00 – 1,500.00.

T-shaped Plains pipe, catlinite, and wooden stem with ornate decorations. The pipe itself is nicely tapered, with a high, round bowl. The stem has quilled designs and brass tacks. Ben Thompson collection, Missouri. Unlisted.

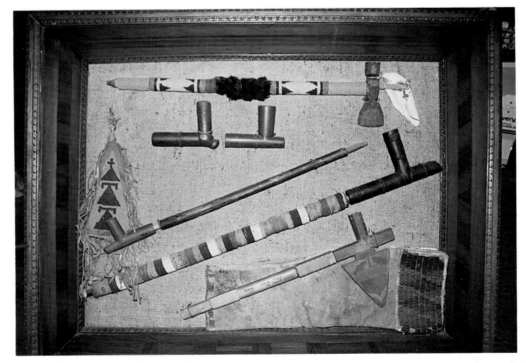

Large frame of Plains type calumet pipes, #V6-1550, all old and in very used condition, ca. 1840 – 1880. The beaded-stem pipe-tomahawk at top carries an old tag, while the beaded-stem large pipe at lower center is from the Tonawanda Reservation, New York. Iron Horse collection. All museum grade.

T-shaped historic Plains pipe and stem, ca. mid-1800s. The pipe is catlinite and the fine wooden stem has a series of thin spools and expanded-center cylinders. A copper bell is fastened near the pipe. The bowl and stem measure 24" long. The set, from South Dakota, bears G.I.R.S. authentication certificate number KD881. Collection of Jim Bickel, Huntington, Indiana. $2,500.00.

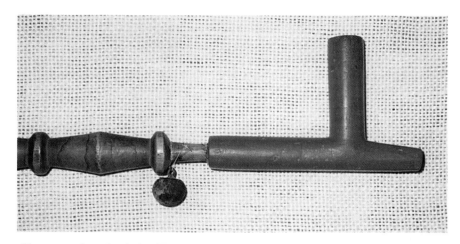

Close-up detail of the T-shaped Plains pipe and stem portion, South Dakota. The copper bell is of interest, so also the careful carving of the stem. The bowl itself is nicely shaped and polished. Collection of Jim Bickel, Huntington, Indiana. $2,500.00.

Classic Plains Indian historic catlinite pipe with partial photo of ornate pipe stem. Ca. 1860 – 1870, the bowl is red catlinite and the stem is hardwood with quill-work, dyed horse-hair, buffalo hair, and mallard duck crown. Overall length is 40" and stem is 30". Bowl size is 5 x 10". This fine set is Lakota (western Sioux). It is shown with a Lakota "possible" bag or tipi bag, ca. 1870. Richard E. Bachman collection, Washington. Pipe and stem $5,500.00.

Cherokee Pipes

The Cherokee people, located in the foothills of the southern Appalachian Mountains, have long been noted pipemakers. The chief material used has always been steatite (soapstone) and several forms were made. Probably influenced by white-manufactured pipes in early historic times, most Cherokee pipes have slender stems with medium-size bowls set at one end.

Some of the pipes, while very nicely made, were of the plain variety. A few have bowls that were made (in imitation of mold-made white-supplied kaolin pipes?) with extremely thin walls. Many such pipes are typical also for smooth surface finishing.

Better known are the Cherokee effigy forms, with miniature re-creations of animals like bears and squirrels. Some of the pipe makers had a good sense of humor, depicting — as did some of the Great Plains makers — people in humorous poses. They also, like certain Northwest Coast pipe makers, occasionally portrayed erotic objects and situations.

Since the Cherokee artisans retained a fairly basic style, it is often difficult to accurately judge the age of some examples. A number can be estimated as historic, early or late, and the information would be fairly accurate. It should also be noted that, like catlinite pipes, some are still being made by Indians today in the older styles.

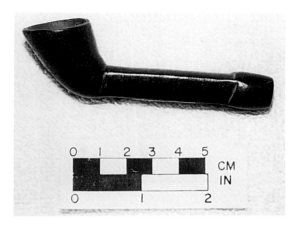

Cherokee pipe, historic, obtuse-angle elbow form with some bowl restoration, ca. 1700 – 1800. This highly polished pipe is from Monroe County, Tennessee. Gary Henry collection, North Carolina. $300.00 – 500.00.

Cherokee pipe, historic, obtuse-angle elbow form with some bowl restoration. It is made of steatite and is ca. 1700 – 1800. It was found in Monroe County, Tennessee. Gary Henry collection, North Carolina. $300.00 – 500.00.

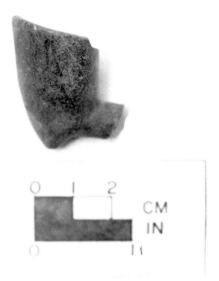

Bowl pipe with short stem, this is probably Cherokee and ca. 1750 – 1835. This pipe was done in imitation of a white-made trade pipe. It has some bowl damage and came from Clay County, North Carolina. Gary Henry collection, North Carolina. $100.00+.

Cherokee protohistoric pipe, winged-bowl form, gray steatite with minute sparkles that may be mica. Stem sides are lightly notched or tallied on this early example, 2½" long. The pipe is slightly out-of-area, being found in Kentucky. Len and Janie Weidner collection, Ohio. $150.00.

Effigy pipe, historic Cherokee, bighorn sheep form, dark steatite. The pipe measures 2⅞" long and the effigy is especially well done. Southern Appalachian Mountain region. Len and Janie Weidner collection, Ohio. $800.00.

Effigy pipe, historic Cherokee, animal form, dark steatite. It is 2⅞" long with reinforced bowl rim. This fine pipe is from the southern Appalachian region. Len and Janie Weidner collection, Ohio. $700.00.

Effigy pipe, historic Cherokee, two snakes extending along the edges of the stem top. These are unusual effigy figures and the pipe, 2½" long, is made of dark steatite. Len and Janie Weidner collection, Ohio. $700.00.

Squirrel effigy pipe, Cherokee, historic, made in black steatite. This polished pipe is 2" long and 1⁵⁄₁₆" high. Ex-collection Stroud, it is from Polk County, Tennessee. Larry Garvin, Back to Earth, Ohio. $250.00.

Effigy pipe, historic Cherokee, squirrel form in dark gray steatite. This pipe is 2⅝" long and the bowl has a rim flange. Southern Appalachian region. Len and Janie Weidner collection, Ohio. $700.00.

Cherokee effigy pipe, squirrel, size 2¼ x 3" long. Material is gray and black steatite and it holds a weathered polish. There is a ring at the stem end; old tag reads "Cherokee Indian Pipe – North Carolina." Larry Lantz, First Mesa, Indiana. $575.00.

Cherokee pipe, historic, squirrel effigy, ca. 1800 – 1900. It is 2¼" long, steatite, and from Blount County, Alabama. Gary Henry collection, North Carolina. $600.00 – 1,000.00.

Cherokee pipe, historic, right-angle elbow form with cross-hatch engraving on stem top. Ca. 1780 – 1820, this 2½" specimen is from Meigs County, Tennessee. Gary Henry collection, North Carolina. $400.00 – 650.00.

Human effigy pipe, view from feet, woman giving birth. This pipe is historic, ca. 1700s, and is made of steatite (soapstone). A Cherokee pipe, this well-done example is 5" long and would be from the southern Appalachian region. Lewis Kruglick collection, California. $800.00.

Human effigy pipe, view from head with child's emerging head visible. Made of steatite, this historic pipe, 5" long, is from the southern Appalachian region. Lewis Kruglick collection, California. $800.00.

Cherokee effigy pipe of historic times, black steatite, 2¾" long and 2" high. The image of an owl is carved between the square bowl and rectangular stem. Alabama-Tennessee border area. Robin Fiser collection, Ohio. $400.00.

Cherokee human effigy pipe, steatite, ca. 1825 – 1835. This historic pipe is nearly 3" long and well carved. It is from Charleston County, South Carolina. Mike Newman collection, Georgia. $850.00 – 1,500.00.

Iroquois Pipes

Half a dozen different groups — Cayuga, Mohawk, Oneida, Onondaga, Seneca, and Tuscarora — made up the Iroquois Confederation. All were pipe makers and users to some degree. The typical Iroquois pipe was trumpet-shaped and the curve was from nearly straight to extreme near the bowl. Most increased gradually in diameter from the mouthpiece to the enlarged bowl; in essence, many Iroquois pipes were tapered tubes.

Some pipes were unadorned but large numbers had incised lines or punctate designs that enhanced the appearance. Effigy forms included those with birds, lizards, and bears or wolves, plus some human forms. A large number of Iroquois pipes were made of pottery.

Pre-Iroquois pipes, around AD 1000, were barrel shaped and a few hundred years later pipes included vase shaped and "puffed-sleeve"

varieties. Still later trumpet-shaped pipes developed that had acorn-shaped or squared bowls, sometimes accented with rings. By 1650, Iroquois types were well established.

One reason pottery pipes were so readily accepted in early historic times in the Northeast United States is the relative ease of manufacture. A coil of clay larger at one end was rolled out, with a strand of fiber cord at the center and the large end hollowed. This was then bent to the desired shape and fired. The heat hardened the clay and burned out the fiber core. Thus a pottery pipe could be completed in far less time than the weeks required for a stone pipe.

Since pottery is quite fragile, collectors especially seek Iroquois pipes that are complete and in good condition. When such pipes are found they are eagerly acquired by knowledgeable collectors.

Iroquois pipe with dot design, very small bowl, ca. 1640 – 1700. It is made of brown pottery and both stem and bowl are 1¼". #SC-32 was found in Erie County, New York. Iron Horse collection. $375.00 – 475.00.

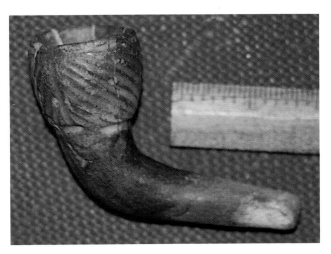

Iroquois chevron design pipe, ca. 1640 – 1700, #SC1-47. The stem is 2½" and bowl height is 2". Made of light brown pottery, this pipe is from Erie County, New York. Iron Horse collection. $300.00 – 400.00.

Iroquois L-type pipe, gray steatite, #1919A. With decorated stem end, the pipe is ca. 1650 – 1750. The stem is 4" long and the bowl 1½" high. Chautauqua County, New York. Iron Horse collection. $300.00 – 400.00.

Iroquois T-type pipe in black steatite, ca. 1640 – 1750. #BT/MC is 2¼" long and 1¼" high. Niagara County, New York. Iron Horse collection. $300.00 – 375.00.

Iroquois hoof-shape pipe with deep engraving, ca. 1600 – 1750. #P-22. It is made of brown pottery; stem is 2¼" long and bowl is 2¼" high. Jefferson County, New York. Iron Horse collection. $500.00 – 750.00.

Iroquoian platform pipe, #HL-6, made of pottery. The stem is 3" long and bowl height is 1½". Ca. 1700 – 1750, this interesting pipe is from Allegany County, New York. Iron Horse collection. $275.00 – 350.00.

Pottery pipe, flared bowl, 5⅝" long. This piece is ca. 1600 and is broken and repaired. The example is Cayuga Iroquois and is marked Venice, New York. Dave Summers, Native American Artifacts, Victor, New York. $300.00.

Iroquois vase-shaped pipe, made of dark hardstone, ca. 1550 – 1650. Nicely shaped and finished, this pipe is #DC-MC and 2½" high. Livingston County, New York. Iron Horse collection. $300.00 – 450.00.

Iroquois square-bowl pipe with line on the edge, red and brown pottery, ca. 1550 – 1650. #279/HL has a 2" stem and bowl height of 1¾". It was found near New Hudson, Allegany County, New York. Iron Horse collection. $200.00 – 300.00.

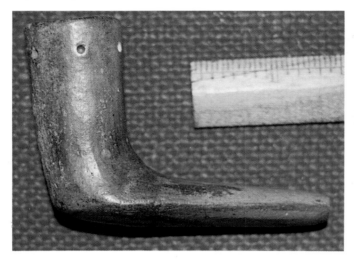

Iroquois covered-bowl pipe with flared mouthpiece, #D-841. Ca. 1500 – 1650, the material is brown pottery; stem length is 2¼" and bowl height is 1¼". This unusual pipe came from the Jamesville region, New York. Iron Horse collection. $375.00 – 425.00.

Iroquois pipe, #CB5, light brown pottery, expanded flat stem and trumpet bowl. Ca. 1680 – 1700, the stem is 3" long and bowl height is 2⅜". Chautauqua County, New York. Iron Horse collection. $275.00 – 350.00.

Iroquois spontoon pipe that once had a short wooden stem, ca. 1700 – 1750. The pottery is black and brown and pipe stem is 2", bowl height 2½". #3217, Allegany County, New York. Iron Horse collection. $350.00 – 400.00.

Iroquois spontoon-type pipe, grit-tempered pottery, #P-59. The stem is 5" long and the bowl height is 3". Ca. 1700 – 1750, this pipe is from Ontario County, New York. Iron Horse collection. $500.00 – 650.00.

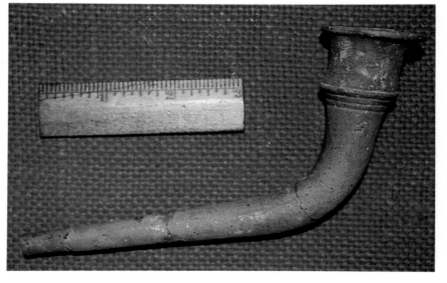

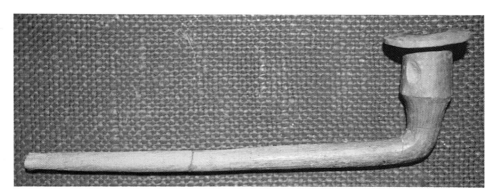

Spontoon-type Iroquoian pipe, #2437, made of red and brown pottery. The stem is 7" long and bowl height is 2½". Ca. 1700 – 1750, the pipe is from Allegany County, New York. Iron Horse collection. $500.00 – 650.00.

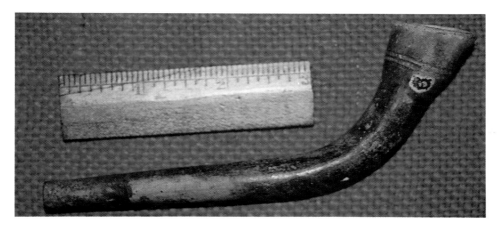

Iroquois hoof-cut trumpet pipe, ca. 1650 – 1750, #1980. It is made of dark brown pottery and has a 4" stem with bowl height of 2½". Monroe County, New York. Iron Horse collection. $450.00 – 550.00.

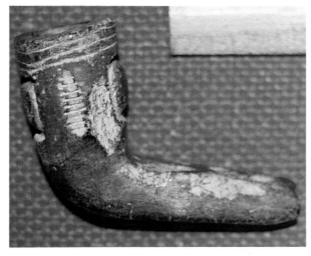

Iroquois designed bowl, ca. 1650 – 1700, gray and brown pottery. The stem on #2016 is 2½" long and bowl height is 2"; note several kinds of decoration on the bowl. Little Valley area, New York. Iron Horse collection. $350.00 – 400.00.

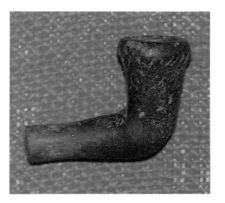

Trumpet pipe with line designs, very small size, Iroquois. This pipe in black pottery is ca. 1600 – 1680 and has a stem 1½" long and bowl 1¼" high. #K-5 was found near Hamburg, Erie County, New York. Iron Horse collection. $125.00 – 250.00.

Iroquois trumpet pipe, burnt-brown pottery, ca. 1600 – 1750. The stem on #2080 is 4" long and the bowl is 2¼" high. Allegany County, New York. Iron Horse collection. $400.00 – 450.00.

Pottery pipe, trumpet shape, with human face toward the smoker. Engraved, this pipe measures 1¼ x 5¼ x 2⅛" high. It is late prehistoric/early historic and came from the Oneida Valley, New York. Bill Mesnard collection, New Jersey. $700.00.

Iroquois trumpet pipe, light brown pottery burned black, ca. 1650 – 1700. #CAL-67 has a 2" stem and the bowl height is 1½". Erie County, New York. Iron Horse collection. $300.00 – 375.00.

Iroquois trumpet pipe, ca. 1500 – 1650, red and brown pottery. #520/2 has a 6" stem and bowl height is 4". The pipe is from Jefferson County, New York. Iron Horse collection. $750.00 – 1,000.00.

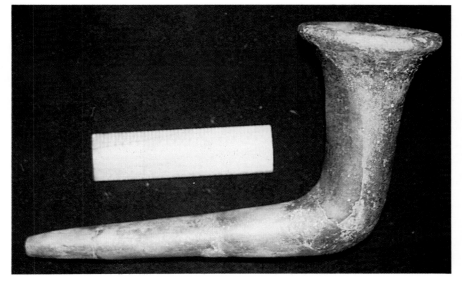

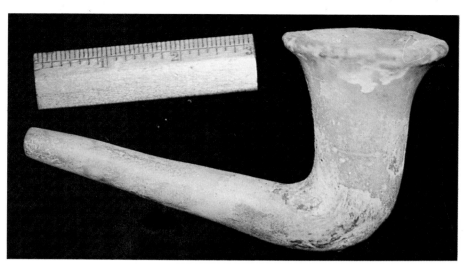

Iroquois large trumpet pipe, ca. 1500 – 1650, in light brown grit-tempered pottery. This pipe, #520/3, has a stem 5" long and bowl height is 3". It was found in Jefferson County, New York. Iron Horse collection. $450.00 – 550.00.

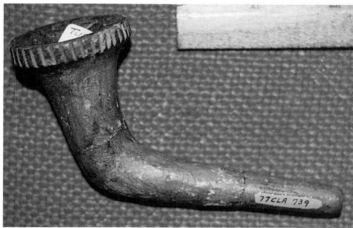

Iroquois trumpet-shaped pipe with rim lines, ca. 1650 – 1750. #77CLA-739 has a 3" stem with the bowl height 2". Jefferson County, New York. Iron Horse collection. $350.00 – 450.00.

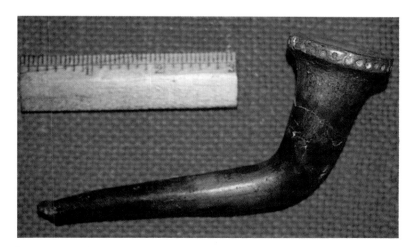

Iroquois trumpet-shaped pipe with dot rim decoration, ca. 1650 – 1750. It is made of brown pottery with a 4" stem and bowl height of 2¼". #106 is from New York. Iron Horse collection. $350.00 – 450.00.

Iroquois trumpet pipe, ring bowl with large dots, ca. 1600 – 1700. Made of light brown pottery, #578 has a stem of 1¾" and the bowl is 2". New York. Iron Horse collection. $375.00 – 475.00.

Iroquois trumpet-shaped pipe with angled lines, ca. 1600 – 1750. This pipe, #P-56, is made of brown pottery and has a 3" stem and 2" bowl. It is from the West Bloomfield area, New York. Iron Horse collection. $400.00 – 550.00.

Iroquois trumpet pipe decorated with lines and dots, ca. 1600 – 1650, red and brown pottery. #AK8-95 has a stem of 4¾" and bowl height of 1¼". Jefferson County, New York. Iron Horse collection. $400.00 – 450.00.

Iroquois plain trumpet-shaped pipe, #3216, ca. 1700 – 1750. The pottery is red and brown and the stem is 4" long, the bowl 2½" high. Allegany County, New York. Iron Horse collection. $350.00 – 400.00.

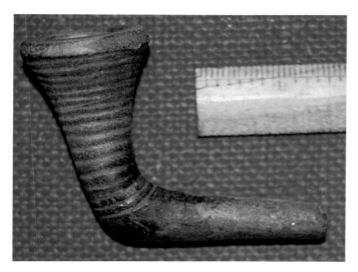

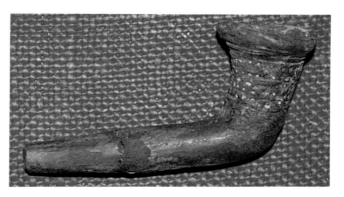

Iroquois trumpet pipe, red and brown pottery, #294. Ca. 1580 – 1650, the stem is 3¼" long and the bowl is 1¾" high. It was found near Watertown, Jefferson County, New York. Iron Horse collection. $250.00 – 350.00.

Iroquois trumpet-shaped pipe, ring design, grit-tempered light brown pottery. This pipe, #RJ/HAU1, is ca. 1650 – 1700 and has an artistic, built-up bowl. Cayuga County, New York. Iron Horse collection. $300.00 – 375.00.

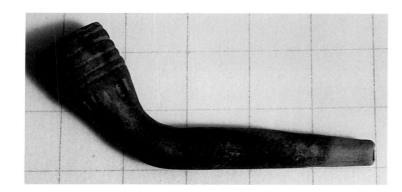

Trumpet pottery pipe, ring bowl, ca. 1670. The pipe is solid and was once in the Wray collection. It is 5¼" long. Seneca-Iroquois and from New York. Dave Summers, Native American Artifacts, Victor, New York. $450.00.

Pre-Iroquois trumpet with line designs, #D-825 is ca. 1450 – 1550. Made of brown and red pottery, the stem is 4½" long and bowl height is 2¾". New York State. Iron Horse collection. $350.00 – 400.00.

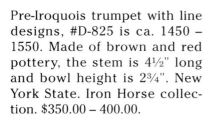

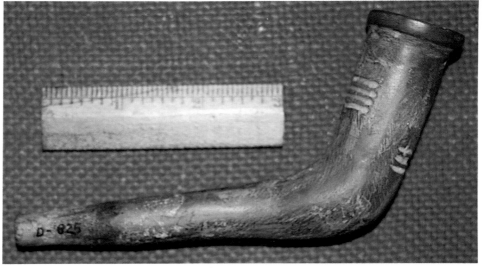

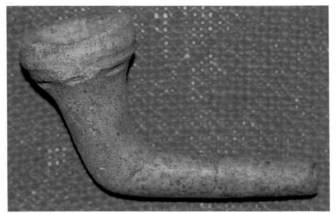

Ring bowl pipe, Iroquois, ca. 1600 – 1680. #K-6 is made of light brown pottery and has a stem 2¼" long and bowl 2" high. It came from near Hamburg, Erie County, New York. Iron Horse collection. $250.00 – 350.00.

Ring bowl pipe, Iroquois, ca. 1600 – 1680. This pipe, #K-4, is made of gray and black pottery with a 4" stem and bowl 2½" high. It was found near Hamburg, Erie County, New York. Iron Horse collection. $350.00 – 400.00.

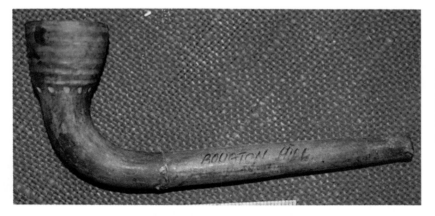

Iroquois ring bowl pipe with dots, ca. 1600 – 1750, gray and black pottery. #2/5 has a stem 6" long and bowl height is 3". From near Victor, New York. Iron Horse collection. $400.00 – 550.00.

Iroquois pipe with large ring bowl, light brown pottery, ca. 1600 – 1750. This pipe, #2/5, has a stem 4½" long with bowl height 2¾". It came from near East Bloomfield, New York. Iron Horse collection. $400.00 – 550.00.

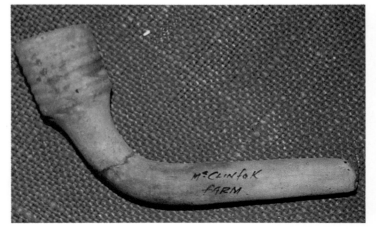

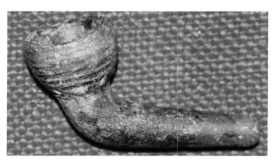

Iroquois ring bowl pipe, ca. 1640 – 1700, dark gray and black pottery. The stem is 3¾" long and bowl height is 2". #SC-99 is from Erie County, New York. Iron Horse collection. $250.00 – 300.00.

Iroquois pipe, ring bowl with dots, ca. 1640 – 1700. The pottery is light brown with black stains and the pipe has a 2" stem with bowl height 1½". #SC-2 is from Erie County, New York. Iron Horse collection. $250.00 – 350.00.

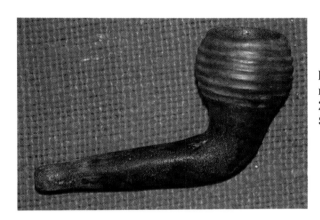

Iroquois pipe, ring bowl, ca. 1640 – 1700. #SC-15 is made of light brown pottery with a 3" stem and bowl 2" high. Erie County, New York. Iron Horse collection. $300.00 – 350.00.

Iroquois ring bowl pipe with dots, ca. 1650 – 1700, #CAL-66. Material is brown pottery with burned black areas; the stem is 4¾" while the bowl is 3" high. Erie County, New York. Iron Horse collection. $450.00 – 550.00.

Iroquois ring bowl pipe with dots, very small, ca. 1650 – 1700. Material is light brown pottery, the stem is 1¼" and bowl height is only 1". #CAL-68 is from Erie County, New York. Iron Horse collection. $400.00 – 550.00.

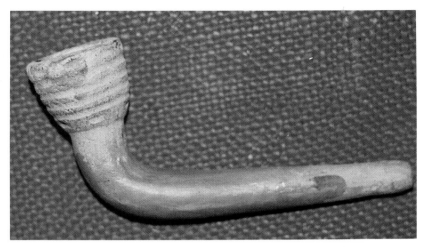

Iroquois ring bowl with dots, ca. 1650 – 1700, #CAL-65. Material is red and light brown pottery, the stem is 4½" and bowl height is 2½". Erie County, New York. Iron Horse collection. $450.00 – 550.00.

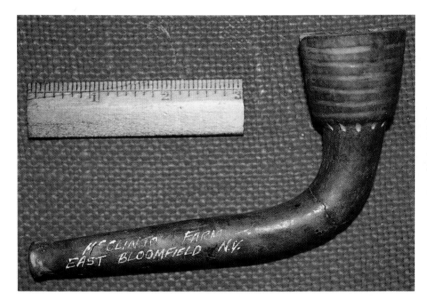

Iroquois pipe, ring bowl with dots, #146. It is ca. 1640 – 1750 and is made of dark brown pottery. The stem is 4½" and bowl height is 2¾". East Bloomfield area, New York. Iron Horse collection. $450.00 – 500.00.

Iroquois (Huron) pipe with large-ring bowl, ca. 1650 – 1750. #MG-63 is made of black and brown pottery, the stem is 3½" and bowl height is 3". Note the slightly expanded stem end. Ontario, Canada. Private collection. $400.00 – 500.00.

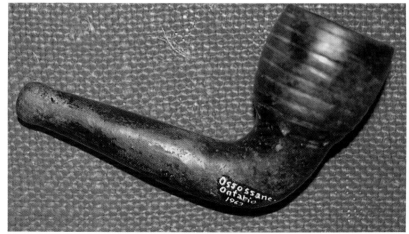

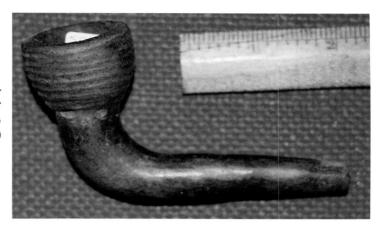

Iroquois pipe, ring bowl with dots, ca. 1640 – 1750. Material is black and brown pottery for #99, stem is 3" and bowl height is 2". Ontario County, New York. Iron Horse collection. $400.00 – 550.00.

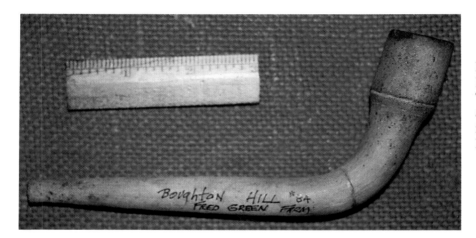

Iroquois pipe with single-ring bowl, light brown pottery, ca. 1600 – 1675. This piece, #84, has a stem of 5¼" and bowl height is 3¼". The pipe is from near Victor, New York. Iron Horse collection. $450.00 – 500.00.

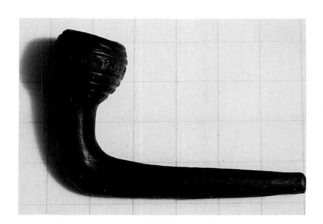

Pottery pipe, bulbous-ring bowl, ca. 1620. Made of tempered black material, this pipe measures 4¾" long and is Seneca Iroquois. Dave Summers, Native American Artifacts, Victor, New York. $900.00.

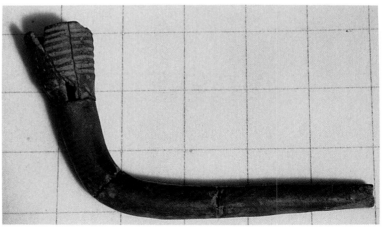

Pottery pipe, trumpet form, ring bowl, ca. 1675. Made of tempered clay, this pipe was broken into eight pieces and glued. It measures 3 x 5½" and is from New York. Dave Summers, Native American Artifacts, Victor, New York. $375.00.

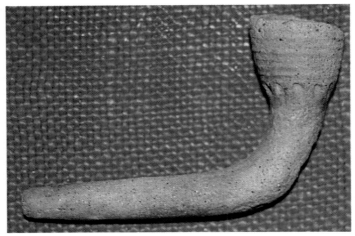

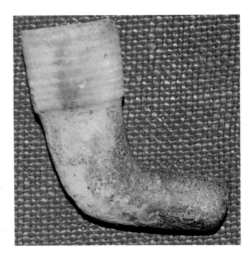

Iroquois ring-bowl with dot decoration, #RXB/1, ca. 1550 – 1650. Material is light brown pottery; stem is 3" long and bowl height is 2¼". New York. Iron Horse collection. $350.00 – 450.00.

Iroquois ring-bowl pipe, #RJ-42, light brown-red pottery. The bowl is 2" high and the stem is 3" long; at one time the stem broke and was ground down and the pipe continued in use. Ca. 1500 – 1650, this pipe is from Jefferson County, New York. Iron Horse collection. $300.00 – 400.00.

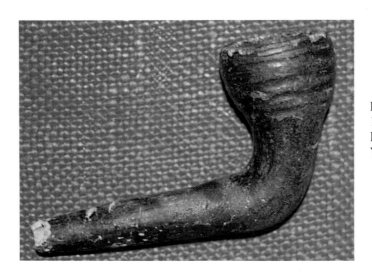

Iroquois ring-bowl pipe, brownish-black pottery, ca. 1500 – 1650. The stem on this pipe, #118/150, is 3¼" long and bowl height is 2⅝". Niagara County, New York. Iron Horse collection. $300.00 – 375.00.

Iroquois ring-bowl pipe, #10/93, ca. 1600 – 1675. It is made of brown-stained black pottery; stem length is 3½" while bowl height is 2¼". Erie County, New York. Iron Horse collection. $350.00 – 450.00.

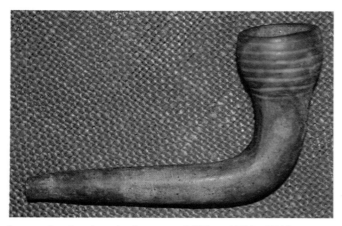

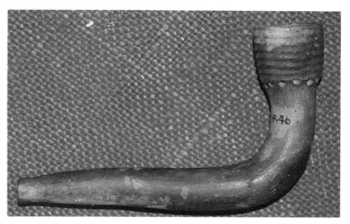

Iroquois ring-bowl pipe, ca. 1600 – 1750, #543. Made of light brown pottery, the stem is 4½" and bowl height is 3". Orchard Park area, New York. Iron Horse collection. $500.00 – 650.00.

Iroquois ring-bowl pipe with dot decoration, ca. 1600 – 1750, #P-40. This pipe is made of dark brown pottery, and the stem is 4¾" plus a 3" bowl. New York. Iron Horse collection. $450.00 – 500.00.

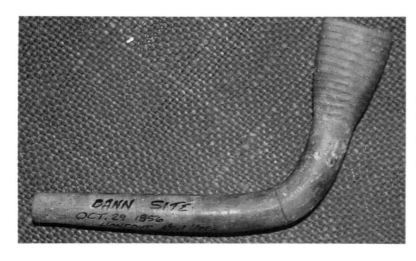

Iroquois ring-bowl pipe, ca. 1600 – 1750, #85. The stem is 4¾" and bowl height is 3⅛". Material is light brown pottery for this piece, from the Genesee Valley, Monroe County, New York. Iron Horse collection. $350.00 – 500.00.

Iroquois pipe, ring bowl with dots, ca. 1650 – 1750. Made of light brown pottery, #2667-HL has a stem 4¾" long with bowl height 2¾". Allegany County, New York. Iron Horse collection. $400.00 – 500.00.

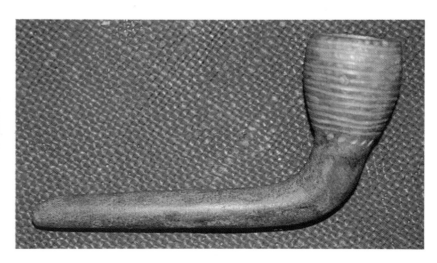

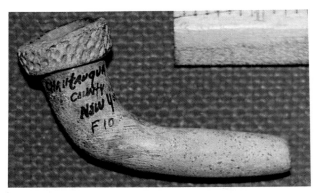

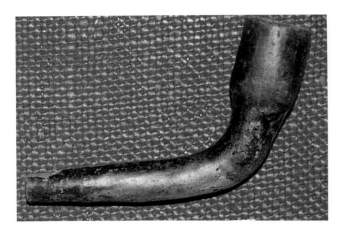

Iroquois flared-rim pipe with dot design, ca. 1600 – 1650. Pipe #F-10 is made of red and brown pottery, with a stem length of 2¼" and bowl height of 1½". Chautauqua County, New York. Iron Horse collection. $250.00 – 350.00.

Iroquois plain flared-bowl pipe, #P-58, in stained light brown pottery. Ca. 1600 – 1750, the stem is 3" long and bowl height is 2¼". This pipe is from the Genesee River Valley, Monroe County, New York. Iron Horse collection. $300.00 – 375.00.

Iroquois flared-bowl pipe with chevron design, #184, ca. 1650 – 1700. Made of brown grit-tempered pottery, the stem is 4" long and bowl height is 2½". New York. Iron Horse collection. $450.00 – 500.00.

Iroquois flared-bowl pipe, triangle design with dots, ca. 1650 – 1750, dark brown pottery. The stem is 4½" and bowl height is 2" for #108, which was found near Stanley, New York. Iron Horse collection. $450.00 – 650.00.

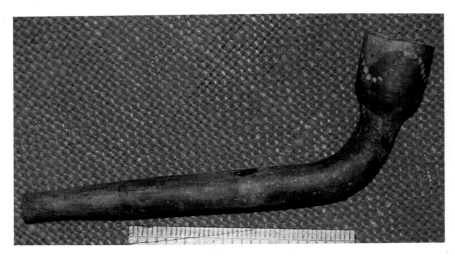

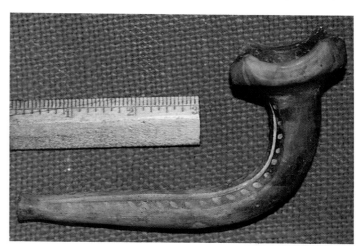

Iroquois pipe with large crown and stitched stem, ca. 1500 – 1700, #180. The stem is 4" and bowl height is 3" on this light brown pottery pipe. From near East Bloomfield, New York. Iron Horse collection. $1,000.00 – 1,300.00.

Iroquois with large crown and stitched stem, ca. 1600 – 1700, #2017. It is made of tan and brown pottery, has a 6" stem and bowl is 3" high. From the vicinity of Holcomb, New York. Iron Horse collection. $1,000.00 – 1,400.00.

Iroquois crown pipe, stitched stem, ca. 1600 – 1700. #P-19 is made of light brown and gray pottery, has a 5" stem and bowl height is 2½". Found near Victor, New York. Iron Horse collection. $950.00 – 1,300.00.

Iroquois crown pipe, ca. 1650 – 1750, light brown pottery. The long stem on #P-50 measures 6" and the bowl is 2⅝" high. From near Hopewell, Ontario County, New York. Iron Horse collection. $750.00 – 1,000.00.

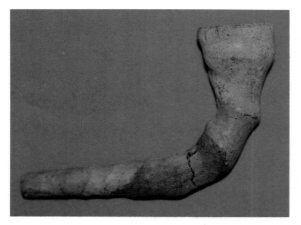

Effigy pipe, snake, Iroquois, ca. 1600 – 1680. Material is red and brown pottery for #K-3, which has a stem 3½" long and bowl height of 3". The pipe is from near Hamburg, Erie County, New York. Iron Horse collection. $550.00 – 750.00.

Effigy pipe, quail, Iroquois, ca. 1600 – 1680. #K-2 is made of light brown pottery and has a stem 3" long with bowl height 3¾". It is from near Hamburg, Erie County, New York. Iron Horse collection. $550.00 – 750.00.

Effigy pipe, Iroquois, otter figure with open mouth and bared teeth plus arrow design, ca. 1680 – 1775. #BB/95 is made of dark brown stone, with 2" stem and bowl height of 2¼". This is an attractive and well-done pipe, found in western New York. Iron Horse collection. Museum grade.

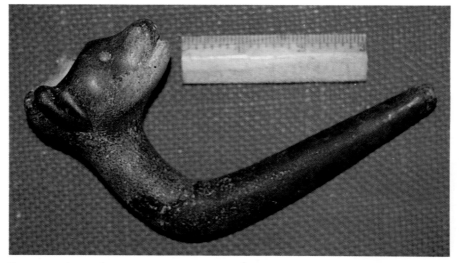

Iroquois bear head effigy pipe, large image, ca. 1600 – 1750. #B/MS is nicely molded, with a 5" stem and bowl height of 3¾". Erie County, New York. Iron Horse collection. $850.00 – 1,200.00.

Iroquois wolf effigy pipe with trumpet bowl, brown pottery, ca. 1600 – 1750. The image is lifelike for this pipe, #2, with stem 2¾" and bowl height 2¼". Genesee River Valley, Monroe County, New York. Iron Horse collection. Unlisted.

Iroquois wolf with open mouth effigy, black pottery, ca. 1600 – 1700. The figure has a copper eye plate, stem length is 2½" and bowl height is 2". #1/19NY, Monroe County, New York. Iron Horse collection. $750.00 – 900.00.

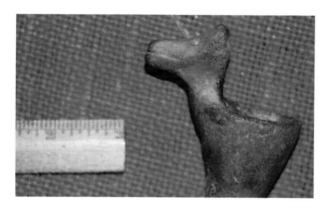

Iroquois wolf effigy pipe, brown pottery, ca. 1600 – 1700. The stem is 4" long and bowl height is 3¼". The pipe, #P-72, was found near Victor in Monroe County, New York. Iron Horse collection. $850.00 – 1,000.00.

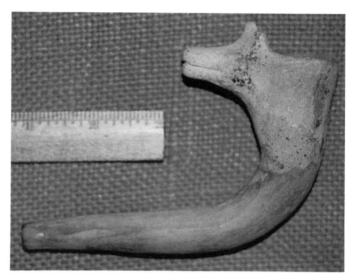

Iroquois wolf effigy pipe, light tan pottery, ca. 1600 – 1750. #RJ/OT has a stem 4" long and bowl height is 3". Genesee River Valley, Monroe County, New York. Iron Horse collection. $850.00 – 1,000.00.

Iroquois wolf effigy pipe, tan pottery, ca. 1600 – 1760. This pipe, #P-70, has a 4" stem and bowl height is 2½". It is from the Genesee River Valley, Monroe County, New York. Iron Horse collection. $1,000.00 – 1,500.00.

Iroquois bird effigy pipe, brown and black pottery, #BC-6, with nicely made bird image. Ca. 1600 – 1700, the stem is 6" long and bowl height is 3". This pipe came from near Watertown in Jefferson County, New York. Iron Horse collection. $900.00 – 1,200.00.

Iroquois human and wolf effigy pipe, angled view, #AK-210, ca. 1600 – 1750, black pottery. The pipe has a stem 4½" long and bowl height is 4". Monroe County, New York. Iron Horse collection. Museum grade.

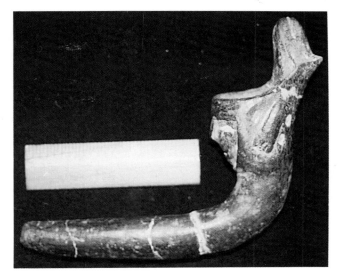

Iroquois human and wolf effigy pipe, side view, #AK-210. The pipe has been published in Beauchamp's *Earthenware of the New York Aborigines*. 1909. Vol. 5 page 131. It was also in Parker's *Archaeological History of New York, Part 1,* 1922, page 152 plate 52 #6. Monroe County, New York. Iron Horse collection. Museum grade.

Blower pipe with stitched stem, Iroquois – Seneca, ca. 1600 – 1700. The fine, large pipe is made of light brown pottery with spots burned black. The stem is 6" long and bowl height is 4". #REA/1200 was found in Finger Lakes region of New York. Iron Horse collection. $1,200.00 – 1,500.00.

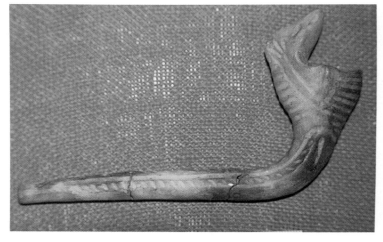

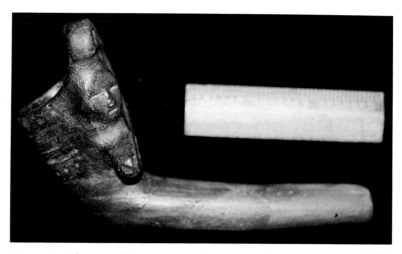

Iroquois human effigy pipe, ca. 1550 – 1700, #P-16, black pottery. It has a stem 2¾" long and bowl height is 2½". Jefferson County, New York. Iron Horse collection. $950.00 – 1,250.00.

Iroquois human effigy moon pipe, escutcheon type, ca. 1600 – 1750. #MO/RM is made of red and brown pottery, has a 4" stem and bowl height is 3¼". Jefferson County, New York. Iron Horse collection. $1,000.00 – 1,350 00.

Iroquois human figure effigy pipe, small human on bowl front facing smoker, #126. Ca. 1600 – 1750, material is red and brown pottery, stem is 1¾" and bowl height is 1¼". Jefferson County, New York. Iron Horse collection. $550.00 – 750.00.

Iroquois human effigy pipe, front view, #519/1. Material is red and brown pottery, the stem is 4½" long and the bowl is 3¼" high. Ca. 1600 – 1750, this pipe is from New York. Iron Horse collection. $1,000.00 – 1,350.00.

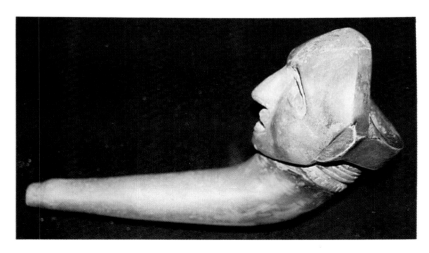

Iroquois human effigy pipe, side view, #519/1. This pipe is a true work of early historic art, ca. 1600 – 1750, with the face carefully shaped and detailed in a naturalistic manner. New York. Iron Horse collection. $1,000.00 – 1,350.00.

Iroquois human effigy pipe, ca. 1600 – 1700, light brown pottery. #1010 has a stem 3½" long and bowl height is 2½". Ontario County, New York. Iron Horse collection. $750.00 – 950.00.

Trumpet style pipe, pottery, human head effigy facing the smoker. The pipe is 5⅜" long and ca. 1670 – 1687. The value listed is what this pipe sold for. From near Victor, New York. Dave Summers, Native American Artifacts, Victor, New York. $1,800.00.

Iroquois pipe, pottery with shell temper, human face toward the smoker. Size for this well-made piece is 1⅜ x 3 x 4¾" high. New York. Bill Mesnard collection, New Jersey. $700.00.

Iroquois human effigy pipe, ca. 1650 – 1750, brown and black pottery. #P-5 has a stem 2¾" long and bowl height is 2⅛". The pipe is from Ontario County, New York. Iron Horse collection. $1,000.00 – 1,800.00.

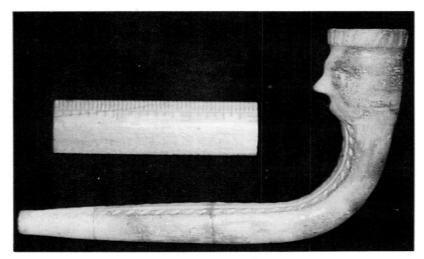

Iroquois human effigy pipe with stitched stem and ring bowl, light brown pottery, ca. 1600 – 1750. #5/19NY has a 5" stem and bowl 3¼" high. It is from near Victor, Ontario County, New York. Iron Horse collection. $1,000.00 – 1,500.00.

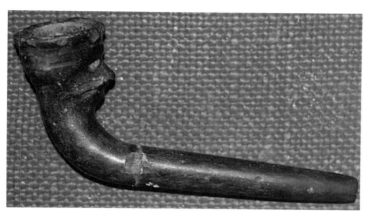

Iroquois pipe, human effigy with catlike (panther) whiskers, #P-55, dark brown pottery. It is ca. 1600 – 1750 and the stem is 4", bowl height 2". It was picked up near East Bloomfield, Ontario County, New York. Iron Horse collection. $1,000.00 – 1,350.00.

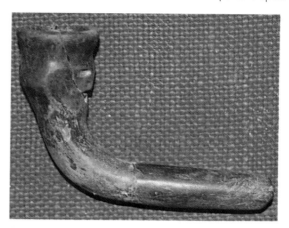

Iroquois human effigy pipe, brown pottery, #P-66, ca. 1600 – 1750. This example has a stem 3½" long and the bowl is 2¾" high. Genesee Valley, Monroe County, New York. Iron Horse collection. $750.00 – 1,000.00.

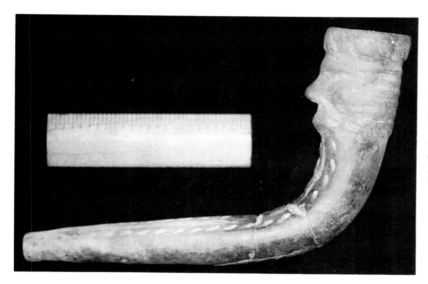

Iroquois human effigy pipe with stitched stem, gray and brown pottery, ca. 1600 – 1750. The stem length is 4¾" and the bowl is 3" high. #226/P-54 is from near Victor, Ontario County, New York. Iron Horse collection. $950.00 – 1,200.00.

Iroquois human-effigy pipe with ringed stem and bowl, light tan pottery, ca. 1600 – 1750. #P-41(2/7) has a stem 4½" long and bowl height is 3". The pipe was found near East Bloomfield, Ontario County, New York. Iron Horse collection. $950.00 – 1,200.00.

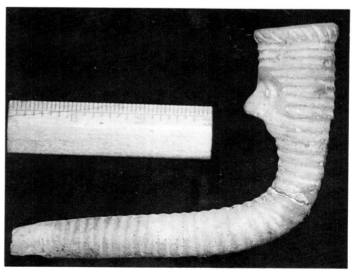

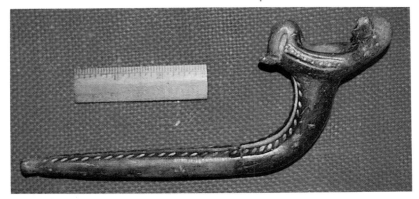

Iroquois reclining human effigy pipe with stitched stem, side view, #132. A Mother of Nations pipe, it is ca. 1600 – 1750 and very well made. From near East Bloomfield, Ontario County, New York. Iron Horse collection. Museum grade.

Iroquois reclining human effigy pipe with stitched stem, #131, side view. A Mother of Nations pipe, the stem is 6" and bowl is 3½". (The Seneca name is *dji-gon-saseh*.) From near East Bloomfield, Ontario County, New York. Iron Horse collection. Museum grade.

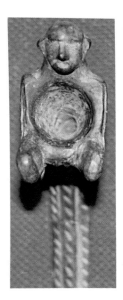

Iroquois reclining human effigy pipe with stitched stem, top view of #131, gray and black pottery. This is a Mother of Nations pipe with a 6" stem and bowl height of 3½". Ca. 1600 – 1750 this pipe is from near East Bloom-field, Ontario County, New York. Iron Horse collection. Museum grade.

Iroquois reclining human effigy pipe with stitched stem, top-side view, #132. This Mother of Nations pipe is made of gray and brown pottery. The stem is 6½" long and bowl height is 3¼". Known by the Seneca as *dji-gon-saseh*, this rare pipe form was found near East Bloomfield, Ontario County, New York. Iron Horse collection. Muse-um grade.

Roebuck human face mask effigy, pot-tery, origin sometime before the year 1535. This rare pipe is 4⅛" long and is broken and glued in two places. The pipe is St. Lawrence Iroquois, northern New York. Dave Summers, Native Ameri-can Artifacts, Victor, New York. $2,700.00.

Face effigy pipe, pottery, probably Iroquois. Size, 2 x 4½". This well-crafted pipe is a type that can be quite expensive when in top condition, as here. Huron County, New York. Private collection, Ohio. $800.00.

Iroquois human effigy pipe with ringed bowl, #P-71, ca. 1600 – 1750. It is made of light brown pottery that has been stained black, has a 5" stem, and bowl height is 2½". It was found near East Bloomfield, Ontario County, New York. Iron Horse collection. $1,000.00 – 1,200.00.

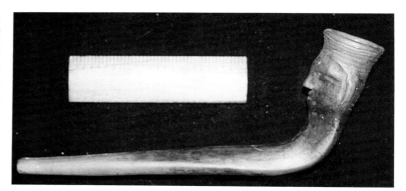

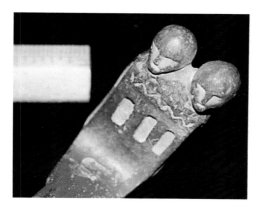

Iroquois double-human effigy pipe, front view, #P-13, ca. 1600 – 1750. This is a rare pipe form with stem 3½" and bowl height of 3". Material is red and brown pottery and the pipe is from near Le Roy, New York. Iron Horse collection. Museum grade.

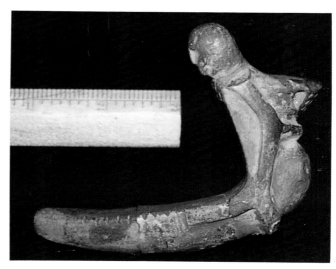

Iroquois double-human effigy pipe, side view, #P-13, ca. 1600 – 1750. This pipe was published long ago, being illustrated in Beauchamp's *Earthenware of the New York Aborigines,* 1898, Vol. 5 page 131. From near Le Roy, New York. Iron Horse collection. Museum grade.

Janus pipe, double faced with what appear to be helmets on the heads, Iroquois, ca. 1600 – 1780. The pipe is made of red pottery that has been burned black. #E-18 was found in the Genesee River Valley, New York. Iron Horse collection. $850.00 – 1,200.00.

Iroquois open-mouth human effigy, frontal/side view, ca. 1600 – 1700, #1320. Material is red and brown pottery, the stem is 3½" long and bowl height is 2½". From near Ellisburg, Ontario County, New York. Iron Horse collection. $1,000.00 – 1,350.00.

Iroquois open-mouth human effigy, top view, pipe #1320. Note the facial and hair details, and how the pipe bowl forms the mouth of the effigy. A finely crafted example, Ontario County, New York. Iron Horse collection. $1,000.00 – 1,350.00.

Iroquois Janus pipe, double-faced human effigies with weeping eyes, ca. 1640 – 1700. It is made from light tan pottery; both stem and bowl are 2½". #SC-14 was found in Erie County, New York. Iron Horse collection. $850.00 – 1,500.00.

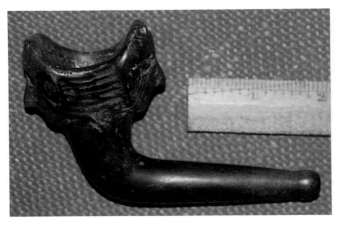

Iroquois Janus pipe, double-faced human effigies with weeping eyes, ca. 1640 – 1700. Material is black, glossy pottery, the stem is 3¼" and bowl height is 2³⁄₁₆". #SC-31 is from Erie County, New York. Iron Horse collection. $850.00 – 1,500.00.

Rare standup-disc pipe, historic Iroquois, engraved. It is marked "L.S.C." meaning League Seneca Chiefs. This is the personal Red Jacket pipe and is 4½" long, 2½" high. This pipe, #390, is made of catlinite and is from near West Candor, Tioga County, New York. Iron Horse collection. Museum grade.

Mic-mac Pipes

This easily recognized type has a high rounded bowl connected to an angled or keeled base by a narrow neck. The stem hole is at one end of the keel, which itself may have one or more small drilled holes for security attachment or decorations. Mic-mac pipes were frequently made of Minnesota catlinite though many other materials including local stone were sometimes selected.

In time, the Mic-mac is late prehistoric into historic eras and seems to have been made for centuries. This, plus a very wide distribution area (much of the eastern United States and north into Canada) makes them an important type, especially since they were also a trade item and went elsewhere. While most Mic-macs are plain, a few effigy examples were made, and a minor number of plain or effigy forms were inset with lead or pewter. All Mic-macs were used with separate stems which were of wood.

At some historic Indian village sites, Mic-mac pipes have been found in abundance. Small, easy to carry and use, the attractive Mic-mac pipe was a personal or individual pipe carried by thousands of Indian and not a few whites.

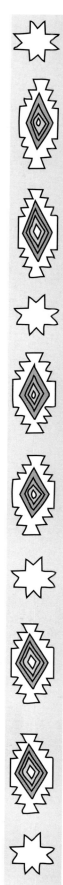

Mic-mac pipe, a variety form, deep red catlinite. The pipe is 1¾" high and carries a rich, mellow patina. It was found in Wisconsin. Len and Janie Weidner collection, Ohio. $300.00.

Mic-mac pipe, deep red catlinite, 2½" high. Like many Mic-macs, this is crisply carved and with the keel suspension hole. It is ex-collections Lackie and Morton and came from Pine County, Minnesota. Larry Garvin, Back to Earth, Ohio. $300.00.

Mic-mac pipe, decorated with large and small dots, #HL/A2. Made of catlinite, it is ca. 1650 – 1750 and 2" high. Allegany County, New York. Iron Horse collection. $500.00 – 700.00.

Mic-mac pipe, with line and triangle designs, ca. 1650 – 1750. It is carved from catlinite and 1⅞" high. #AK/88, the pipe is from Ontario County, New York. Iron Horse collection. $500.00 – 700.00.

Mic-mac pipe, hole for thong or decoration in keel bottom, ca. 1650 – 1700. #15 is made of unusual material for a Mic-mac, black steatite, and measures 2" high. Gang Mills area, New York. Iron Horse collection. $300.00 – 450.00.

Mic-mac pipe, ca. 1650 – 1750, fine-grained sandstone, 1¾" high. The pipe has the letter "R" on the keel, which has a drill hole located on the keel bottom center. #E-1245/AK88, Ontario County, New York. Iron Horse collection. $350.00 – 475.00.

Mic-mac pipe, quite plain, hole just started, ca. 1650 – 1750. Material is polished light brown sandstone and the pipe is 1⅛" high. #E-745 is from Ontario County, New York. Iron Horse collection. $375.00 – 450.00.

Mic-mac pipe, catlinite, ca. 1600 – 1780. The pipe, #E-2158, has the bowl top inlaid with pewter and is 3¼" high. Ex-collection Dr. Hugh Young, the pipe is from Kansas. Iron Horse collection. $375.00 – 650.00.

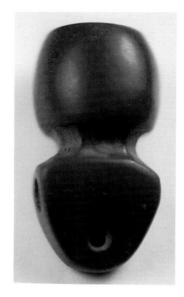

Mic-mac style pipe, historic period, this example made of dark red catlinite. This pipe is 2¾" high and came from Michigan. Lee Hallman collection, Pennsburg, Pennsylvania. $500.00.

Mic-mac pipe, keel with suspension hole, made of pale red catlinite. Probably early historic, this example came from the Miami River area of Ohio. Collection of and photograph by Duane Treest, Illinois. $300.00+.

Mic-mac type pipe, red pipe-stone, nicely carved. This pipe, in two shades of catlinite, is ex-collection Swann and is from Minnesota. Larry Garvin, Back to Earth, Ohio. $475.00 – 500.00.

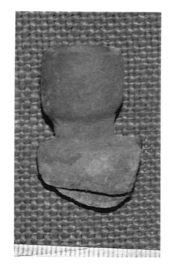

Mic-mac pipe, #HL-55, very plain and with no keel hole, gray and brown sandstone. Ca. 1650 – 1750, this pipe is 2¼" high. Allegany County, New York. Iron Horse collection. $300.00 – 450.00.

Mic-mac pipe, with hole in keel plus dot and ring designs, ca. 1650 – 1750. Pipe #RJ-11 is made of polished dark brown sandstone and measures 2⅛" high. Ontario County, New York. Iron Horse collection. $375.00 – 475.00.

Mic-mac pipe, faceted keel with hole, polished fine-grained sandstone, ca. 1650 – 1750. #RJ-10 is 2¾" high and was found in Ontario County, New York. Iron Horse collection. $400.00 – 500.00.

Mic-mac pipe, square-based keel, ca. 1650 – 1750. #HS/10 (P-42/I-92) is made of fine-grained sandstone that was polished. Only 1¾" high, the pipe was found near Seneca Lake, Ontario County, New York. Iron Horse collection. $300.00 – 400.00.

Mic-mac pipe with triangular designs and keel hole, ca. 1650 – 1750. Material is unusual, being a brown hardstone, and the pipe is 2¼" high. #P-43 is from the Onagee area, Ontario County, New York. Iron Horse collection. $375.00 – 450.00.

Mic-mac pipe, early historic period, pottery, probably a copy of catlinite pipes from the same region. The bowl is ¾" in diameter and the overall height is 2¼". It is from northern Illinois. Collection of and photograph by Duane Treest, Illinois. $125.00 – 175.00.

Mic-mac pipe, early historic period, this example made of pottery. The overall pipe is 1¾" high. Probably made as a copy of catlinite Mic-macs, it is from northern Illinois. Collection of and photograph by Duane Treest, Illinois. $100.00 – 150.00.

Mic-mac pipe, left front view, 1⁷⁄₁₆" long and 1¹⁄₁₆" wide. Found by the owner along the Meramec River in Missouri, it was said by Gregory Perino to be the second nicest Mic-mac pipe he had seen. This artifact has been published in the journal of Central States Archaeological Society, Vol. 39 No. 3, July 1992. Brian Andrews collection, Missouri; photograph by Tony Clinton. Museum quality.

Mic-mac pipe, right front view, historic period, 2" high. Material is deep red catlinite and the pipe was drilled with holes (now filled with pewter) for attachment to the stem. Note suspension hole at bottom center of the keel. This was a personal find of the owner on 8-31-91 in St. Louis County, Missouri. Brian Andrews collection, Missouri; photograph by Tony Clinton. Museum quality.

Mic-mac pipe, late historic era, made of dark brown pipestone. The well-shaped pipe is 1⁷⁄₈" high and 1⁷⁄₈" long. This piece is Chippewa, from Minnesota. Jim Maus collection, North Carolina. $300.00.

Steatite pipe, Mic-mac influence, ca. 1880 – 1890. The pipe with three suspension holes is 3" high and 6¾" long, including the thin wooden stem. This is a Blackfoot pipe. Sam Merriman collection, Oregon. $700.00.

Mic-mac keel-type pipe, inlaid with lead and pinned, ca. 1600 – 1700. #AK/42 is made of green banded slate and is 2" high and 1¾" long. It was found in northern Ohio, near Lake Erie. Iron Horse collection. $350.00 – 475.00.

Disc Pipes

Disc pipe design is another form that transcended eras, being used both in late prehistoric and in historic times. Made very often of catlinite, this is a two-level pipe with the large disc and central bowl hole set above the elongated keel base with a stem hole at one end. While most discs were rounded, as the name suggests, a few were oval and at least one squared example is known.

Many pipes of this type were some 2½ x to 4" long, with disc diameter about half the length of the pipe. Disc pipes also had a wide distribution, from the Rockies east to the Atlantic. A few were used with long handles as Plains pipes, but these are not common.

One variety has an angular disc extension over the keel, and this form is known to have been placed in some Omaha war bundles. Varieties of disc pipes include large and small discs, thick and thin discs, and below-disc keel lengthening that forms a handle.

Some of the disc pipes in catlinite are very attractive because they are carefully made and the disc surface, especially, is highly polished. Sometimes this type is also called the sun-disc pipe because of the shape and color of the disc.

Disc pipe made of gray pipestone with chip from edge of disc. It is late prehistoric/historic and measures 2 x 2 x 1" high. This pipe was found April 24, 1954, in Indiana. Bill Mesnard collection, New Jersey. $200.00.

Disc pipe, late prehistoric period, 1½ x 4½". This is a fine example of the elongated disc form, made of Ohio pipestone. It is highly polished and in perfect condition. Meade County, Kentucky. Private collection, Ohio. $1,000.00.

Disc pipe, dark catlinite, nicely designed over-all with the wedge-shaped base and circular pipe rim. In fine condition, the pipe measures 3¾" long, 1" high, and 2¼" across the bowl. Mason County, Kentucky. Bill Mesnard collection, New Jersey; Sarah Bones, photographer. $400.00.

Disc pipe, short-stem type made of weathered limestone. The pipe is 1½" long and 1¼" high. Kentucky. Len and Janie Weidner collection, Ohio. $350.00.

Disc pipe, late prehistoric – historic peri-od, made of light-colored limestone with polish. The pipe is 3⅞" long while the disc is 1⅝" in diameter. Kentucky. Len and Janie Weidner collection, Ohio. $650.00.

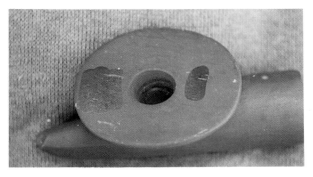

Disc pipe, very late prehistoric and ca. 1400, catlinite. The length is 3¼" and the pipe is 1⅞" across the bowl. This pipe was found by T. Watson in Van Buren County, Iowa. Dale and Betty Roberts collection, Iowa; Betty Roberts photograph. $350.00.

Disc pipe, late prehistoric – early historic, with oval or oblong bowl, pipe 2¼" long. Material is light brown stone and the pipe came from Humphreys County, Tennessee. Len and Janie Weidner collection, Ohio. $400.00.

Disc bowl pipe, late prehistoric and early historic, red and yellow catlinite. The example is 1½ x 3¾" and came from Holt County, Missouri. A burrowing rodent has gnawed away much of the bowl rim, leaving toothmarks. Mike George collection, Missouri. $50.00 – 100.00.

Disc bowl pipe, red catlinite, late prehistoric and early historic period, from Holt County, Missouri. It measures 2¾" across the bowl and is 3⅛" long. Mike George collection, Missouri. $450.00.

Disc pipe, engraved along sides of the keel and with disc reworked and angular, 5" long. This late prehistoric – early historic pipe, #287, was found in Defiance County, Ohio. Iron Horse collection. $500.00 – 750.00.

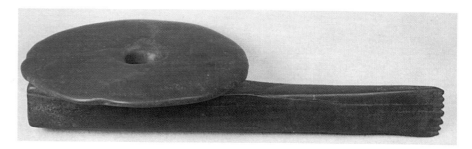

Disc pipe, late prehistoric – early historic, 2" across the disc. Formerly in the Dr. Meuser collection, this is pipe #288/3511/5 from near Eaton, Preble County, Ohio. Iron Horse collection. $350.00 – 450.00.

Disc pipe, long-handled, large size at 6⅞" with disc diameter 3¾". Probably historic, deep red stone with good surface polish and patina. One of the better disc pipes. Trempealeau County, Wisconsin. Larry Lantz, First Mesa, Indiana. $1,850.00.

Disc pipe, late prehistoric, made of limestone. The stem was broken long ago. The pipe is 1¾" long and the bowl is 1½" across. This pipe came from Henderson County, Kentucky. Collection of and photograph by Duane Treest, Illinois. $75.00 – 125.00.

Disc pipe, made of black, slate-like stone, late prehistoric period and found in central Wisconsin. It measures 2½" long and the bowl is 1" in diameter. The disc surface is quite polished. Collection of and photograph by Duane Treest, Illinois. $300.00+.

Disc pipe, Mississippian to protohistoric, made of brown steatite. The disc is 1¾" in diameter and the pipe is 2¾" long. This pipe came from Macon County, Georgia. Private collection, Georgia. $400.00.

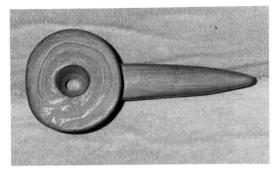

Disc pipe, Mississippian to protohistoric period, with carved serpent on face of disc. Material is brown stone for this example which is 2¼ x 3½". It came from Aberdeen, Ohio. Frederick DeWitt Ufford collection, Georgia. $925.00.

Disc pipe, Mississippian into protohistoric times, material red catlinite. The bowl or disc diameter is 1½" and pipe length is 2½". With good polish, this pipe is from Kentucky. Private collection, Georgia. $550.00.

Disc pipe, late prehistoric – early historic, with large side line that may represent a bird beak. Material appears to be very dark, highly patinated catlinite. The pipe is 3¼" long with disc 1½" across, and bowl diameter with a ⅜" hole. Found in three pieces, the repaired pipe is from Union County, Kentucky. Dennis Link collection, Ohio. $1,000.00.

Disc pipe, top view, catlinite, probably historic, 1" high and 3½" long, with disc 1¾" in diameter. Material is brick-red with pink flecks and there is high, glossy use polish. Larry Lantz, First Mesa, Indiana. $565.00.

Disc pipe, side view, in brick-red catlinite. It has a suspension hole at the keel end of this nicely polished historic pipe. Larry Lantz, First Mesa, Indiana. $565.00.

Tubular Pipes

As a more-or-less single, specific pipe style, Great Pipes kept their distinctive shape for the longest period of time. But as a general form and a broad style, tubular pipes lasted even longer. Tube pipes in fact existed for the entire pipe-making period in North America, from roughly 1500 BC to AD 1500 and beyond.

This is 3000-plus years of manufacturing and steady use. As a quite direct and simple style, tubular pipes may even have been rediscovered from time to time in different regions. At the beginning, in the Late Archaic, tubular pipes were made by the Glacial Kame people of the eastern Midwest and the Poverty Point Indians of the South.

The Adena of Early Woodland times kept the style alive with their many tubular forms — the tapered, the cylinder, the blocked-end, the flared-mouthpiece. Here and there across the country, in Middle and Late Woodland times (BC 500 – AD 100 or so) a few other tube pipes seem to have been used. As already mentioned, some of the Northeastern pottery pipes were essentially tubes with some degree of bend. The Northwest had many tubular styles, some quite late in time. The Southwest had tubular forms in both stone and pottery.

Part of the appeal of tubular pipes was the exquisite simplicity of style and manufacture. For stone examples, the bowl and stem openings were in-line, aiding in grinding, polishing, and drilling. With the bowl an extension of the stem, and vice-versa, the design was easy to use and, probably, quick to clean.

For this, the first pipe form or type in what is now North America, it would be fascinating to know what inspired this design in the first place. Perhaps a burning stick with a hollow center was lifted from a campfire. Or, tubular pipes may have been made of organic material, bone or antler, with no trace now remaining.

Tubular pipe, brown pottery, 3½" long. This is a well-made example with medium polish on the exterior. Washington County, Tennessee. Larry Garvin, Back to Earth, Ohio. $200.00.

Tubular pipe, orange pottery, 2⅛" long. Very well shaped, the side is marked "Cliff Dwellers, ARIZ." Len and Janie Weidner collection, Ohio. $225.00.

Pottery tubular pipes, both Meadowood and Middle Woodland for the region. Left, #2/19-NY, 2¾" long, Kipps Island, New York. $350.00 – 400.00. Right, #102, 4" long, Genesee Valley, New York. $350.00 – 375.00. Iron Horse collection.

Tubular pipe, Archaic period, made of gray steatite. It is 1⅜" wide and 3⅞" long. This early form was found in a rock shelter near New London, Connecticut, in 1948. H . B. Greene II collection, Florida. $100.00.

Tubular pipe, probably Late Archaic, made of tan fine-grained sandstone. The pipe has a chip out of the mouthpiece and the bowl end, and measures 1⅜" in diameter, 3⅝" long. It is from Coshocton County, Ohio. Bill Mesnard collection, New Jersey. $250.00.

Tubular pipe, Glacial Kame of the Late Archaic and ca. 1500 BC. It is made of banded glacial slate and was found in Huntington County, Indiana, along Majenica Creek. This is the earliest known pipe form or type in the Midwest. Collection of Jim Bickel, Huntington, Indiana. $900.00.

Tubular pipe, fine-grained sandstone, Red Ochre Indians, Late Archaic – Early Woodland period. This example, 6¹⁄₁₆" long, was found in 1933. Lawrence County, Ohio. Len and Janie Weidner collection, Ohio. $2,500.00.

Tubular pipe, sandstone, 6¹⁄₁₆" long. It is Red Ochre of Early Woodland times and one of the better examples done in close-grained sandstone. It was found by A. Blackwell in 1933 near the Hanging Rock region of Lawrence County, Ohio. Len and Janie Weidner collection, Ohio. $3,000.00.

Tubular pipe, fine-grained sandstone, Red Ochre people of Late Archaic – Early Woodland times. The expanded mouthpiece, as seen, was in use at a fairly early date. This example, 8½" long, came from Lawrence County, Ohio. Len and Janie Weidner collection, Ohio. $3,500.00.

Tubular pipe, Late Archaic – Early Woodland timespan, 2" long. Material is a brownish stone and this basic pipe form was found in Wisconsin. Collection of and photograph by Duane Treest, Illinois. $100.00 – 150.00.

Tubular pipe, gray-brown sandstone, with "railroad track" incising on exterior. This Late Archaic pipe is 3⅛" long and came from Summit County, Ohio. Len and Janie Weidner collection, Ohio. $1,800.00.

Tubular pipe, Glacial Kame Indians of the Late Archaic, made of close-grained sandstone. The pipe measures 4" long and has a polished exterior. Wayne County, Ohio. Len and Janie Weidner collection, Ohio. $1,200.00.

Tubular pipe, Archaic period, made of dark stone. This basic pipe type is 1" in diameter and 3¼" long. The pipe was acquired from Lee County, Mississippi. Wilfred Dick collection, Mississippi. $400.00 – 550.00.

Tubular pipe, Glacial Kame people of Late Archaic times, ca. 1500 BC, made of banded glacial slate. The pipe is 4" long and 1⅜" at maximum thickness. An outstanding example of an early pipe, it is from Wayne County, Ohio. Len and Janie Weidner collection, Ohio. $1,200.00.

Cloudblower tubular pipe, Late Archaic period, 4½" long. The majority of Late Archaic tubular pipes in the glaciated upper eastern Midwest were made of banded slate, so this pipe in green granite-like hardstone is very unusual. This was a personal find of the owner on March 6, 1991. Clinton County, Indiana. Tom E. Smith collection, Indiana. Unlisted.

Glacial Kame (Late Archaic) tubular pipe, this superb example made of limestone. It measures 1½ x 8" and is one of the larger examples from the state. Hardin County, Ohio. Private collection, Ohio. $1,200.00.

Tubular pipe, Glacial Kame people of the Late Archaic, made of fine-grained tan-brown sandstone. The exterior has some peck marks and abrading marks plus a small amount of polish. The pipe is 1⅜" across and 3¾" long. Kentucky. Bill Mesnard collection, New Jersey; Sarah Bones, photographer. $350.00.

Tubular pipe, Glacial Kame Indians of the Late Archaic, tan sandstone. This pipe measures 4⅛" long and has incised lines which can be seen on the lower side, somewhat like tally marks. The pipe is marked "OHIO." Len and Janie Weidner collection, Ohio. $1,300.00.

Tubular pipe, Glacial Kame people of the Late Archaic period, 4" long. The material is dark hardstone and the pipe was found in Hardin County, Ohio. Len and Janie Weidner collection, Ohio. $500.00.

Tubular pipe, Late Archaic period and ca. 1000 BC, made of close-grained sandstone. The origin of this pipe is unknown but it is probably Tennessee. Gary Henry collection, North Carolina. $250.00 – 350.00.

Tubular pipe with side hole, Late Archaic – Early Woodland period, 2⅜" long. This is an unusual form in dark hardstone, from the Green Bay region of Wisconsin. A longer but similar example is shown in Hart's *Prehistoric Pipe Rack*, page 262, top. Collection of and photograph by Duane Treest, Illinois. $200.00 – 300.00.

Tubular pipe, Glacial Kame and Late Archaic, ca. 1500 BC. This is an extremely fine expanded-tube pipe in dark banded slate, 6¾" long, well polished. Eastern Midwest. Len and Janie Weidner collection, Ohio. $1,500.00.

Tubular pipe, green banded slate, 4½" long. The mouthpiece end has a thin band for extra strength, and the pipe is thin walled and nicely polished. Greenup County, Kentucky. Len and Janie Weidner collection, Ohio. $750.00.

Tubular pipe, Early Woodland period, made of a minority material for the time, catlinite. In solid maroon, this pipe measures 3⅜" long. Ex-collection Payne, it is from Hopkins County, Kentucky. Len and Janie Weidner collection, Ohio. $850.00.

Adena tubular pipe with flared mouthpiece, 1¾ x 3½" long. A scarce pipe form, it is made of Ohio pipestone and was found in Ross County, Ohio. Private collection, Ohio. $1,200.00.

Tubular pipe, blocked-end subtype, Adena people of the Early Woodland. The pipe is 4¼" long and is made of dark, fine-grained sandstone. It was found near Chillicothe, Ross County, Ohio. Len and Janie Weidner collection, Ohio. $700.00.

Adena tubular pipe, blocked-end type, 6" long. #SRB/1 is ca. 800 – 100 BC and is made of limestone. The pipe has an unusual side ventilation hole for controlling substance burn. This piece was found near the Seneca River in Seneca County, New York. Iron Horse collection. $1,000.00 – 1,500.00.

Adena (Early Woodland) blocked-end tubular pipe, cream-colored Ohio pipestone with bowl opening to the left. This example came from Scioto County, Ohio, a region with many Mound-builder earthworks and artifacts. Lee Hallman collection, Pennsburg, Pennsylvania. $350.00 – 550.00.

Adena blocked-end tubular pipe, Early Woodland and ca. 800 – 100 BC, #MS/ELL. Material is greenish-gray steatite with a medium polish and the pipe is 3⅞" long. It was found near Ellington, Chautauqua County, New York. Iron Horse collection. $400.00 – 750.00.

Woodland tubular pipe, #MCL-2500, ca. 500 BC – AD 500, green banded glacial slate. It is 5½" long and nicely shaped with artistic banding. Iron Horse collection. Museum grade.

Woodland banded slate tubular pipe, ca. 500 BC – AD 500, green banded glacial slate. #AK-GF, this nicely tapered pipe is 4½" long and from the Seneca River area near Montezuma, New York. Iron Horse collection. $1,500.00+.

Woodland banded slate tubular pipe, ca. 500 BC – AD 500, banded glacial slate in shades of green. Pipe #2HL is 3⅜" long and came from Seneca County, New York. Iron Horse collection. $950.00 – 1,300.00.

Tubular pipe, Adena period, greenish pipestone. The pipe is fully drilled and the stem end has a rounded contour. This superb example is 5⅜" long and is from the eastern Midwest. Len and Janie Weidner collection, Ohio. $1,350.00.

Tubular pipe, Adena (Early Woodland) period, 2½" long. Well polished in yellow-tan Ohio pipestone, this artifact was a prehistoric export, being found in Huntington County, Indiana. Collection of Jim Bickel, Huntington, Indiana. $350.00 – 450.00.

Long tubular pipe, Adena and Early Woodland, made of pipestone. It measures 12½" long and is ex-collections Ritter, Snyder, and B. W. Stephens. Loudon County, Tennessee. Dale and Betty Roberts collection, Iowa; Betty Roberts photograph. $1,150.00.

Tubular pipe, Adena of Early Woodland times, 1¹⁄₁₆ x 3⁷⁄₈" long. While the stem end has a small drill hole, the bowl end is large. The material is gray pipestone which retains a beautiful, glossy finish. Fayette County, Kentucky. Len and Janie Weidner collection, Ohio. $750.00.

Flattened-stem Adena tubular pipe, Early Woodland period, 1 x 3" long. Well shaped and with a medium polish, this scarce type is from Lawrence County, Ohio. Private collection, Ohio. $1,300.00.

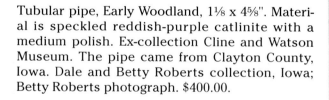

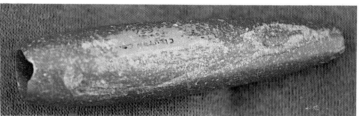

Tubular pipe, Early Woodland, 1⅛ x 4⅝". Material is speckled reddish-purple catlinite with a medium polish. Ex-collection Cline and Watson Museum. The pipe came from Clayton County, Iowa. Dale and Betty Roberts collection, Iowa; Betty Roberts photograph. $400.00.

Blocked-end tubular Adena pipe, Early Woodland, 1¼ x 5". The mouth-piece end is shown, with the other section (bowl opening) considerably larger. Material is Ohio pipestone. Bedford County, Pennsylvania. Private collection, Ohio. $1,600.00.

Tubular pipe, Adena of Early Woodland times, 5¹⁄₁₆" long. Material is greenish-tan pipestone and the exterior is highly polished. The narrowed portion is the stem end for this high-grade piece. Ohio. Len and Janie Weidner collection, Ohio. $1,200.00.

Adena tubular pipe, bowl view. It is the blocked end variety, made of close-grained sandstone and 2⅝" long. Mercer County, Kentucky. Dale and Betty Roberts collection, Iowa; Betty Roberts photograph. $300.00.

Adena tubular pipe, Early Woodland period, mouth-piece view. This sandstone pipe is ex-collections Albert, Davis, and Watson Museum. Mercer County, Kentucky. Dale and Betty Roberts collection, Iowa; Betty Roberts photograph. $300.00.

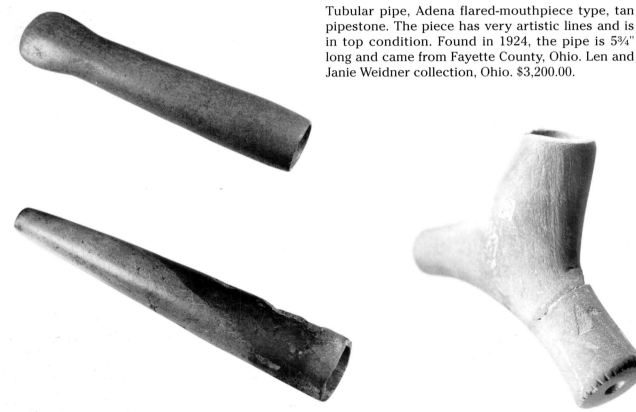

Tubular pipe, Adena flared-mouthpiece type, tan pipestone. The piece has very artistic lines and is in top condition. Found in 1924, the pipe is 5¾" long and came from Fayette County, Ohio. Len and Janie Weidner collection, Ohio. $3,200.00.

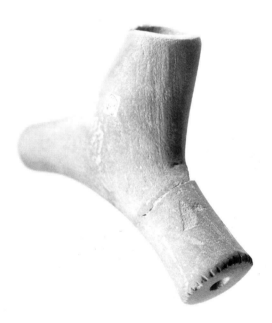

Tubular pipe, tapered for length, Adena people of Early Woodland times. This very fine example is made of greenish pipestone and at some time incurred fire damage. It is 6¾" long, from the eastern Midwest. Len and Janie Weidner collection, Ohio. Museum grade.

Modified blocked-end Adena tubular pipe, a very rare form. It is made of close-grained sandstone, one of the favored materials of Adena craftspeople. It is 4 x 5" and is tally marked around the stem hole. This pipe is from the Cynthiana area of Kentucky. Private collection, Ohio. Museum grade.

Modified tubular pipe, Adena people of Early Woodland times, made of tan medium-hard stone. The projection to the side is the stem, with the main body 4⅛" long. This rare form is probably Middle Adena. Ohio. Len and Janie Weidner collection, Ohio. $2,500.00.

Adena modified tubular pipe (with side stem), ca. 800 – 100 BC. Made of light brown sandstone, tube length is 8¼" and stem (not bowl) height is 2". #SRB/2 was found near the Seneca River, Seneca County, New York. Iron Horse collection. $1,000.00 – 1,500.00.

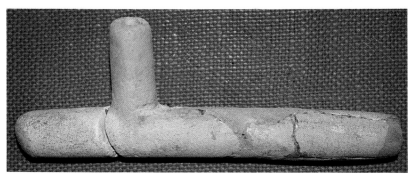

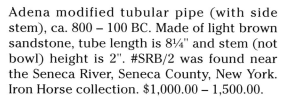

Tubular pipe in unusual material, finely shaped catlinite, 2¾" long. Ex-collections Phillips and Wagers, the pipe is from Manitowoc County, Wisconsin. Len and Janie Weidner collection, Ohio. $475.00.

Flare-rim tubular pipe, historic, ca. 1600 – 1750. It is pottery and very late Occaneechi culture, 2⅜" long. This pipe is from eastern Virginia. Jim Maus collection, North Carolina. $100.00.

Tubular pipe with expanded bowl rim, black steatite, pipe tapered and 1¼ x 3½". Very thin walls and exterior well polished with three thin lines around the pipe. Possibly late prehistoric; Polk County, Tennessee. Larry Lantz, First Mesa, Indiana. $750.00.

Blocked-end tubular pipe, probably Early Woodland period, #H-461, black speckled steatite. This fine pipe with ring enhancement of the stem end measures 6¼" long and is from the Saltsville area of Virginia. Iron Horse collection. Museum grade.

West Coast Pipes

In late prehistoric and early historic times Indians of the West Coast northward had many tubular forms, with descriptive names given them by today's collectors such as wine glass or cigar-holder. Many West Coast pipes were made of steatite and were long, slender, and tapered.

Such pipes are also noted for being made of material combinations, like wood and stone. Sometimes these are so carefully fitted together that the sections can easily be seen but the joint itself is nearly invisible. Other examples may be enhanced with bits of shell glued on with asphaltum or natural tar and incised lines.

West Coast pipes may further be decorated with raised rings and enlarged mouthpiece ends for bowl rims. Many are also spectacular due to length or finish, some being polished to a high gloss. The entire West Coast region, from southern California north through Oregon and Washington into Canada, produced a large number of tubular forms. It was here that tubular pipes reached a high state of development, at least insofar as the use of steatite was concerned.

Effigy tubular pipes were done but they are few since long, narrow designs have limited effigy applications. Sometimes fish or sea mammals are portrayed in other pipe styles, and for some reason pipes shaped like killer whales were frequently made.

Tubular pipe, medicine form, with holes drilled in the pipe body. Ca. 800 – 1300, the steatite pipe measures 1 x 6½" long. It came from Santa Barbara County, California. E. Woods collection, California. $750.00.

Tubular pipe, single flange, ca. 500 – 1500. Nicely polished, it is made of steatite and measures ⅞ x 4" long. The pipe came from Contra Costa County, California. E. Woods collection, California. $450.00.

Tubular pipe, phallic form, made of steatite. This pipe is ca. 700 – 1300 and measures 1 x 4" long. It is from San Diego County, California. E. Woods collection, California. $550.00.

Tubular pipe, phallic form, made of steatite. This unusual pipe is ca. 800 – 1400 and measures 1 x 7". It was acquired from San Diego County, California. E. Woods collection, California. $800.00.

Medicine pipe, tubular form, well developed and decorated. It is inlaid with clamshell disc beads and has incised lines. Ca. 1000, the pipe measures 1 x 6" and came from Los Angeles County, California. E. Woods collection, California. $1,200.00.

Tubular pipe, small single-flange type, ca. AD 500 – 1500. The material is green steatite and size is ¾ x 1¾". It was found in Contra Costa County, California. E. Woods collection, California. $150.00.

Tube pipe with rim, medium polish, in black steatite. This nicely designed pipe is ca. AD 700 – 1400 and measures 1 x 8". It is from Sacramento County, California. E. Woods collection, California. $1,100.00.

Steatite and wood tubular pipe, Hupa Indian of California and areas north, ca. 1900. This historic pipe has a short steatite bowl and long wooden stem; it is ⅞" in diameter and 4⁵⁄₁₆" long. Though a simple form it is carefully fitted and nicely polished. Sam Merriman collection, Oregon. $800.00.

Tubular cloudblower double-flanged pipe, black steatite, Augustine pattern/Estero facies. It is ca. 500 – 1500 and measures about 1⅖ x 3". The larger flange is 1¹⁄₁₀" across. This pipe type usually had bird bone or reed stems secured with asphaltum or pitch. This lovely flared tube pipe is from Marin County, California. M. Hough collection, California. $425.00.

Steatite pipe, tubular form, with wooden handle/stem. Ca. 1900, it is Hupa Indian from the California and areas north region. The well-shaped and highly polished pipe is 6⅜" long. Sam Merriman collection, Oregon. $800.00.

Tube pipe, simple design, made of green steatite. This pipe is Augustine pattern/Hotchkiss facies, ca. AD 500 – 1500. It measures 3¾ x ⁹⁄₁₀" and the interior was partially blocked with a rounded stone filter. Contra Costa County, California. M. Hough collection, California. $400.00.

Tubular pipes, simple design, both in micaceous hardstone and both ca. 500 – 1500. Usually the small end had a larger bone mouthpiece. Augustine pattern/Hotchkiss facies; Contra Costa County, California. Left, ⁹⁄₁₀ x 2". $200.00. Right, ⁷⁄₁₀ x 1". $125.00. M. Hough collection, California.

Tube pipe, double flanged, Augustine pattern/Hotchkiss facies, made of black steatite. It is ca. 500 – 1500 and size is ⁹⁄₁₀ x 2⅖" long. The larger flange is about ⅘" across. Bird bone or reed stems were often used, applied with asphaltum or pitch. Contra Costa County, California. Private collection, California. $250.00.

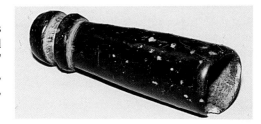

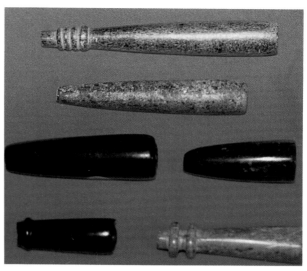

Side view and frontal view of California tubular pipes, six specimens in six different styles. The longest example is 8". The dark pipes are steatite while the lighter pipes (mottled pale green) are made of serpentine. All are nicely shaped and polished. Artifacts formerly in the Jim Cressey collection, California. Private collection. All unlisted.

Tube pipe, single flange, made of black steatite. It is Augustine pattern/Hotchkiss facies, ca. AD 500 – 1500. This graceful example measures $9/10$ x 4" long, with the flange about $1 1/10$" in diameter. These pipes were often used with a rounded stone which acted as a filter. Contra Costa County, California. M. Hough collection, California. $400.00.

Tubular pipes, simple design, both Augustine pattern/Hotchkiss facies, ca. AD 500 – 1500. Usually the smaller end had a larger hollow bone mouthpiece extension. Both are made of black steatite and are from Contra Costa County, California. Left, $4/5$ x $1 9/10$". $150.00. Right, $7/10$ x $1 3/4$". $150.00. M. Hough collection, California.

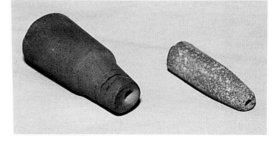

Tube pipe, ringed and with knurling on the raised area, $6 3/4$" long. This is a highly developed tubular form, with California county unknown. David Singer collection, California. $800.00.

Tubular pipes. Left, graduated-tube, fine-grained hardstone, ca. 3000 – 500 BC. Originally a bird bone or reed stem was inserted. It is 2" long, from Pershing County, Nevada. $250.00. Right, simple-tube, lava stone, ca. 200 – 1500. It too once had a bird bone or reed stem. This pipe is $1 1/2$" long, from Modoc County, California. $100.00. M. Hough collection, California.

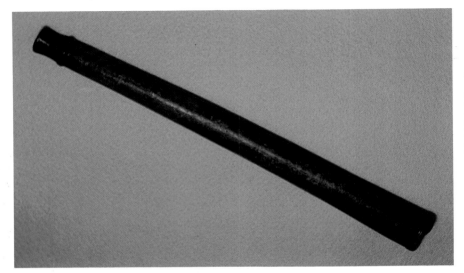

Tube pipe with single ring, delicate and extra-long at 9⅝". It is late prehistoric – Chumash and made of black steatite. Beautifully shaped, this ex-collection Heye Foundation pipe is from Los Angeles County, California. David Singer collection, California. $900.00.

Tube pipe with reed stem, pipe with inlaid clamshell beads set in asphaltum. It is late prehistoric – Chumash and the material is black steatite. This 5⅜" long pipe was formerly collected by the Heye Foundation. Los Angeles County, California. David Singer collection, California. $400.00.

Tubular pipe, narrow variety, beautifully tapered and thin walled. The mouthpiece end has incised circles and the interior was worked out beyond drill width. Pipe is 5⅞" long; made of black steatite, it came from California. Len and Janie Weidner collection, Ohio. $1,200.00.

Tubular pipe, slender and delicate wine glass type, 8½" long. Material is gray steatite for this example which came from the Lower Klamath River Valley, California. Len and Janie Weidner collection, Ohio. $1,500.00.

Tubular pipe, black steatite, 1¼ x 7¼". The interior opening tapers from 1¼" at the tobacco end to ½" at the mouthpiece end. The mouth end also has an expanded ring 1¼" in diameter. This piece was collected along the San Joaquin River west of Fresno, California. Larry Lantz, First Mesa, Indiana. $875.00.

Tubular pipe, very highly polished black steatite, 5" long. With greatly flared mouthpiece, this pipe was found northwest of Sacramento in 1973. California. Len and Janie Weidner collection, Ohio. $1,500.00.

Cloudblower tubular pipe, Augustine pattern/Hotchkiss facies, ca. AD 500 – 1500. Material is hard sandstone for this example, which is pictured in plate #30 of *Introduction to California Archeology* by Lillard, Heizer, and Fenenga. M. Hough collection, California. $300.00.

Tubular pipe, 5" long, black steatite with high polish. Most of the surface has long and short engraved lines. In cross-section the pipe is oval, with two flattened sides and in diameter the pipe tapers from ½" to 1". Some age patina for this piece from northern California. Larry Lantz, First Mesa, Indiana. $650.00.

West Coast pipe in two stones, larger portion in black California steatite and smaller stem section in light red catlinite-like stone. Total pipe length for this very unusual nearly-miniature specimen is 4" with greatest diameter of ¾". Expanded ring decoration is on both pieces and both have high polish. Larry Lantz, First Mesa, Indiana. $675.00.

Tubular pipe, wine glass style, Pacific Northwest Coastal region. This graceful example is made of steatite and has a line-inscribed flared bowl and expanded mouthpiece at the small end. It is 5¹⁄₁₆" long. Zell Adams collection, California. $450.00 – 600.00.

California tube pipes, prehistoric. Top, northern California, black steatite, highly polished. Center, northern California, black steatite, 12" long. Bottom, central California, unpolished, green and black steatite. Artifacts formerly in the Jim Cressey collection, California. Private collection. All unlisted.

Tubular pipe, prehistoric, from the Pacific Northwest region. This delicate and carefully made example is steatite, 6½" long. Mike George collection, Missouri. $850.00.

Tubular pipe, flared bowl, green slate, wine glass variety. The pipe is 3¼" long and came from the Columbia River area of northern Oregon. Len and Janie Weidner collection, Ohio. $450.00.

Stone tubular pipe from the mid-Columbia River area of Washington State. Ca. 1200 – 1700, it is made from gray metamorphic stone. The pipe is 3" long and 1¼" in diameter. It was obtained from a private collection in Oregon in 1991. J. Steve and Anita Shearer collection, California. $300.00.

Tubular pipe, black steatite, 1" across at the bowl end, 2⅞" long. The bowl side was broken and is now glued, and the exterior has moderate polish. Harney County, Oregon. Bill Mesnard collection, New Jersey; Sarah Bones, photographer. $250.00.

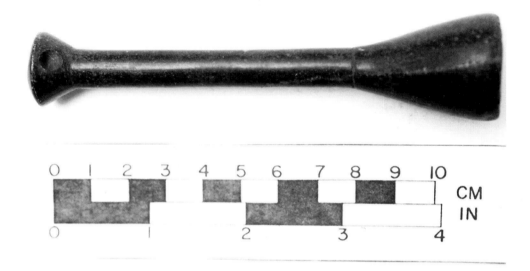

Pacific Northwest pipe, wine glass style, probably pre-1500 in time. This is a delicate and graceful piece in steatite, nearly 5" long. Columbia River area. Gary Henry collection, North Carolina. $900.00+.

Tubular pipe, wine glass style, green-black steatite. The pipe is 3" long and has a small security hole beside the mouthpiece main hole. Originally a cord would have gone through the smaller hole. Gracefully shaped, the pipe is from British Columbia, Canada. Len and Janie Weidner collection, Ohio. $650.00.

Mississippian Pipes

The Mississippian lifeway, which varied time-wise in different parts of the country but can be considered as beginning ca. AD 800 and lasting some six or eight hundred years, once covered much of North America east of the Rocky Mountains. Centered along the Mississippi Watershed, there was an emphasis on mound-building, agriculture with corn, squash, and beans, and a great deal of ceremonialism.

Major population and ritual centers developed, among them Cahokia (Illinois), Etowah (Georgia), and Spiro (Oklahoma). Pottery was made in large quantities, trade networks flourished, and bows and arrows were widely used.

Pipes were also made in huge quantities, many materials, and in almost any imaginable shape. Some of the elbow forms even resembled pipes of earlier times and may have been copied from them. Manifestations of the so-called "Southern Cult" sprang up, with basic Mississip-pian beliefs but with regional adjustments.

Large and heavy effigy pipes were designed, made of materials like sandstone, bauxite, and limestone. These often portrayed people in important activities, working a field, playing the discoidal game, or prepared for battle. One specific pipe form is termed the "bound prisoner" type, a kneeling man with arms tied behind his back. Warfare seems to have been a constant preoccupation, if not an actual practice.

Smaller pipes, perhaps individually made and used, existed throughout the Mississippian cultural area. Often these were somewhat rudimentary, being a bowl with a stem hole in the lower side. Material was almost any suitable stone, with sandstone widely employed. Pottery pipes were also made. The size, materials, and style range is greater for the Mississippian than pipes of any other prehistoric period in North America.

Circular pipe, Mississippian period, 1" thick and 2¼" in diameter. Material is light-colored mudstone; the pipe came from Decatur County, southern Georgia. Collection of Bruce Butts, Winterville, Georgia. $500.00.

Spud-shaped pipe, with some exterior polish, 1¾ x 1½". Made of tan close-grained sandstone, this effigy form is Ft. Ancient in origin and was found in Brown County, Ohio. Patrick Welch collection, Ohio. $800.00 – 1,200.00.

Pipe, late prehistoric, tan-colored fine-grained sandstone which is coated with red ochre. Engraving consists of angled parallel lines. This pipe with unusually large bowl for size may have been inspired by the Mic-mac style. It is 2⅝" high and the body is 1½ x 1¾". Jefferson County, Ohio. Bill Mesnard collection, New Jersey; Sarah Bones, photographer. $175.00.

Barrel-type pipe, fine-grained sandstone with much engraving. Parallel lines are obvious and there is an unknown animal figure. This Mississippian piece (Ft. Ancient) is 1" in diameter and 1⅞" high. Ohio. Bill Mesnard collection, New Jersey. $200.00.

Fort Ancient squared vase pipe, Mississippian period, banded glacial slate. The pipe measures ⅞ x 1¾" and was found in Shelby County, Ohio. Dennis Link collection, Ohio. $250.00.

Fort Ancient rectangular pipe, Mississippian period, made of sandstone. This pipe measures 1¹⁄₁₆ x 3" and came from Fairfield County, Ohio. Dennis Link collection, Ohio. $225.00.

Barrel pipe, sandstone, with incised banding or rings, minor repair to bowl rim. It is 2" high and 1¼" in diameter, and was found in western Ohio. This is a Fort Ancient piece, Mississippian period; sandstone was often used for Fort Ancient pipes in Ohio. Collection of and photograph by Larry G. Merriam, Oklahoma. $100.00 – 150.00.

Elbow pipe, red sandstone, heavily incised with X-shaped marks on stem and bowl. This Ft. Ancient pipe is 1⅞" long and 1⁵⁄₁₆" high. It was found in northern Kentucky. Patrick Welch collection, Ohio. $500.00.

Elbow pipe, tan sandstone, Ft. Ancient people, 2¾" long and 2⅛" high. Brown County, Ohio. Patrick Welch collection, Ohio. $500.00.

Elbow pipe, obtuse angle, Mississippian period, made of banded glacial slate. It is 2½ high and has G.I.R.S. authentication certificate number C89-55. Scioto County, Ohio. Collection of Jim Bickel, Huntington, Indiana. $500.00.

Elbow pipe, stone, Mississippian, bowl 1¾" across and pipe 3" long. Made of tan stone this example is from Pennsylvania. Collection of and photograph by Duane Treest, Illinois. $150.00 – 225.00.

Elbow pipe, Mississippian period, carefully shaped. The material is olive-green mottled pipestone and the piece is ex-collection Wehrle. Just 1¾" high, it is from Meigs County, Ohio. Len and Janie Weidner collection, Ohio. $275.00.

Elbow pipe, polished gray hardstone, bowl ¾" in diameter and the pipe 2¼" long. Probably Mississippian, this pipe came from the Cahokia area of Illinois. Collection of and photograph by Duane Treest, Illinois. $200.00 – 250.00.

Vase-type pipe, Mississippian period, made of dark brown unknown stone. The example is well made with thin walls and is ⅞" across, 1¾" high. The bottom is flattened and the bowl itself is rounded. Logan County, Ohio. Bill Mesnard collection, New Jersey; Sarah Bones, photographer. $125.00.

Vase-type pipe, Ft. Ancient and Mississippian period, brown fine-grained sandstone. The stem hole is angled downward at about 135 degrees. This pipe is ¾" in diameter, 1¾" high. Bath County, Kentucky. Bill Mesnard collection, New Jersey; Sarah Bones, photographer. $175.00.

Vase-shaped pipe, Mississippian period, made of cream-colored stone with brown inclusions. The pipe is 1½" high and bowl is ¾" across. It came from Sandusky County, Ohio. Collection of and photograph by Duane Treest, Illinois. $75.00 – 100.00.

Vase-shaped pipe, Mississippian period and Ft. Ancient people, brown sandstone. It is 1¾" high and came from Ross County, Ohio. Ted McVey collection, Ohio. $165.00.

Vase-shaped pipe, Mississippian period, fine-grained sandstone. It measures 1⅜" wide and 1¾" high, and is ex-collection Dr. Meuser. This pipe, #E-1084 (A/M), is from Gallia County, Ohio. Iron Horse collection. $300.00 – 400.00.

Bowl-type pipe, eroded red sandstone, with bird in flight engraved on the side. This example, Ft. Ancient culture, is 1¾ x 1 x 1¾" high. It was found in Kentucky near the Ohio River. Bill Mesnard collection, New Jersey. $150.00.

Pipe, vase type, pink and brown pipestone. This pipe measures 2¼" high and was found in Logan County, Ohio. Larry Garvin, Back to Earth, Ohio. $200.00.

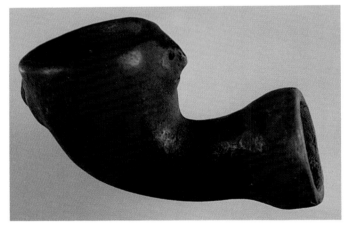

Effigy pipe, Mississippian period, biconical, gray pottery, 3" high. The bowl has two small faces on opposite sides, one facing the smoker. Lee County, Arkansas. Larry Garvin, Back to Earth, Ohio. $275.00.

Vase-type pipe decorated with incised lines around the bowl, 1⅜" high. This Mississippian piece is made of brown hardstone and came from Ohio. Len and Janie Weidner collection, Ohio. $275.00.

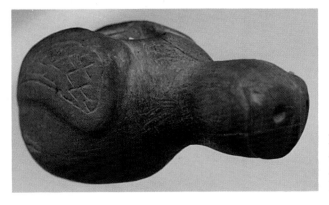

Effigy pipe, owl, 3¼" long. It is carefully made with detailed face and feather-incised wings, and with stem hole at the rear. This is a Fort Ancient pipe, from Kentucky. Larry Garvin, Back to Earth, Ohio. $500.00.

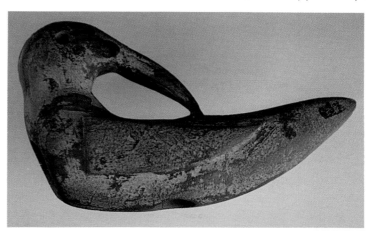

Pipe bowl, barrel configuration, Late Mississippian period, 1⅞" high. The pipe is made of brown hardstone with a medium polish. Eastern Midwest. Len and Janie Weidner collection, Ohio. $250.00.

Effigy pipe, late prehistoric period, large size at 5" high. This pipe, formerly in the famous Dr. Young collection in Tennessee, is made of a yellow-brown unknown stone. It originally was found in Muskingum County, Ohio. Larry Garvin, Back to Earth, Ohio. Museum grade.

Bowl pipe, vase-shaped, Mississippian period, made of sandstone. It is 1¾" high and the same diameter. The simple form is decorated with various incised lines; this is a Tennessee pipe. Collection of and photograph by Duane Treest, Illinois. $75.00 – 150.00.

Bowl pipe, Fort Ancient people of Mississippian times, 1⅛" high. The material is greenish-tan stone and the pipe was found in Adams County, Ohio. Larry Garvin, Back to Earth, Ohio. $200.00.

Stone bowl pipe, Mississippian, light brown sandstone. #1799 is 1⅜" across and 2⅜" high. It is from Ohio. Iron Horse collection. $175.00 – 235.00.

Vase-type pipe, fine-grained brown sandstone. The artifact measures 3⅛" high and width varies from 1¼ to 1½". This is a basic Mississippian period pipe without polish. Bill Mesnard collection, New Jersey; Sarah Bones, photographer. $150.00.

Vasiform or bullet-shaped pipe with rim, Ft. Ancient people, made of limestone. Size is 1½" top diameter with height of 3⅜". This is a well-shaped late prehistoric pipe from the Ohio Valley region. Patrick Welch collection, Ohio. $650.00.

Effigy flattened vase pipe, Mississippian period, dark slate-like stone. It has the image of a wild turkey incised on the wide side with marks on the opposite side. It is 2¼" high and was made by the Whittlesey people, south of the eastern part of Lake Erie. Cuyahoga County, Ohio. Len and Janie Weidner collection, Ohio. $750.00.

Vase-type pipe with dramatically flared rim, 1 x 2". This is a Ft. Ancient piece, Mississippian period, made of Ohio pipestone. Scioto County, Ohio. Private collection, Ohio. $600.00.

Vase-like pipe of truncated or cutshort cone form, Fort Ancient people, 1⅞" high. Material is mottled gray pipestone and the piece was found in Kentucky. Len and Janie Weidner collection, Ohio. $550.00.

Vase type pipe, Mississippian, 1⅝" high and 1¼" in diameter. The pipe is made of dark steatite and once took a bone or wood stem. Clermont County, Ohio. Dennis Link collection, Ohio. $200.00.

This engraved Fort Ancient (Mississippian era) pipe is made of light brown cotton rock or loess, fine windborne particles. Ex-collections Dr. Mahan, Almgren, and Ahlstrom, the pipe is from Adams County, Ohio. Larry Garvin, Back to Earth, Ohio. $400.00+.

Highly developed late Ft. Ancient calcite pipe from Highland County, Ohio. This shows the graceful taper from body to neck to rim and the glossy polish that still remains after hundreds of years. Ted McVey collection, Ohio. $1,500.00 – 2,000.00.

Effigy bowl-type pipe with raised figures of turtles on each side of the bowl. It is made of greenish-brown hardstone and is Fort Ancient in origin. This 2" high pipe is from Brown County, Ohio. Len and Janie Weidner collection, Ohio. $450.00.

Fort Ancient pipe, late prehistoric period, possibly a foot effigy. One end of the pipe has lines that may indicate toes. This pipe is made of sandstone and is 1¾" long with bowl ⅞" high. Ex-collection Weidner, Clermont County, Ohio. Dennis Link collection, Ohio. $200.00.

Animal effigy pipe, bear's head, pecked finish with some smoothing and grinding around the bowl rim. In fine-grained sandstone the bear's features are only lightly indicated giving it a ghostly appearance. It is 2⅜ x 3⅜ x 1⅜" high. Mississippian period, Montgomery County, Kentucky. Bill Mesnard collection, New Jersey. $250.00.

Face effigy vase type pipe, Mississippian period and Whittlesey people of northeastern Ohio. Close-grained brown sandstone is the material, and the pipe is 1½ x 1¾ x 1⅞" high. The stem hole is the mouth and eyes are impact crushes. Very interesting pipe, Tuscarawas County, Ohio. Bill Mesnard collection, New Jersey. $300.00.

Swan effigy pipe with bird incised on pipe sides, pipe 2⅜" high. Material is dark sandstone for this piece, probably Mississippian. It came from a rock shelter in Tennessee. Larry Garvin, Back to Earth, Ohio. $250.00.

Beaver effigy pipe, with flattened tail protruding over the head at right, made of fine-grained sandstone. Size is 3¼ x 4¼". Pickaway County, Ohio. Private collection, Ohio. $1,300.00.

Other Indian Pipes

Besides the major chapter designations in this book, there are other pipe forms familiar to collectors. Certainly one would be certain Hopewell pipes of the eastern United States, a topic worth a book itself. This is because of quality, not quantity. Only a few hundred classic Hopewell effigy platform pipes were ever made.

The effigy pipes were simple enough, with the bowl set near the center of a flattened platform. In early years the platform tended to be fairly straight, but it curved more as the style developed. The bowl was the effigy — bird, animal, or human — and the tobacco hole was usually centered in the effigy. A narrow stem hole began at one end of the platform.

Material was usually pipestone from nearby quarries; Ohio pipestone in various hues came from the lower Scioto Valley in that state, while Illinois pipes were often produced in the greenish pipestone quarried there. The effigy figures were depicted naturalistically and the whole pipe was highly polished. As a class these are among the smallest of Indian pipes and, conversely, have some of the highest values. One of the first major depictions of these pipes was in the Squier and Davis 1848 publication, *Ancient Monuments of the Mississippi Valley.* The pipes were famous thereafter.

Also in the eastern United States, in the Late Woodland period, the Intrusive Mound people made beautiful pipes in another platform style. Most of these were plain, not effigy, and the bowl was set at one end of the long, flattened platform.

At times the platform was so thin, a ridge or elongated raised section had to be left above the stem hole for reinforcement. Pipes were up to a foot long and the material of choice was steatite, mainly obtained from southern regions. The pipes were widely distributed in prehistoric times and can be found well away from quarry sources.

Alate or winged pipes had long stems with side projections or wings, and the bowl was set at an obtuse angle to the stem. These were also made of steatite and some examples had engraved designs on the wings, stem, or bowl. This was another form from the Late Woodland.

Still another pipe form was the constricted-center tube, sometimes called a medicine tube pipe. These began in the BC centuries of Early Woodland times, and range in size from a few inches to well over a foot in length. The type had two reamed-out cone-shaped openings opposite one another, connected by a center hole. Here too the material was usually steatite.

The above three pipe types were almost always made of steatite. Despite this material being widely available across much of the country, in the eastern portion this usually indicates a southern orientation if not origin. A few rare examples of Intrusive Mound and winged pipe types were made of materials like serpentine and chlorite.

Bowl type pipe, steatite, probably Cherokee and late prehistoric – early historic, ca. 1450 – 1830. This small pipe is from Buncombe County, North Carolina. Gary Henry collection, North Carolina. $75.00 – 125.00.

Top left, Mic-mac style steatite pipe bowl, 2 x 2½", probably early historic, gray and black stone, engraved rectangles on bowl sides. Meigs County, Tennessee. $385.00. Right, probably late prehistoric elbow pipe, also steatite, 3¼ x 4", faded black stone. Well made and with patina, it is from Jefferson County, Ohio. $875.00. Larry Lantz, First Mesa, Indiana.

Miniature pipe, dark pottery, 2½" long. Late prehistoric, this piece is ex-collection Morse and was found in New York. Robin Fiser collection, Ohio. $125.00.

Elbow pipe, human head effigy, sandstone, 4 x 4¾". Probably Woodland, this piece is ex-collection Albert Davis and Watson Museum. Mahoning County, Ohio. Dale and Betty Roberts collection, Iowa; Betty Roberts photograph. $500.00.

Pipe with mid-bowl incised decoration, gray steatite, bowl only remaining after stem was broken away. Thickness is only ¹⁄₁₆" at the rim which means the bowl itself is even thinner. This well-made example is ⅞" across, 1¾" high. Essex County, Virginia. Bill Mesnard collection, New Jersey; Sarah Bones, photographer. $100.00.

Cone pipe, a rare joining of artifact types, Woodland period. It began as a hematite cone and was later converted into a pipe with small stem hole in the side at the broken area. From Kentucky, the pipe is 1⁵⁄₁₆" in diameter. Zell Adams collection, California. $200.00 – 275.00.

Discoidal pipe, Late Woodland – Mississippian period, made of unknown hardstone. This is a rare item, being originally a discoidal and later a pipe, hence a double artifact. It is 3¹⁄₁₆" in diameter and is from Missouri. Zell Adams collection, California. $325.00 – 450.00.

Prehistoric salvage examples, pipe sections repaired for further use. Left, steatite, pipe engraved on four sides, drilled holes for dowels and adhesive. Right, chlorite, two holes for dowels and adhesive. Both Ohio. Private collection. Unlisted.

Ridged-bowl pipe, 1¼" in diameter. This interesting form is made of gray steatite and was collected in Union County, Pennsylvania. Richard Savidge collection, Pennsylvania. $350.00.

Platform pipe, high bowl and small base, possibly done in a monolithic axe effigy form. The pipe is 1¾" high and made of dark green serpentine. Ca. 1200, Etowah phase, it is from Northumberland County, Pennsylvania. Richard Savidge collection, Pennsylvania. $400.00.

Unusual Pueblo pipe made of carved antler, 3 x 3¼", with old wooden stem 9¾" long. Here, bowl is up and longest projection is actually the stem receptacle. This may be historic. Northern Arizona. Larry Lantz, First Mesa, Indiana. $595.00.

Pueblo pipe bowl, prehistoric, orange-tan sandstone. Size is 2¾ x 3¾" for this early pipe which is thick and heavy. Unusual pipe, northern New Mexico. Larry Lantz, First Mesa, Indiana. $375.00.

Pueblo pipe, unknown period, 3 x 5¾". It is made of a material resembling sandstone, has incised decorations, and traces of old paint. This is a scarce and well-done example from a region not usually noted for pipes. Northern New Mexico. Larry Lantz, First Mesa, Indiana. $750.00.

Broken face effigies from early sites, many from pipes or figurines, with materials being pottery, catlinite, and steatite. Ca. 1500 – 1675, frame #EFF/15 has artifacts with an average height of 2¼". The fifteen pieces are from various counties in New York. Iron Horse collection. Frame, $2,500.00 – 3,200.00.

Dipper-type pipe, miniature form, polished steatite. This tiny pipe measures only 1⅞" long and came from the area of Augusta, Virginia. Larry Garvin, Back to Earth, Ohio. $175.00.

Bowl-type pipe, Mississippian period, made of brown sandstone. It is 3" high and 2¼" in diameter. This pipe was found in Pike County, Mississippi. Wilfred Dick collection, Mississippi. $175.00 – 250.00.

Club-head pipe, gray hardstone with exterior groove. This rare form is 2¾" high. Though the exact timeframe is unknown, it is probably late in prehistory. Miami County, Ohio. Larry Garvin, Back to Earth, Ohio. $250.00.

Expanded barrel pipe, gray-brown solid-color slate with sides almost egg-shell thin near the bowl top. This pipe is very nicely made, probably early historic, with bowl 2½" high. The pipe is marked with a collector number plus "Ohio." Len and Janie Weidner collection, Ohio. $350.00.

Human head effigy pipe, probably Mississippian, 3" high. It is made of catlinite and has an upper security hole for attachment to the stem. Hart County, Kentucky. Larry Garvin, Back to Earth, Ohio. $450.00.

Platform pipe, Woodland period, brown hardstone. This pipe measures 2¾ x 4¾" and came from Arkansas. Collection of and photograph by Duane Treest, Illinois. $300.00 – 400.00.

Pipe made of light tan stone, possibly historic and ca. 1700s. It measures 3¾" long and was found in Missouri. Pipes like this, with features suggesting both historic times (overall style) and Woodland (material, low bowl), can be difficult to place in time. Collection of and photograph by Duane Treest, Illinois. $175.00 – 300.00.

Biconical pipe or Medicine tube pipe, 5¾" long. It is made of steatite and is ex-collection E. K. Petrie. Banks County, Georgia. Dale and Betty Roberts collection, Iowa; Betty Roberts photograph. $750.00.

Wide-stemmed pipe, tan-brown hardstone, Woodland period. This pipe is fully drilled and was found near Ferrum, Virginia, in 1963. Broken in two places and glued, this fine pipe is 3½" high and 10¼" long. Larry Garvin, Back to Earth, Ohio. $1,500.00.

Elbow pipe, Woodland period, 2¾" high and 4¹⁄₁₆" long. The pipe was found in 1872, in Fayette County, Tennessee. Larry Garvin, Back to Earth, Ohio. $375.00.

Elbow pipe, brown sandstone, 1¾" high. This pipe would be for basic, utilitarian use; it is from the Mt. Carroll area, Illinois. Len and Janie Weidner collection, Ohio. $200.00.

Elbow pipe, squared cross-sections for bowl and stem, Late Woodland or Mississippian period. It measures 3½" high and is made of close-grained sandstone. Illinois River area, Illinois. Len and Janie Weidner collection, Ohio. $500.00.

Tapered-stem pipe, probably Woodland period, made of gray steatite. The pipe came from a farm family in Tennessee, and measures 1¹⁵⁄₁₆" high and 10¼" long. Larry Garvin, Back to Earth, Ohio. $650.00.

High-bowl Hopewell platform pipe, Middle Woodland, an extremely rare form. This artifact measures 3 x 4" and is made of pipestone. Very carefully made and finished, this pipe is from St. Louis County, Missouri. Private collection, Ohio. $3,000.00.

Miniature platform pipe, Hopewell and Middle Woodland period, 2⅜" long. The short bowl has an expanded base and flanged bowl top, while the platform has a typical gentle curve. This rare pipe is made of mottled green and tan pipestone and came from Ohio. Len and Janie Weidner collection, Ohio. $ 8,500.00.

Platform pipe, Woodland period, with engraving on the platform bottom. It is made from black steatite and measures 2¾ x 1½ x 1⅜" high. The bowl was broken off and glued and a small piece of the bowl is missing. Provenance includes a newspaper clipping from 1949 describing the pipe find. Massachusetts. Bill Mesnard collection, New Jersey. $700.00.

Hopewell platform pipe, Middle Woodland period, made of green steatite. The bowl was chipped and reworked in ancient times. It measures 1⅛ x 3¼" and is now only ⅞" high. This pipe came from Henry County, Indiana. Bill Mesnard collection, New Jersey. $700.00.

Hopewell plain platform pipe, Middle Woodland period, made of well-finished fine-grained brown sandstone. The pipe measures 1¼ x 4 x 1½" high. Union County, Illinois. Bill Mesnard collection, New Jersey. $1,200.00.

Hopewell platform pipe with engraved and angled parallel lines on the bowl exterior, made of reddish brown material. Possibly Ohio pipestone, size is 1¼ x 2¹⁵⁄₁₆" by 1⅝" high. This came from Muskingum County, Ohio. Bill Mesnard collection, New Jersey. $1,400.00.

Platform pipe, Hopewell Indian, Middle Woodland. High polished, this rare example is made of blue-gray Ohio pipestone. The material is famous for holding a polish, as evidenced here. Washington County, Ohio. Len and Janie Weidner collection, Ohio. $6,500.00.

Frog effigy pipe, Middle Woodland, broken in half and with restoration. It is made of brown pipestone and is ex-collection B. W. Stephens. This Hopewell pipe is from Calhoun County, Illinois. Bill Mesnard collection, New Jersey. $3,500.00.

Hopewell platform pipe, mottled greenish-gray and maroon Ohio pipestone. This fine pipe is 2½" long and is highly polished overall. Licking County, Ohio. Robin Fiser collection, Ohio. Museum grade.

Hopewell platform pipe, measuring 1¾ x 1¾ x 3" long. It is made of green pipestone from either Illinois or Ohio. Still with a high polish, this fine example was found by Herman Henke in 1897. Wisconsin. Bill Mesnard collection, New Jersey. $2,500.00.

Hopewell platform pipe, Middle Woodland period, made of mottled blue-gray pipestone. One corner has an old break, but otherwise this rare pipe is complete. It is 3½" long, from Ohio. Len and Janie Weidner collection, Ohio. $4,000.00.

Hopewell platform pipe, Middle Woodland period, made of dark Ohio pipestone. This beautiful and classic example measures 2½ x 3½" and is highly polished. It was found in that great center of Hopewell activity, Ross County, Ohio. Private collection, Ohio. Museum grade.

Platform pipe, Late Hopewell period, blue-green steatite. This example, formerly in the Payne collection, measures 4⅝" long and 2⅜" high. Note the striations inside the bowl from the wide drill revolutions. The pipe was found in Rutherford County, Tennessee. Len and Janie Weidner collection, Ohio. $2,500.00.

Hopewell pipe, Middle Woodland period, curved-base platform type. The bowl is 2½" high with overall pipe length of 4¾". As pictured, the stem hole is on the right side of the platform, and stem sides are tally marked. This beautifully polished pipe is made of mottled gray-green Ohio pipestone. Eastern Midwest. Len and Janie Weidner collection, Ohio. $15,000.00.

Hopewell platform pipe, Middle Woodland period, highly polished. It is made of olive pipestone and is 2¾" long. This is a rare specimen in original condition. Ohio. Len and Janie Weidner collection, Ohio. Museum grade.

Platform pipe, Hopewell and Middle Woodland period, 2⅜" long. This is a salvaged example which continued in use after part of the platform was broken. The remainder is incised with straight lines, and tally marked around the bowl rim. The pipe was picked up in 1979 in Carroll County, Illinois. Len and Janie Weidner collection, Ohio. $1,200.00.

Platform pipe, rare deeply curved Hopewell type, with bowl 2⅞" high. Material is brown-gray hardstone for this extraordinary piece. Ohio. Len and Janie Weidner collection, Ohio. $1,800.00.

Platform pipe, a rare Hopewell highly arched form, pipe 3" high. Material is attractive amber-tan pipestone for this very unusual type. Interestingly, the pipe was obtained in England, but the origin is Illinois. Len and Janie Weidner collection, Ohio. $8,500.00.

Hopewell pipe, Middle Woodland timeframe, an extremely rare example of a raised-center platform pipe. The repaired pipe is made of gray-green Ohio pipestone and the bowl is 3" high, with overall pipe length of 5¼". It is one of the few such pipes in private collections. Eastern Midwest. Len and Janie Weidner collection, Ohio. $8,000.00.

Intrusive Mound platform pipe, side view, ca. AD 500 – 1100, #T-1086. This Late Woodland example is made of black steatite; platform is 6½" and bowl height is 1⅝". A large and superior example, it is from Ontario County, New York. Iron Horse collection. Museum grade.

Intrusive Mound platform pipe, top view, ca. AD 500 – 1100. #T-1086 is carefully shaped and finished, with a thin bowl-rim reinforcing ring. This is a prime specimen from a superb pipe-making era, Late Woodland times. Ontario County, New York. Iron Horse collection. Museum grade.

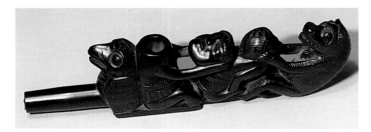

Northwest Coast figured pipe, featuring the Bear Mother myth. Ca. 1860 – 1880 the material is black argillite and size is 8¼" long and 2¼" high. The argillite came from a quarry on the Queen Charlotte Islands. This pipe with intricate carving was collected from a private collector/dealer in Ottawa, Canada, in 1993. J. Steve and Anita Shearer collection, California. $3,500.00.

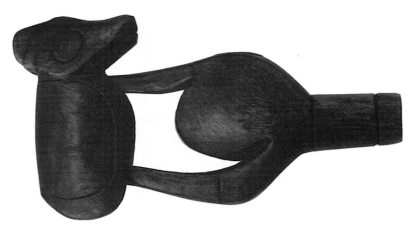

Historic pipe, Inland Tlinget and ca. 1840 – 1860. This pipe was made from a musket stock and measures 5" long. Pipe material is walnut and brass for this interesting example in Pacific Northwest style. Jeb Taylor collection, Idaho. $3,000.00 – 5,000.00.

Elbow pipe, steatite, 2¹⁄₁₆" long. This is probably a protohistoric pipe, ex-collection Dauphin, with exterior unpolished. Pennsylvania. Richard Savidge collection, Pennsylvania. $200.00.

Vase-shaped pipe, medium-dark stone, possibly historic and ca. 1700s. The pipe is 2½" high and the bowl is 1¼" in diameter. This is an unusual style. Collection of and photograph by Duane Treest, Illinois. $100.00 – 150.00.

Decorated pipe, probably historic, tan sandstone with paint. Most of the pipe is pale green while the bowl top is painted red. A large pipe at 1¾ x 3 x 6" long, it came from Arizona. Bill Mesnard collection, New Jersey. $400.00.

Bird effigy pipe, historic period, steatite. This pipe measures 2½" both long and high and came from Washington County, Maine. Hogan Gallery Inc., Naples, Florida. $250.00.

Tubular pipe, probably Mandan, originally with a bone or wood stem. It is 2¾" long and has the stem end reinforced with brass, possibly from a cartridge case. Ca. 1850 – 1880, the pipe came from near Bismark, North Dakota. Jeb Taylor collection, Idaho. $700.00 – 1,000.00.

Cherokee council or four-directions pipe, 2¾" high and with bowl 3" in diameter. Historic period, the pipe is made of orange-brown pyrite-tempered pottery. Cherokee County, Georgia. Larry Garvin, Back to Earth, Ohio. $500.00.

Historic pipe, an ornate form made of steatite with heart-shaped cutout and drilled holes. It is 4½" in diameter and came from Perry County, Tennessee. Collection of and photograph by Duane Treest, Illinois. $400.00 – 500.00.

Carved woman's pipe, birchwood bowl and stem, ca. 1870 – 1880. The bowl is 1½" high and the stem is 10½" long. This unusual pipe set was obtained at an Indian show in Los Angeles from the great grandson of an Ojibwa woman captured in Canada in the 1870s and brought to Minnesota to live with the Chippewas. The pipe is from Minnesota. J. Steve and Anita Shearer collection, California. $500.00.

Human face effigy pipe, gray stone, proto-historic period. This large and well-made pipe is 2¼" high and 4½" long. Andrew County, Missouri. Mike George collection, Missouri. $350.00 – 450.00.

Catlinite pipe, late prehistoric – early historic period, 1¼" high. This fine small pipe has a security hole, and is ex-collections Frank and Dwight Shipley and Coulter. Erie County, Ohio. Private collection, Ohio. $400.00.

Catlinite pipe, 1⅛ x 2", with original 14" wooden stem that bears traces of old green color. This 1880s set is nicely matched and both have good patina from use. Grand Traverse Bay, Michigan. Larry Lantz, First Mesa, Indiana. $985.00.

Buffalo or bison effigy pipe, dark red Catlinite, this example recently made and marked "Omanico." The 2" scale indicates size. Lee Hallman collection, Pennsburg, Pennsylvania. $175.00.

T-shaped red Catlinite pipe, recently made and initialed "FE," with 2" scale. This nicely polished example has ring decorations. Lee Hallman collection, Pennsburg, Pennsylvania. $75.00.

Modern bear effigy pipe, polished limestone, 7" long. This fantasy piece was made in eastern Arkansas to sell at a trading post and does not copy any known Indian-made pipe form. Collection of and photograph by Larry G. Merriam, Oklahoma. Unlisted.

T-shaped catlinite pipe, recent make and probably 1950s, 2½ x 4⅛" and with 16" wooden stem. This pipe was made by the Comanche in Montana and was obtained from a relative of the maker. The two white strips are unusual. Collection of and photograph by Larry G. Merriam, Oklahoma. $115.00 – 165.00.

Souvenir pipe-tomahawk pipe, catlinite with stem of the same material. The stem is 9¼" long and the pipe head measures 3⅝ x 6½". From the Midwest, the head is dated 1899. Collection of Elizabeth Allais Hill. $900.00.

Tomahawk style pipe with floral designs and stem with star decorations. Both are made of red catlinite and the set is ca. 1880 – 1900. Pipe bowl is 2" high while the stem measures 1½" wide and 13" long. These were collected in 1985 at San Juan Capistrano, California. J. Steve and Anita Shearer collection, California. $1,300.00.

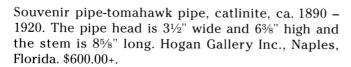

Souvenir pipe-tomahawk pipe, catlinite, ca. 1890 – 1920. The pipe head is 3½" wide and 6⅜" high and the stem is 8⅝" long. Hogan Gallery Inc., Naples, Florida. $600.00+.

Pipe Facts

This is a compilation of facts about pipes. Some are widely known within the collecting field, while others are of a more specialized, even obscure, nature. The main criteria for inclusion in the chapter is that the facts should be informative, interesting, and a help for those who want to know more about Indian pipes.

Tube pipes were made in various shapes and sizes, with most boldly tapered types being from the Late Archaic period. One example in banded slate, 2¾" long, came from Huntington County, Indiana. An unusual curved tube pipe from the same county was made of Ohio pipestone, with a length of 2½". (*Central States Archaeological Journal.* Vol. 36 No. 4. October 1989, p 186.)

Historic Plains-like pipes were sometimes salvaged by means of careful repair. "Many of the Calumets of the Great Lakes region are ornamented with geometric designs, inlaid with lead or silver. In almost any collection may be found pipe-bowls that have been broken and mended by cutting grooves and filling them with lead." (West, George A. *Tobacco, Pipes and Smoking Customs of the American Indians*, Part I, Text. 1934, p 269.)

The bitumen used to glue some bone mouthpieces to tubular stone pipes in California may have come from famous tar pits. These were the Rancho La Brea deposits in Los Angeles, which seeped to the surface of the ground. Many early birds and animals in the form of fossil bones were also preserved. (Gnidovec, Dale M. "Tar Pits Preserve Fossil Trove," *The Columbus Dispatch.* April 20, 1997, p 7-B.)

A fine large frog effigy pipe was unearthed from a Mississippian house feature in St. Louis County, Missouri. Recovered in several pieces, it measured 4⅛" high and 3" wide. This is a good example of an important cultural artifact that was salvaged for further study. (*CSAJ/The Archaeology of Missouri and Greater St. Louis.* Vol. 37 No. 4. October 1990, p 135.)

Some prehistoric pipes seem to have been so treasured that, once damaged or broken, they were still kept in use. Other pipes were transformed from one artifact type to another. Such an artifact was listed in the Dr. Meuser catalog as item #C-2164. Originally it was a platform pipe of bluish Ohio pipestone. The top of the bowl was broken off, ground down, and grooved to become an earspool 1½" in diameter. It is interesting to speculate whether — since earspools were usually made in pairs — there is a twin or mate somewhere. (Meuser, Dr. Gordon F. *Catalogue of the Archaeological Collection...* 1914/1970.)

Here are some thoughtful observations on the survivability of prehistoric pipes. "Bearing in mind that our stone pipes were usually provided with reed or wood stems, we shall understand that a perfect stone pipe would be the rule, and that a perfect pottery pipe would be the exception as bowl and stem were all formed in one piece, and, owing to the fragile character, easily broken by the combined effects of frost and water, as well as by the tools of the cultivator." (Dustin, Fred. "Indian Pipes Collected in Saginaw County, Michigan," reprint from *Papers of the Michigan Academy of Science, Arts and Letters.* Vol. XIV. 1930, published 1931, pp 36 – 37.)

Some of the Great Lakes pipe-heads in black or red pipestone have projections in front of the bowl or above the bowl's stem to form a comb or crest. These, sometimes done in artistic designs, served two purposes. They were decorative and served as a holder for fingers when the pipe bowl became hot.

An unusual Great Pipe made of steatite, from Scott County, Virginia, was a double effigy form. The forward head, in the usual position, represented a duck. The opposite end of the pipe terminated in an owl's head. This pipe was 6" high and 10" long. (Fundaburk, Emma Lila, and Mary Douglass Foreman. *Sun Circles and Human Hands.* 1957/1985, plate 104, top left.)

Catlinite stems for Plains-type calumet pipes do not seem to be as old as wooden stems. "Apparently the idea of long detachable stems made of stone is entirely a modern idea. In fact it seems to have been developed only within relatively recent times and is largely the outgrowth of tourist and curio store demand. It is safe to say that all Calumet stems up to perhaps the middle of the last century (1850) were made of wood, instead of stone." (West, George A. *Tobacco, Pipes and Smoking Customs of the American Indians,* Part I, Text. 1934, pp 247 – 248.)

Pipe bowl sizes, and the amount of smoking material they would hold, varied greatly. "The most diminutive pipes now used (1912) are those of the Alaskan Eskimo. Those of the greatest capacity are the flat-bottomed monitor pipes, found along the Atlantic coast and inland to Ohio and Tennessee." (Hodge, Frederick Webb. *Handbook of American Indians North of Mexico*, Part 2. BAE Bulletin 30. 1912, p 258.)

The Indian word for smoking material in some linguistic groups in historic times was "Kinnikinnick," meaning something that was mixed. A mixture was preferred for several reasons, among them the typical high cost of imported or traded tobacco. Straight tobacco was considered too harsh by some users, who also enjoyed the aromatic addition of certain plant parts.

A general comment on Indian pipes: "In no one article was so much ingenuity displayed by aboriginal natives as in pipe making. Many of the pipes are formed with much taste, and are designed to be representations of animals with which they were familiar." (Lapham, I. A. *The Antiquities of Wisconsin,* Smithsonian Contributions to Knowledge. Vol. VII. 1855, p 85.)

One variety of disc pipe was the heavy type, used in the war bundles of the Omaha (and several other tribes). There it seems to have been mainly for ceremonial use. Disc pipes with thin discs are probably older than those with thick discs. (West, George A. *Tobacco, Pipes and Smoking Customs of the American Indians,* Part I, Text. 1934, pp 206-207.)

Mic-mac pipes often had one or more holes drilled through the narrow, keel-like basal platform. If one hole, it was used to secure the pipe to the stem. Additional holes were used for ornamentation or decoration. (Hodge, Frederick Webb. *Handbook of American Indians North of Mexico*, Part 2. BAE Bulletin 30. 1912, p 259.)

Four Indian pipes once belonged to United States President Andrew Jackson and eventually went to the Museum of the American Indian in New York City. All the pipes came from Tennessee. A black slate effigy pipe was 8¼" long, while a dark-green steatite effigy pipe was 8½" long. There were also two plain elbow pipes of greenish-black steatite, 3" and 4⅛" long, respectively. (*Indian Notes.* Museum of the American Indian/Heye Foundation, Vol. 2 No. 2. April 1925, pp116 – 118.)

Some regions do not seem to have large numbers of pipes (here, eastern Pennsylvania) compared to others, and one theory attempts to give a reason for this. "The comparative rarity of aboriginal smoking pipes is easily explained by the fact that they were not discarded as were the weapons, when those by whom they were fashioned entered the iron

age. The advances of the whites in no way lessened the demand for pipes, nor did the white substitute a better-made implement; therefore, the pipes were retained, and used until worn out or broken...." (Moorehead, Warren K. *Prehistoric Relics*, quoting Dr. C. C. Abbott in *Smithsonian Report.* 1875, p 343.)

Very little has been written about finding prehistoric pipes to the north of the adjoining United States, so two sentences here are of uncommon worth: "In every village site broken clay pipes are frequently found. Stone pipes are more usually surface finds." (Orr, Rowland. "Smelser-Orr Collection," *Annual Archaeological Report.* The Legislative Assembly of Ontario. 1908 – 1911, p 54.)

A nearly outdated term, "monitor," is applied to certain platform pipes. These are the plain platform type with a round bowl near the center. The word comes from the Civil War (battle, 1862) when a Union iron-clad gunboat was named the Monitor. The deck was low and flat, with a single large revolving cannon turret. It was also referred to as "the cheesebox on a raft."

The prehistoric Indians of northern California and southern Oregon often used the bones of water birds (such as the pelican) for stems in tubular pipes. (Howe, Carrol B. *Ancient Tribes of the Klamath Country.* 1968/1972, pp 180 – 181, figure 139.)

Some pipes had, besides stems, other organic additions that may not have survived to the present. "The walls of some California Tube Pipes are very thin and in order that they might be comfortably held in the hand, when being smoked, it was a common practice to wind a cord of some vegetable fibre around the bowl or some other part of the pipe." (West, George A. *Tobacco, Pipes and Smoking Customs of the American Indians*, Part I, Text. 1934, p 136.)

Fake pipes or modern replicas offered as old and authentic are a problem today, and here are two examples: "Spiro-like pipes are made of soapstone today, but the originals were made of red bauxite. The Great Pipes of the Eastern mountains have been reproduced in numbers far exceeding the number of authentic pipes of that type." (Perino, Gregory, "Points & Barbs," *Central States Archaeological Journal.* Vol. 30 No. 3 July 1983, p 157.)

One of the unusual aspects of large Mississippian human-figure pipes is that they provide more than classy examples of the pipe makers' art. The positions of figures and associated objects (like hoes or chunkee stones) tell us something about late prehistoric activities. In some cases clothing is carefully depicted, as are hairstyles and incised lines that may indicate tattooing.

Some pipes in the Upper Midwest, later made in catlinite, were earlier made of materials such as limestone. Some of the examples are believed to be quite old, before the Indians began extensively working the Minnesota quarries.

The word "calumet" originally meant only the highly decorated long stem of the Plains-type pipe. Now, it refers to both the stem and attached stone pipe bowl. (King, J. C. H. *Smoking Pipes of the North American Indian.* 1977, p 9.)

A stone elbow pipe found in a Texas Panhandle Pueblo ruin in Texas contained the unidentified remains of a smoking substance. Ca. AD 1200, the pipe measures 1½ x 2¼" and had incised markings. (Parker, Wayne. "A Pipe With Charred Smoking Material," *Artifacts.* Vol. 8 No. 1. 1978, p 14.)

Some pipe bowls were enlarged after the initial drilling by simply using a larger (wider) drill and reboring the same hole. Other times the bowl hole was enlarged by gouging or scraping with other tools, a method commonly used with tube pipes. (West, George A. *Tobacco, Pipes and Smoking Customs of the American Indians,* Part I, Text. 1934, p 345.)

It is difficult to compare the artistic (or even basic, mechanical) skill of prehistoric pipe makers with those of more recent workers because, for one thing, the pipes were often different types. Yet comparisons have been made. "In investigating the arts of the ancient pipe makers, and thereby endeavoring to ascertain the status for the prehistoric tribes in the scale of civilization, we have for many years carefully observed the work of the pipe makers among the historic tribes. We have patiently watched the Dakota Indians when they were engaged in carving and polishing their fine catlinite pipes, generally with the aid of no better tools than common pocket knives. The art of pipe carving was one of the few prehistoric Indian arts that remained after the advent of the Europeans, and after the art of making pottery and flint implements had been forgotten." (Thruston, Gates P. *The Antiquities of Tennessee.* 1890, p 209.)

For all of North America there are perhaps 30 basic pipe types, each with from several to many sub-types or variations.

In addition to the well-known red pipestone of Minnesota and elsewhere, there is also mention of a black pipestone from the Lake Huron region and a white pipestone from St. Josephs Island, Lake Huron. (McGuire, Joseph D. "Pipes and Smoking Customs of the American Aborigines," *Report of U. S. National Museum.* 1897, p 480.)

Henry Shetrone, author of one of the important early books on Indians who constructed mounds, commented briefly on the use-range of pipes: "The distribution of native American tobacco pipes is very broad, but their frequency of occurrence rapidly declines toward the Southwest and the Mexican border. In the Pueblo region and southward the simple tubular pipe, resembling in form the modern cigar-holder, is typical, while in Middle and South America the smoking of tobacco, where it occurred, seems to have been in the form of cigarettes and cigars, the prototypes of the modern pipeless methods of smoking." (Shetrone, Henry Clyde. *The Mound-Builders.* 1930, p 161.)

Hopewell effigy platform pipes, if broken in prehistoric times, were repaired in one of three ways. Commonly, the broken area (usually part of the platform) might be ground down and use continued with the pipe in a different and shorter form. Occasionally a copper strip or band was wrapped to "heal" the break, especially at the base of an effigy. Rarely the break surfaces were drilled and held together with small copper dowels.

Two major collectors of years past had numbers of pipes that would be very impressive today. The author George A. West had about 600, while John A. Beck of Pittsburgh had about 1,800. (Moorehead, Warren K. *The Stone Age in North America,* Vol. II. 1910, p 30.)

Some students of Amerind lifeways consider that pipes were used only for important occasions, but this is just one person's view. "There have been discovered (in Kentucky) a large number of pipes which could likely have been used for ceremonial purposes alone, but there are still greater numbers of small individual pipes which, from their very make-up, demonstrate that they were used for personal and not for public service." (Young, Col. Bennett H. *The Prehistoric Men of Kentucky.* 1910, p 272.)

Of all American Indian pipes, the one with the greatest distribution area is that of the tubular form. "*Tubes* are found over a greater area than any other form of Pipe. The Mississippi and Ohio Valleys appear to have been the original home of the Tube, as its greatest development is found there." (West, George A. *Tobacco, Pipes and Smoking Customs of the American Indians*, Part I, Text. 1934, p 355.)

Regarding material used for southern Great Pipes, several dense, close-grained stones were often selected. "While steatite appears to be the most common mineral employed in making these pipes, chlorite and serpentine were also used at times." (McGuire, Joseph D. "Pipes and Smoking Customs of the American Aborigines," *Report of the U. S. National Museum.* 1897, p 443.)

West made a careful distinction between prehistoric and historic Indian pipes. The former he referred to as "archeological" and the latter, "ethnological." His archeological pipes were "truly aboriginal, and which show no modern influence." (West, George A. *Tobacco, Pipes and Smoking Customs of the American Indians.* Part I, Text. 1934, p 381.)

Fire clay — the old name for eastern Midwest

pipestone — is generally thought to be from the well-known deposits near Portsmouth in southern Ohio. However, there are other sources in Forest County, Pennsylvania, and probably elsewhere in that region. (Mayer-Oakes, William J. *Prehistory of the Upper Ohio Valley.* 1955, pp 58, 60, and 63, plate 18.)

Most Indian pipes had additional stems for ease of smoking. Since many of the stems were made of organic materials, few or no traces of the stems remain. Examples: "The enlargement of the smaller end of this tube is evidently for the purpose of inserting a mouthpiece of wood, or bone, or possibly even of stone. The California pipes had mouthpieces of bird bones held firmly in place with bitumen, similar to those of the cliff dwellers which were held with gum of the greasewood. These mouthpieces served the purpose of preventing in a measure the tobacco or plant consumed from escaping into the smoker's mouth." (McGuire, Joseph D. "Pipes and Smoking Customs of the American Aborigines," *Report of U. S. National Museum.* 1897, p 385.)

Authorities have commented about the ability of New England Indians to make (by casting) metal pipes in the 1600s. There is agreement that some lead and pewter pipes were made, but doubt exists as to whether brass was cast.

Pipes in general seem to have always been used as pipes, that is as smoking instruments. An occasional example does indicate use for another purpose as well. Two large, bulky sandstone double-conoidal pipes — one from Ohio, another from West Virginia — have a deep groove on their bottoms as if for shaping or sharpening tools. (McGuire, Joseph D. "Pipes and Smoking Customs of the American Aborigines," *Report of the U. S. National Museum.* 1897, pp 529 – 530.)

Calumet or Plains type pipes were made of different materials, mainly of course catlinite from Minnesota. Other materials include catlinite-like stone from Wisconsin, calcite, steatite, black Canadian pipestone (steatite?), and several kinds of glacial slate.

Tubular stone pipes were once widely available for sale, with many probably from the Midwest: "Red stone, 1⅞ x 2¼", polished, good — $2.75. Brownish slate, 1⅜ x 3⅝", tapered nicely, very fine — $8.00. Banded green slate, 1½ x 3½", all polished, very fine — $7.00. Brown stone, 1¾ x 3½", smooth, fine — $3.75. Tan stone, 1½ x 4½", tapers to ½" at small end, glossy polish, very fine — $10.00." (Grutzmacher, A. D. *Stone Age, Ancient Indian and Mound Builder Relics.* 1940, p 27.)

Fossilized coral, occasionally used as pipe raw material, was found in several locations. One was at major deposits south of Louisville, Kentucky.

In early historic times white-made pottery pipes were favored items for barter or trade. "The readiness and cheapness with which Europeans were enabled to mold, burn, and sell the trade pipe caused it to be produced in great quantities, and the trader could afford to sell it at a price which brought it within the reach of all." (McGuire, Joseph D. "Pipes and Smoking Customs of the American Aborigines," *Report of U. S. National Museum.* 1897, p 503.)

Pipestone is a generic term that could refer to materials from different parts of the country. Quarries were located in Barron County, Wisconsin, in Yavapai County, Arizona, in southwestern Minnesota (the famous catlinite), in Scioto County, Ohio, and in South Dakota. (Fredrickson, A. G. "More on Pipestone from Wisconsin and Other States," *Central States Archaeological Journal.* Vol. 28 No. 4. October 1981, pp 173 – 174.)

The longest all-stone pipes unearthed in North America were those from the Great Temple Mound, LeFlore County, Oklahoma. These platform pipes, with one or two bowls, measured from 5 to 31" long. (*North American Indian Relic Collectors Association.* Vol. 1 No. 8. March 1936, pp 3, 5.)

Long stone tubular pipes found in California often have small shaped stones as filters in the bore near the mouth-piece end. Such pipes may reach 16½" in length. (Howe, Carrol. "The Filter Pipes of Nightfire Island," *The Redskin.* Vol. 8 No. 2. 1973, pp 48 – 50).

A pipestone much used by Canadian people was described as being gray in color and found between layers of lime slate. It was soft enough to cut with a knife. Upon exposure to air or sunlight the stone became yellow. To darken the stone, the pipes were coated with grease and held above a fire, where upon the pipe became the desired black with this color maintained by smoking. (McGuire, Joseph D. "Pipes and Smoking Customs of the American Aborigines," *Report of U. S. National Museum.* 1897, pp 497 – 498.)

Historic-era Sioux Indians became adept at using lead with catlinite pipe heads. Lead was melted and shaped in pre-cut grooves. This work was done for three reasons. Lead was used purely for decoration, or to hold together two separate sections, or to repair a broken pipe. (West, George A." The Aboriginal Pipes of Wisconsin," *The Wisconsin Archeologist.* Vol. 4 Nos. 3 & 4. April – August 1905, p 89.)

Quillwork was sometimes done on the stems of early Plains pipes. "*Wrapping.* This is the simplest method of applying quills and is used to cover long, slender objects, like pipe stems, or strands of leather fringe. The method was to bend the moistened quills around the object to be decorated, beginning with several overlapping rounds of wrapping to cover the end of the quill. As new quills were added, their ends were twisted around the old ones with a half turn which was concealed by the next wrapping." (*Quill and Beadwork of the Western Sioux.* Lyford, Carrie A. U. S. Office of Indian Affairs. 1940, p 44.)

Pipes that have a small hole drilled below the bowl or above or below the stem probably had this feature for cord attachment, so the bowl could not be dropped. This may have been done to prevent loss in snow, so the main regions of pipe distribution are noteworthy. "Pipes of this type are commonly found throughout the territory adjoining Lakes Ontario and Erie down through Ohio, Indiana, and Kentucky, and into Tennessee and North Carolina, and along the coast up to the British possessions." (McGuire, Joseph D. "Pipes and Smoking Customs of the American Aborigines," *Report of U. S. National Museum.* 1897, pp 627 – 628.)

Argillite, a relatively soft dark stone somewhere between shale and slate in hardness, was used for Northwest Coast pipes. Some were carved in elaborate styles. "Many of these souvenir pipes were made by the Haida Indians of the Queen Charlotte Islands of argillite, a stone which is soft on excavation and so easily worked. Argillite is a form of carbonaceous shale found eight miles from Skidegate in the Queen Charlotte Islands at a place called Slatechuck mountain; only the Skidegate Eagle clan had rights of mining the argillite in the nineteenth century." (King, J. C. H. *Smoking Pipes of the North American Indian.* 1977, pp 27 – 28.)

Pipes in prehistoric America were made in a great number of types and sub-types, in different sizes, and from many kinds of materials. Probably no other artifact class as a whole is so wide ranging and individualistic.

Joseph McGuire, in his study of Indian pipes, remarked on the great beauty of certain tubular effigy pipes in particular and stone pipes in general. This was when they were contrasted with "extremely rude efforts" of the effigies incised or engraved on some pipes. He felt that the pipes and marking on the pipes could not have been done by the same people. (A good example would be the obtuse-angle or alate pipes which were often incised after completion.) (McGuire, Joseph D. "Pipes and Smoking Customs of the American Aborigines," *Report of U. S. National Museum.* 1897, pp 400 – 401.)

Some pipestone, fairly easy to work and attractive when shaped and polished, is not always as durable or stable as hardstone. The following account emphasizes this, and also provides a clue as to how pipe stems were holed: "The problem of locating stone pipes [Hopewell platform pipes] where the sites are composed of clay is that most crumble when drying. Two other pipes made of Ohio pipestone found in these mounds crumbled when they dried. One of the pipes that disintegrated had a piece of an obsidian drill in the stem hole." (Perino,

Gregory. "A Brief History of Two Woodland Pipes and a Mississippian Pipe," *Central States Archaeological Journal.* Vol. 24 No. 1. January 1977, pp 28 – 29.)

Various substances were mixed with tobacco, and an early account mentions one such example "Kin-Ne-Ne-Kah (arbitrary name) Sumac: They [the Indians] consider it a principal article, next to tobacco, in the stores for the pipe; mixed with about an equal part of tobacco, it forms one of their most fashionable treats." (Hunter, John D. *Manners and Customs of Several Indian Tribes Located West of the Mississippi.* 1823/1957, pp 389 – 390.)

Joseph McGuire's Indian pipe study noted the attention to finish on most pipes: "If we examine any collection of ancient American pipes the extreme care with which they have been finished is noticeable, though it is seldom that a polish of any kind is met with in any implements of aboriginal art north of Mexico." (McGuire, Joseph D. "Pipe and Smoking Customs of the American Aborigines," *Report of the U. S. National Museum.* 1897 p 414.)

Terminology can be confusing when pipe materials are mentioned, especially in accounts from the past. "Fired clay," for one, is pottery, molded in the plastic state and baked to hardness; it is a ceramic. "Fireclay," on the other hand, is pipestone, a naturally occurring hard substance usually mined and that was carved into the final form.

The so-called file marks early writers sometimes mentioned as having been seen on pipes were then considered to be marks made by the whites' iron file. They were actually the signs of prehistoric tool use. The location of these marks was on those parts of the pipe surface that were most awkward to reach and polish. In other words, the marks were difficult to remove in these areas and remained to mislead early investigators. (McGuire, Joseph D. "Pipes and Smoking Customs of the American Aborigines," *Report of the U. S. National Museum.* 1897, p 522.)

When studying drill holes in stone pipes, it is sometimes noted that the holes slightly change in diameter along the interior of the stem. This is because the first drill became worn out (or was resharpened, in the case of flint and chert drill tips) and a slightly smaller drill was next used. Also, the presence of smooth-sided drill holes in genuine, old pipes does not mean a steel drill bit was used. Likely, a thin copper rod was employed which somewhat polished the sides as it revolved and advanced.

The important investigator of mound-building cultures, Henry Shetrone, felt that the alate (winged) or obtuse-angle pipe might represent "...a highly conventionalized bird." (Shetrone, Henry Clyde. *The Mound-Builders.* 1930, p 159 figure 90.)

Argillite or carbonaceous shale was much used in the Pacific Northwest for carvings, including pipes. Found in the Haida region, the pipes (and other objects) were made exclusively for trade. (Due to the nature of the materials, pipes were not smoked.) Some pipe examples were quite ornate and in traditional styles. (Gunther, Erna. *Art in the Life of the Northwest Coast Indians*. The Ford Foundation. 1966, pp 185 – 186.)

Salvage of damaged pipes was sometimes done in prehistoric times. One example, about 2" long, began as a Hopewell platform pipe, and was picked up near O'Fallon, Missouri. This piece, made of green pipestone, consisted of the bowl and part of the platform. The platform had several drilled holes, probably for thongs or sinew fastenings to the missing section(s). (*CSAJ/The Archaeology of Missouri and Greater St. Louis*. Vol. 37 No. 4. October 1990, p 111.)

The Hopewell platform pipes, mainly from the Midwest and in plain or effigy form, are said to require no additional stem or mouth piece since the stem already exists in one part of the platform. There are three reasons why this may not be correct. Tooth marks are usually not found on the stone stems. And smoking many of the pipes in the usual way would place the pipe bowl very close to the smoker's nostrils, too close for comfortable use. Finally, at least one collector with an experimental mind actually smoked a damaged prehistoric pipe. He remarked that the pipe very quickly became too hot for use.

Much more has been written about pipes than pipe stems, though many of the former would be useless without the latter. "Tubular pipes were generally smoked by means of bone, wood, or even stone stems, inserted in the smaller end of the tube, as is indicated by its interior enlargement. In California, and among the Pueblos and cliff dwellers, these mouthpieces were held in position by means of bitumen or gum, though there is little direct evidence as to the method employed in the eastern portion of the United States to hold the tubular pipestems in place; similarity in shape of tube would suggest like methods. Pipestems of wood — round, flat, curved, bent, and carved, long and short — are common from the Rocky Mountains to the Atlantic Ocean, the Indian being governed in the character of stem largely by the supply of material in the territory to which he had access whether personally or through trade." (McGuire, Joseph D. "Pipes and Smoking Customs of the American Aborigines," *Report of the U. S. National Museum*. 1897, p 436.)

In the case of some catlinite Plains pipes, the bowl might be made of catlinite from one block of stone, the stem from another block. So, while a bowl and stem do not necessarily need to match in color, they should indeed match in style and proportion and wear and polish if they are truly a paired set.

There are some short, even stubby, tubular pipes that follow longer pipes in having the added mouthpiece inserted at the smaller end. The follow description refers to such a stone pipe found in New Jersey, measuring about $1^{15}/_{16}$ x $2\frac{1}{2}$": "It closely resembles the long tubular pipes so characteristic of the islands off the coast of California. While many of the latter are three and four times as long as this specimen, others are of about the same length, and so almost, if not entirely, lose their tubular character, and are simply elongated pipe-bowls." (Abbott, Charles C. MD. *Primitive Industry*. 1881, pp 329 – 330.)

A side benefit of pipe smoking may have been some medical use: "He-Ne-Pis-Ka (Fire gone out) Ashes: The ashes of tobacco, and the mountain laurel, are applied with considerable advantage, to ill-conditioned ulcers." (Hunter, John D. *Manners and Customs of Several Indian Tribes Located West of the Missisippi*. 1823/1957, p 369.)

Gray sandstone, used for some pipes in Minnesota, may have come from several locations. One was the Upper Cambian layers from southern Minnesota. The other was from Wisconsin. (Winchell, N. H. *The Aborigines of Minnesota*. The Minnesota Historical Society. 1911, p 484.)

West reported that some 2,000 catlinite pipes were made by whites for trade with Indians in the late 1700s. Characteristics of such pipes are said to be extra large size, a base without a comb or crest between the bowl and stem end, and stem holes and bowl holes of the same cylindrical size because they were made with the same steel drill bits. Also, upon receiving these pipes, some were reworked by the Indians to become somewhat different. (West, George A. *Tobacco, Pipes and Smoking Customs of the American Indians*, Part I, Text. 1934, pp 327 – 328.)

Long, wooden pipe stems of the calumet type pipes of the Plains and Great Lakes areas were decorated in various ways. Some were artfully carved in a spiral or puzzle design with cutouts so that it was difficult to know where the stem hole was located. Others might be painted, covered partially or entirely with quillwork or beadwork, or have attached feathers, fur, horsehair, or cloth streamers. Inlaying the stems with bone, shell, or stone was occasionally done.

Iroquois late prehistoric and early historic pipes have attracted interest due to the skill with which they were made and the large number crafted. "Pipes of stone are much more varied in shape than are pipes of clay. The clay pipe of the East and North is based on the plain tube, the prevailing modification being the development of the bowl and the addition of a trumpet-like mouth. The tube is not straight, but is bent at the base of the bowl at angles varying from a few degrees to a right angle or even more." (Holmes, W. H. "Aboriginal Pottery of the Eastern

United States," *Twentieth Annual Report of the Bureau of American Ethnology*. 1903, p 174.)

Colonel Raymond Vietzen had an informative caption in one of his books describing a photograph with four metal historic pipes. All were fairly plain, with thin stems and flared bowls set at right angles (3) or obtuse angle (1). "Trade pipes of lead, pewter, and German silver found in western Ohio and Indiana along the Maumee, Auglaize, and Wabash rivers. Pipes of this type found their way to Fort Wayne and Vincennes. A few were forged of iron and many pottery trade pipes were in use as traders became numerous in the Northwest Territory." (Vietzen, Colonel Raymond C. *Their Fires Are Cold*. 1984, p 123.)

A relatively small number of pipes were made of ultra-hard material like quartzite. And they tend to be purposely made as pipes from the beginning. A few pipes, however, are the result of salvage from what originally were other, and different, artifacts. One such, formerly in the Dr. Meuser collection of Columbus, Ohio, began as a bell pestle made of cream quartzite. It evolved into a pipe when part was ground down and drilled for a bowl hole and stem hole. The pestle-pipe was from Clermont County, Ohio. In a sense, such scarce examples are double artifacts. (Meuser Auction catalog. Garth's Auctions, Delaware, Ohio. 1974, no. 5/1786.)

Several kinds of pipestone from the Upper Midwest have been called catlinite. "The Minnesota catlinite of which most of the Elbow Pipes of that region were made was near at hand and easily mined, which is probably a reason why such a great number of so-called Siouan Pipes were made of that material. Others, showing considerable age, are made of the brownish [Barron County] Wisconsin catlinite." (West, George A. *Tobacco, Pipes and Smoking Customs of the American Indians*, Part I, Text. 1934, p 278.)

While certainly a generality, McGuire has a worthwhile observation on stone pipes in one geographic area. "Until the coming of the whites most New York pipes were of clay, the Narragansetts making those of stone, but with the use of steel tools stone pipes became common." (McGuire, Joseph D. "Pipes and Smoking Customs of the American Aborigines," *Report of the U. S. National Museum*. 1897, p 433.)

Certain beliefs once held that prehistoric Indians were incapable of some kinds of work. In terms of pipes, this meant that prehistoric pipes could not have been made in ancient times but must have been the result of influence or contact with whites. For effigy pipes, the figures were thought to be too European for primitive people to create. Gouge marks inside bowls, and finishing marks left on pipe surfaces, were thought to be the signatures of white-supplied metal tools. And, high surface polish on some pipes was thought to be an European trait.

Pipes of the Pacific Northwest, while sometimes related in form, were made of many materials. "All along the western and northwestern coast of America a most curious style of pipe is found, commonly of very grotesque form and made of a great variety of material, such as wood, stone, antler, and of these materials in combination with metal, bone, and mother-of-pearl. North of California almost all the pipes found not only indicate quite modern origin but, in a measure, are suggestive of being made for sale to the whites...." (McGuire, Joseph D. "Pipes and Smoking Customs of the American Aborigines," *Report of the U. S. National Museum*. 1897, p 584.)

The word *calumet* is often used to mean the historic long-stemmed peace pipe, ceremonial or social pipes of the Plains Indians. The word is sometimes applied to the pipe head itself, often made of catlinite. Actually the word was originally used to mean the long and often elaborate or decorated wooden pipe stem, with the T-shaped or L-shaped pipe head itself often being of secondary importance.

Pipes have long been made in the southern Appalachian area, so age at times can be uncertain. "The historic tribes of the region, and especially of the Carolinas, have always been great pipe makers and have for at least a hundred years practiced the art with much ardor, using the product in trade with neighboring tribes and with the whites. ...We are led by this circumstance to question the age of all the more ornate forms of pipes not found in associations that prove them to be ancient." (Holmes, W. H. "Aboriginal Pottery of the Eastern United States." *Twentieth Annual Report of the Bureau of American Ethnology*. 1903, p 140.)

Smoking pipes in many United States regions seem to become more common in later prehistoric times. For example, at a Ft. Ancient (Mississippian period) site in southern Ohio many pipes were recovered, these made of various materials. "Most of them were made from the limestone of the region. Some were of sandstone, while a small number were of other varieties, including serpentine and red pipestone. Two or three rude pipe bowls were found made from sections of deer antler, also fragments of four or five pottery pipes, fashioned of fine clay of a kind very different from that used by the inhabitants in making pottery." (Willoughby, Charles C. "Artifacts from the Site," *Indian Village Site and Cemetery Near Madisonville, Ohio. Peabody Museum*. 1920, p 73.)

Gray serpentine or gray pipestone was apparently much used in the Minnesota region for pipes, and sources are here located: "The gray serpentine used by the northern tribes was obtainable at a number of places in northern Minnesota and in the adjoining portions of Canada. One place is on the shore of a bay at the south side of Bassimenan Lake [while] another is at Pipestone rapids, in a steep cliff, on the east side, and at a point a short distance above the rapids, on the right bank." (Winchell, N. H. *The Aborigines of Minnesota*. The Minnesota Historical Society. 1911, p 487.)

Astute observers like Moorehead felt that artistic decorations on pipes were more than mere artwork. "...The decoration seems to be the essential thing in pipes. The idea of the maker was to portray something on the pipe or to have the pipe stand for more than a mere receptacle in which tobacco was smoked. No other conclusion is possible when we consider the high percentage of decorated and ornamented pipes, and the surprising number of pipes worked into effigies." (Moorehead, Warren K. *The Stone Age in North America*, Vol. II. 1910, p 57.)

In historic times, and possibly a carry-over from late prehistory, some pipes were not considered to be "empowered" or complete until the bowl and stem were joined. This is especially true of certain Plains types.

While the effigy symbolism of most prehistoric pipes will never be really known or understood, images were usually positioned in certain ways. "A striking characteristic of pipes is that figures on stems or bowls from a given area commonly face in one direction." (Hodge, Frederick Webb. *Handbook of American Indians North of Mexico*. Part 2, BAE Bulletin 30. 1912, p 258.)

Some of the pottery tubular pipes so often found in Pueblo region of the American Southwest had incised lines or crosshatching about the middle of the tube. These may have served as decoration, but they also may have created a non-slip surface for holding when the pipe was used. (McGuire, Joseph D. "Pipes and Smoking Customs of the American Aborigines," *Report of the U. S. National Museum*. 1897, pp 378 – 379.)

Different substances were used at various times for smoking, either alone or in mixture with others. Examples of plant materials are the bark or inner bark or leaves of sumac, dogwood, willow, ironwood, and laurel. In late historic times true tobacco might be combined with other substances and only rarely was tobacco alone used.

The Copena people, centered in northern Alabama, were named after two of the materials often used for artifacts, copper and galena. With a combination of Adena and Hopewell traits, these Indians were responsible for some of the large effigy steatite pipes that have been found in the South, and some were even exchanged with Ohio's Hopewell people. (Evans, E. Raymond. "Copena: A Middle Woodland People/100 B. C. to 400 A. D.," *The Redskin*. Vol. 8 No.

2. 1973, p 66.)

McGuire, one of the more knowledgeable students of Indian pipes a century ago, still believed that pipes found in Hopewell mounds were probably the result of at least indirect white contact. He based this on some faulty reasons: The presence of "file marks"; certain earspools that appeared to be absolutely round; and, silver found in a few mounds. He also believed that "delicate finish and artistic merit" of effigy platform pipes was beyond the capabilities of Mound Builders. (McGuire, Joseph D. "Pipes and Smoking Customs of the American Aborigines," *Report of U. S. National Museum*. 1897, p 522.)

A. E. Douglass, one of the major American collectors, passed away in 1901. His collection contained, in part, 209 bannerstones, 721 celts, 419 grooved axes, and 375 pipes. (Smith, Harlan I. "Andrew Ellicott Douglass," *The Wisconsin Archeologist*. Vol. 1 No. 2. 1902, p 42.)

Very little is known about prehistoric pipe-stems in the great pipe-making area known as the Mississippi Valley or Watershed, but educated observations have been made. "The great Calumets of the so-called southern type, although found throughout the Mississippi Valley, have large stem cavities indicating heavy and long stems. Many of these stem cavities are conical in shape and would not hold fast a stem unless the same was lashed to the pipe-bowl. (West, George A. *Tobacco, Pipes and Smoking Customs of the American Indians*, Part I, Text. 1934, pp 266 – 267.)

One does not usually think of pipe stem holes as being particularly important, but some indeed are. "Large funnel-shaped stem holes, sometimes even larger than the pipe bowls, appear to the author to have been one of the distinguishing characteristics of southern clay and stone pipes, and we suggest to antiquarians the importance of this feature in the proper classification of these objects." (Thruston, Gates P. *The Antiquities of Tennessee*. 1890, p 178.)

Changes in pipe form can be important markers over time. "Pottery is the primary and the best indicator of cultural change, and pipes are also quite sensitive to changes in style." (Mayer-Oakes, William J. *Prehistory of the Upper Ohio Valley*. 1955, p 25.)

George A. West, early authority on Indian pipes, believed the disk or disc pipe was used in a certain fashion. "This is a most interesting class of pipes, the typical examples having a circular face, widened out, in some cases, to extravagant proportions. When in use the disk faced the smoker, which probably accounts for its often having a finer finish than does the remainder of the pipe, and for its being often ornamented with engraved figures." (West, George A. "The Aboriginal Pipes of Wisconsin," *The Wisconsin Archeologist*. Vol. 4 Nos. 3 & 4. April – August, 1905, p 130.)

Interest in the steatite Great Pipes remains high,

and these observations should be helpful; it should be kept in mind that a few Great Pipes have been found in the last two decades. "The great pipes were all cut from either a cylinder blank or a rectangular blank. ...Conclusions from the collected data reveals a total number of 11 known full winged great pipes. Five of these pipes are in museums or institutions, leaving about six in private collections." (Baldwin, John. "The Eiker Pipe," *The Redskin.* Vol. 10 No. 1. 1975, p 18 – 19.)

A final word of good advice to collectors of pipes: "If, in your possession, you retain a pipe from the prehistoric period, make every effort to investigate old written history or pictures of the past. This study will establish its entrance into known time, and make possible the authentication of your pipe. Protect this object to retain its original form that it may be studied by pipe researchers of the distant future when more advanced knowledge plus improved scientific instrumentation will be available. In so doing, you will enhance a part of the heritage of our country." (Hart, Gordon. *Hart's Prehistoric Pipe Rack.* 1978, p 18.)

Pipe Finds

With the coming of large-scale agriculture, construction activities of many kinds and natural erosion from wind and water, it was and is inevitable that Indian pipes would be found. Some of the pipes were picked up many years ago while others are recovered to this day.

Some pipes are as whole and unmarked as the day they were made hundreds or thousands of years ago. Other specimens were dropped or damaged in use, or broken by modern farming implements.

In terms of all other kinds of prehistoric Indian artifacts, pipes tend to be scarce no matter the kind of pipes or location where they are found. Any such smoking instrument is a rare treasure from the past, one that the collector can be proud to own and protect for the future.

A Bound Prisoner effigy human pipe was found in Mississippi County, Missouri, prior to April of 1980. Made of greenstone, the well-crafted example was 4½" high and 4½" long. (*Central States Archaeological Journal.* Vol. 27 No. 3. July 1980, p 135.)

Picked up near Port Gibson, Claiborne County, Mississippi, one of the largest and heaviest prehistoric stone pipes was made to resemble a frog or toad. The Port Gibson pipe was made of weathered sandstone and measured 11⁷⁄₁₀" long and weighed 19 pounds. (Brown, Calvin S. *Archeology of Mississippi.* Mississippi State Geological Survey. 1926, p 251 figure 212.)

After extensive flooding, a large Mississippian platform pipe was recovered in St. Louis County, Missouri, in 1983. Known as the Davis Pipe, it represents a squirrel eating a nut or similar food. Made of reddish-brown siltstone-like material, the pipe may be from the Stirling phase, ca. AD 1050 – 1150. (*CSAJ/The Archaeology of Missouri and Greater St. Louis.* Vol. 37 No. 4. October 1990, p 133.)

An unusually fine pottery effigy pipe was found at the Strickler Site, Lancaster County, Pennsylvania, nicely made of clay baked to dark yellowish-red. The bowl depicted an owl effigy facing the smoker, with the bowl in the owl's back. The pipe was 11" long. (Cadzow, Donald A. *Archaeological Studies of the Susquehannock Indians of Pennsylvania.* Pennsylvania Historical Commission, Vol. III. 1936, pp 62, 77 – 78, plate 31.)

The state of Delaware had a major artifact collector, Joseph Wigglesworth, who also had an unusual find of pipes: "One of the rarities in his collection was a series of tobacco pipes carved from slate and adorned with animal effigies which a steam shovel had gutted out of the earth in Accomac County, Virginia." (Weslager, C. A. *Delaware's Buried Past.* 1944, pp 45, 58.)

A beautiful owl effigy Hopewell platform pipe came from Calhoun County, Illinois. Made of brown and gray Ohio pipestone, the well-polished pipe was 3 x 4". (*The Redskin.* Vol. 10 No. 1. 1975, p 26.)

In 1976 an interesting effigy pipe was found in New York on a late prehistoric site. Made of white steatite or soapstone in the form of a bear, the object had 24 indented sections which had once held inlays, of which four remained. Two were made of copper, one was shell, and one possibly made from a seed. Adhesive retained in the eye-sockets indicates these too had inlays. The pipe measures 2" high, 1" wide, and 3" long. (Mania, Sam. "An Inlaid Bear Effigy Stone Pipe," *Central States Archaeological Journal.* Vol. 30 No. 3. July 1983, p 131.)

Picked up around 1900, a fine Hopewell effigy platform pipe came from near Davenport, Iowa. Made of green Ohio pipestone, the image probably represented a hawk. Very carefully made and polished, the pipe had eyes of small river pearls. The platform base was 1½ x 3³⁄₁₆" and the pipe height was 2". (Grimm, R. E. *Prehistoric Art.* The Greater St. Louis Archaeological Society. 1953, pp 50 – 51.)

One of the finest Adena tubular pipes came from near Chillicothe, Ohio. Made of banded slate and with a gracefully flared mouthpiece, it was 1¹⁄₁₀" in diameter and 13" long. (Fowke, Gerard. *Archaeological History of Ohio.* 1902, p 577.)

Constricted-center steatite tube pipes can be as small as 4" long, with one such example found in Park County, Tennessee. (*Indiana Archaeological Society Yearbook.* 1974, p 12.)

After careful searching, the nine pieces of a superb pipe (revealed by the fall of a great beech tree) were finally assembled into a complete pipe. Made of dark hardstone, the tubular effigy

form had what appeared to be a wolf's head at one end, with the right-angle bowl about in the shoulder area. The pipe was 16¾" long and weighed 7½ pounds. (Young, Col. Bennett H. *The Prehistoric Men of Kentucky.* 1910, pp 285 – 286, 288, 291.)

One of the most unusual tubular pipes was a flared-end tube, Adena in origin, from Wolfe Plain, Ohio. It was 5½" long, ¾" across at the body, and 2" wide at the flattened mouthpiece end. The material was wood covered with sheet copper. (McGuire, Joseph D. "Pipes and Smoking Customs of the American Aborigines," *Report of the U. S. National Museum.* 1897, p 383.)

A large Mississippian period limestone pipe in an owl-like form came from Madison County, Illinois, in 1951. The pipe was 4" high and 6" long. (Wiemers, Tim. "Worth the Trip," *Central States Archaeological Journal.* Vol. 35 No. 1. January 1988, pp 34 – 35.)

One of the longer tube pipes made of Minnesota catlinite was found in Winnebago County, Wisconsin. It measures 1⅖" wide by just over 11" long. (West, George A. *Tobacco, Pipes and Smoking Customs of the American Indians,* Part II, Plates. 1934, p 540, plate 30 figure 1.)

A Red Ochre culture tubular pipe was recovered near St. Charles, Missouri, ca. early 1940s. It was the tapered type with one end larger than the other. Made from compact dark brown stone, it measures 1⅛ x 4⅞". (Titterington, Dr. Paul. "Some Non-Pottery Sites in St. Louis Area," *Illinois State Archaeological Society/50th Anniversary Issue.* Vol. 33 No. 4. October 1986, pp 291, 294.)

Tate County, Georgia, was the find-locality of a very large talc-steatite elbow pipe in the early 1900s. It was 7" high, 4" wide, and 10" long. (*Prehistoric Artifacts.* Vol. 20 No. 2. 1986, p 6.)

Two of the better Hopewell (Middle Woodland period) effigy platform pipes came from Pike County, Illinois. One is known as the Gilcrease Raven, and was made of green pipestone. The other, the Bedford Beaver, was carved from black pipestone; it had inset pearls for eyes and inset beaver incisor sections for teeth. (*Illinois State Archaeological Society/50th Anniversary Issue.* Vol. 33 No. 4. October 1986, p 322, plate 55.)

Henderson County, Kentucky, was the regional location for a very large catlinite disc or sun-disc pipe. Associated with eight chipped points or knives, the fine pipe was 7¼" long and had a disc diameter of nearly 3⅞". (*Central States Archaeological Journal.* Vol. 39 No. 3. July 1992, p 133.)

The year 1940 saw the finding of a famous pipe, a tubular effigy form known as the Blind Wolf Pipe. It was plowed up in the Tennessee hills and was made of dark green steatite with gold mica flecks. The very artistic pipe, with a wolf-like animal laying atop and straddling a large tube, measured an unrivaled 22¼" long, with the tube itself about 2½" in diameter. The effigy portion was 14" long. The name came about because the facial features were present except for the eyes. (Berner, John F. "The Magnificent Blind Wolf Pipe," *Prehistoric Artifacts.* Vol. 20 No. 3. 1986, pp 14-15.)

An effigy pipe representing a kneeling human with a large container held in the arms was found in Mississippi County, Arkansas. The open container was the pipe bowl, and material was a gray quartzite. This pipe measures 2½ x 3¼". (*The Redskin.* Vol. 4 No. 1. January 1969, p 31.)

A pipe find: "James Duncan, while husking corn in a field near the No. 11 school house, East of Millwood, in this county (Kansas) recently noticed a round looking object on the ground that appeared to be something out of the ordinary and, picking it up, found that it was a curiously carved stone smoking pipe. He took it to a local antiquarian at Porter, who pronounced it an ancient Indian pipe. It was made of yellow sandstone and will not hold much more than a thimble-full of tobacco." (Remsburg, George J. "Miscellaneous Notes," *The Archaeological Bulletin.* Vol. 6 No. 1. January – February 1915, p 11.)

Seven Adena blocked-end tubular pipes in a cache were found in an undisclosed region, along with other artifacts made of flint, copper, and slate. The pipes were skillfully made in gray Ohio pipestone and ranged in length from 3¾ to 10⅜". (Munger, Lynn. "Adena Cache," *The Redskin.* Vol. 13 No. 3. 1978, pp 84, 86.)

A fine biconical pipe was found in eastern Tennessee in 1974, made of brown and green steatite flecked with mica. The pipe had good overall polish and measures 2⁷⁄₁₆ x 12½". (Cruse, Amon H. "Great Surface Find of the 1970s," *Prehistoric Art/Archaeology "80."* Vol. 15 No. 1. 1980, pp 8 – 9.)

In 1958 a late prehistoric trumpet type pipe was discovered in New York. The material used was rare, a red and brown chlorite. Well polished, the pipe was 2¼ x 2½". (*The Redskin.* Vol. 14 No. 1. 1979, p 19.)

The seated human figure pipe known as "Big Boy" was one of the heaviest Midwestern pipes. It was recovered during commercial excavation at the Craig Mound, Spiro, Oklahoma. Made of red bauxite, the seated male figure wearing a feathered cape was once covered with red paint. The effigy weighed a remarkable 11½ pounds. ("The 'Big Boy' Pipe," *Central States Archaeological Journal.* Vol. 24 No. 4. October 1977, pp 162 – 163.)

Blocked-end tube pipes made by the Adena (Early Woodland) people were exported from the eastern Midwest into the New England area. One example, made of shale-like material, was found near Swanton, Vermont. It was 11¾" long. (Mohrman,

Harold. "New England Tube Pipes," *Central States Archaeological Journal*. Vol. 32 No. 1. January 1985, p 17.)

Cass County, Indiana, in the 1920s produced a high-bowl platform pipe with a large bowl set about one-third from the undrilled end. Material was a red-brown stone with light bands, probably a pipestone. This pipe was 2 x 5⅜". (Kistler, Jack. "The Swisher Pipe," *The Redskin*. Vol. 9 No. 3. 1974, pp 114 – 115.)

One of the largest and finest of the effigy Hopewell platform pipes came from Hardin County, Illinois. Somewhat similar to the Gilcrease Raven pipe, the example is known as the Rutherford Site Raven. The material was highly unusual, being a conglomerate stone, and the pipe measured 4¾" long. (*Illinois State Archaeological Society/50th Anniversary Issue*. Vol. 33 No. 4. October 1986, p 325, plate 58 figure 1.)

A very large steatite Great Pipe was found ca. 1929 near the Holston River, close to Knoxville, Tennessee. In blackish steatite, the effigy was that of an extended bird and the pipe was just over 18" long. (West, George A. *Tobacco, Pipes and Smoking Customs of the American Indians,* Part II, Plates. 1934, p 654, plate 87.)

One of the better Hopewell plain platform pipes was found in Franklin County, Ohio, prior to 1974. Made of gray-green Ohio pipestone, the example had a thick, slightly curved base and spool-shaped bowl. Now in the Baldwin collection, the classic piece measured 1⅞ x 4½". (Hothem, Lar. *Ancient Art of Ohio*. 1994, p 232 no. 598.)

An unusual Adena tubular pipe was recovered from a rock shelter in Tennessee. Made of green, slate-like stone, it measured 3½" long and was the blocked-end variety typical of Adena manufacture in the Ohio Valley. The bowl rim was notched and the expanded body incised with crossed lines. (*Central States Archaeological Journal*. Vol. 29 No. 1. January 1982, p 3.)

One of the very few bird effigy tubular Adena pipes was found in Montgomery County, Ohio. It represented a duck, the expanded bill being the mouthpiece, and a long neck formed the tube and bowl. Made of limestone, the pipe was 6¼" long. (*The Redskin*. Vol. 5 No. 4. October 1970, p 101.)

Elegant and streamlined, a Late Woodland long-stemmed pipe with high bowl and flanged rim was found in Wythe County, Virginia. The pipe was made of gray steatite and measured 3¾ x 8⅛". (*The Redskin*. Vol. 8 No. 1. 1973, p 3.)

The Canadian province of Ontario sometime before 1915 produced an unusual animal pipe. The material is unlisted for the pipe, which measured 2" high, 3½" wide, and 4½" long. Rows of protrusions along the back on either side of the pipe bowl suggested the image of a porcupine. ("New Accessions in Museum," *Twenty-Seventh Annual Archaeological Report/1915*. The Legislative Assembly of Ontario. 1915, p 91.)

Smyth County, Virginia, was the find-area for an extremely fine alate or winged Late Woodland pipe with a high bowl. The material was green steatite, very well polished, and the wide stem was quite thin. Pipe width was 4⅗" and length was 13⅕", while bowl height was 9⅗". (West, George A. *Tobacco, Pipes and Smoking Customs of the American Indians*, Part II, Plates. 1934, p 990, plate 255.)

A large Woodland biconical or indented center tubular pipe was found in Hardin County, Tennessee. Made of steatite, the pipe had some modern damage at one end and was 7¾" long. (Wilkes, Jeff. "Hunt Your Surface Sites," *Central States Archaeological Journal*. Vol. 29 No. 4. October 1982, p 208.)

Especially in the eastern Midwest and other areas that were heavily glaciated, many pipes were manufactured from banded slate. This material was once called ribbon slate or lined slate. Banded slate seems to have originated in southern Canada, was scattered into the United States by glacial action, and was found in the glacial drift by prehistoric artisans. (Webb, William S. *The Parrish Village Site*. University of Kentucky. Vol. 7 No. 6. February 1951, p 431.)

Darke County, Ohio, produced a bear effigy elbow pipe made of brown sandstone. Eye, nostrils, and teeth were accented in the specimen. Length of the pipe was about 2¾". (*The Redskin*. Vol. 5. No. 1. January 1970, p 10.)

In Cocke County, Tennessee, an artistic bird effigy Great Pipe was plowed up prior to October 1969. Found near the Pigeon River, it was 3¾" high and 9" long. (*Central States Archaeological Journal*. Vol. 16 No. 4. October 1969, p 164.)

Limestone was the raw material used for a tubular pipe picked up (along with a limestone gorget) in a Kentucky rock shelter. The pipe was 5¾" long. (*The Redskin*. Vol. 4 No. 1. January 1969, p 33.)

Near-matching pairs of Hopewell platform pipes are almost unheard of, but such a pair indeed exists. Found before 1933 in Illinois, the curved-base plain pipes were made of spotted pipestone in olive green and were highly polished. Each pipe measured 5⅛" long, and shared a height of 3". The similarity is so striking they may well have been made by the same prehistoric artisan. (Grimm, R. E. *Prehistoric Art*. The Greater St. Louis Archaeological Society. 1953, pp 62 – 63.)

An unusual 1931 find of a stone human effigy pipe from the Mississippian period was made in Jackson County, Illinois, which depicted a warrior crouching behind a rectangular shield. The pipe was about 4" high. (*Illinois State Archaeological Society/50th Anniversary Issue*. Vol. 33 No. 4. October

1986, p 318, plate 53.)

A fine Mississippian stone pipe was discovered in Kingston, Tennessee, before the turn of the century. It illustrates a kneeling or crouching human figure, and is 6" high and 5" long. Quite well known, the pipe was illustrated in Thruston's *Antiquities of Tennessee* and Moorehead's *Prehistoric Implements,* among other publications. (Townsend, Earl C. Jr. "A Fine Tennessee Effigy Pipe," *Central States Archaeological Journal.* Vol. 31 No. 1. January 1984, pp 14 – 15.)

Highly unusual, a human effigy pipe with a bowl above the head made of dark green Ohio pipestone was collected before 1876 by a doctor in Ohio. The figure had a face on both the front and back of the pipe, which represented a standing human. It had a height of 4¼". (*The Redskin.* Vol. 4 No. 1. January 1969, p 30.)

An effigy pipe which depicted a panther was found in 1886 in Chicot County, Arkansas. Made of ivory-hued limestone, the stem hole was at the rear and the bowl was in the middle of the animal's back. The pipe was 4⅜" high and 5" long. (Perino, Gregory. "Three Late Middle Mississippi Effigy-Pipes," *Central States Archaeological Journal.* Vol. 12 No. 3. July 1965, pp 105, 107.)

Chlorite is a scarce material for bannerstones and a rare material for pipes. Such an example, a platform pipe with a tall, centered bowl, was found in Richland County, Ohio. It measured 2 x 7" long. (*The Redskin.* Vol. 6 No. 3. July 1971, p 86.)

A beautiful platform pipe was once in the possession of Frank Burdett of Dayton, Ohio. A Late Woodland Intrusive Mound pipe, probably in dark steatite, it had a wide, thin base with ridged stem hole and high, narrow bowl. Originally collected by W. K. Moorehead in Mason County, West Virginia, the polished pipe was 10¼" long. ("Outstanding Artifacts From Burdett Collection," *Ohio Indian Relic Collectors Society/Ohio Archaeologist.* Vol. 1 No. 1. April 1951, inside front cover & p 1.)

A large elbow-type pipe was found in Giles County, Tennessee. With biconical drilling, the pipe bowl measured 5" high; it was made of sandstone. (Rost, R. L. "A Tennessee Stone Pipe," *Central State Archaeological Journal.* Vol. 16 No. 4. October 1969, pp 170 – 171.)

Highland County, Ohio, was the recovery area for a large Mississippian human effigy pipe. It portrayed a crouching female and measured 2 x 7½ x 7½"; the pipe was made of close-grained sandstone. The pipe was displayed at the 1876 Philadelphia Exposition and the Pan American Exposition, 1901, at Buffalo, New York. (Hothem, Lar. *Ancient Art of Ohio.* 1994, p 270 no. 690.)

One of the finest tall-bowl platform pipes, Intrusive Mound culture, was found in 1830 near the town of Manchester, Ohio, on the Ohio River. Made of highly polished black steatite, the pipe bowl rim was squared, and a human face on the side of the bowl faced the smoker. This extraordinary pipe was 9" long and 4½" high. (Grimm, R. E. *Prehistoric Art.* The Greater St. Louis Archaeological Society. 1953, pp 134 – 135.)

A constricted-center steatite tubular pipe was found in 1982 along the Collins River, Warren County, Tennessee. Nicely polished, the pipe was nearly 9" long. (*Central States Archaeological Journal.* Vol. 35 No. 4. October 1988, p 212.)

In 1878, more than a century ago, a very large frog effigy pipe was found in Arkansas. Late Woodland to Mississippian in time, it was made of close-grained sandstone and the size was 6¾ x 8½". The weight was 7 pounds. (Hart, Gordon. "The Dr. Rollin Bunch Frog Pipe," *The Redskin.* Vol. 9 No. 3. 1974, pp 86 – 89.)

Perhaps the largest and finest Late Woodland alate or winged obtuse-angle pipe was found in Smyth County, Virginia. In perfect condition and made of brownish steatite, this pipe with line incising along the stem top measured 4⅖" wide and a startling 20⅖" long. (West, George A. *Tobacco, Pipes and Smoking Customs of the American Indians*, Part II, Plates. 1934, p 988, plate 254.)

An eagle effigy pipe in black steatite came from Kentucky about the year 1920. It measured 2½" high, 2⅛" wide, and was 6" long. The pipe was in fine condition and had excellent workstyle. (McCoy, Mike. "A Rare Bird Pipe," *Central States Archaeological Journal.* Vol. 31 No. 1. January 1984, p 22.)

Ohio's most famous single pipe is undoubtedly the Adena Pipe. It was found in a mound at Adena, the estate of Thomas Worthington and which became the type site for the Adena culture. Made of multicolored Ohio pipestone, the back was orange-red while the front was gray. This is an effigy tubular pipe representing a human with physical deformities such as short legs and a thickened neck. The fully drilled artifact, about 8" high, has the bowl between the feet and the mouthpiece at the top of the head. Photographs of this rare pipe have appeared in many publications since the discovery in 1901. (Baby, Dr. Raymond S. "The Adena Pipe," *Artifacts.* Vol. 2 No. 2. April 1972, pp 12 – 13.)

Christian County, Kentucky, contains rock shelters that have produced hardstone "torch-holder" type tubular pipes. One pipe had a protruding stem made of bone. (*Central States Archaeological Journal.* Vol. 13 No. 3. July 1966, p 98.)

A bird effigy Great Pipe was found along the Allegheny River in Pennsylvania in 1924. It was made of green steatite with pink veining and measured 1¾" high, 5½" wide, and 8" long. (Feldser, William. "The

Giles Thomas Flying Eagle Pipe," *Prehistoric Artifacts*. Vol. 19 No. 1. 1985, p 17.)

A very large Hopewell plain platform type pipe was picked up in Richland County, Ohio, in 1911. It was made of gray Ohio pipestone and measured 2¼ x 6½". (*The Redskin*. Vol. 2 No. 3. July 1967, p 114.)

An excellent bird effigy Great Pipe came from Cumberland County, Tennessee. The material was black steatite, the bird head was large and well done for type, and the pipe overall length was 13½". (*Prehistoric America*. Vol. 28 No. 4. 1994, p 13.)

In the 1880s a large frog effigy pipe was found in Illinois. Made of red bauxite, the bullfrog-like image, 5" high, appears to be holding a rattle. This Mississippian pipe, known as the Rattler Frog Pipe, is the finest of the type found in the state. (*Illinois State Archaeological Society/50th Anniversary Issue*. Vol. 33 No. 4. October 1986, p 250 plate 35.)

One of the best Adena tubular pipes in the eastern Midwest was picked up on Blennerhassett Island in the Ohio River. Found in 1889, it was made of gray Ohio pipestone and measured 8" long. (*The Redskin*. Vol. 2 No. 3. July 1967, p 113.)

A cache or grouping of superb steatite pipes was located in 1989 in North Carolina. The finds included a large bird pipe measuring 4½ x 9½", a squirrel effigy pipe 1½" high and 5" long, a platform pipe 2½" high and 3⅜" long, and a greenstone gorget 6" long. (Finder, The. "The Find of a Lifetime," *Prehistoric Artifacts*. Vol. 23 No. 4. 1989, pp 26 – 29.)

One of the largest effigy Hopewell straight platform pipes, made of tan Ohio pipestone, probably came from Darke County, Ohio. Rather than the bowl being part of the animal effigy, it was plain and one end of the platform had been shaped into the effigy form. Broken and restored, the pipe measured 1⅞ x 6⅝". (*The Redskin*. Vol. 5 No. 3. July 1970, p 87.)

Long-stemmed animal effigy pipes in "fire-clay" or pipestone are unusual, and a fine example was found on Plum Island in the Susquehanna River, Pennsylvania, in 1907. Probably late prehistoric, it was 5" high and 12" long. (Laidlaw, Col. George E. "Effigy Pipes in Stone," *Thirty-Fourth Annual Archaeological Report*/1923. The Legislative Assembly of Ontario. 1924, p 72.)

Olive-green Ohio pipestone was the material selected for a Hopewell platform pipe found in Wayne County, Ohio. Highly polished, the pipe had a reinforced rim and measured 1¼ x 3". (Fincham, Glenval. "A Fine Curved Base Hopewell Platform Pipe," The Redskin. Vol. 9 No. 3. 1974, pp 104-105.)

In Whiteside County, Illinois, an historic pipe made of limestone was recovered from a stream bank. It was a raised-bowl type, 4½" long and 3½" high, with incised decorations. (Miller, Doug. "Rock River Pipe," Central States Archaeological Journal. Vol. 41 No. 1. January 1994, p 13.)

A bird effigy elbow pipe, with the bowl shaped as a bird head and neck facing the smoker, was found in Wayne County, Ohio. Made of gray banded slate, size was 2½ x 3½". (*The Redskin*. Vol. 2 No. 4. October 1967, p 150.)

An historic-era Mic-mac pipe was fairly recently found in St. Louis County, Missouri. It was made of catlinite and measured 1⁷⁄₁₆" long and 2" high. Five drilled holes were lead filled, for stem attachment. (Andrews, Brian. "Mic-mac by the Meramec," *Central States Archaeological Journal*. Vol. 39 No. 3. July 1992, p 112.)

In the late 1800s an outstanding biconical pipe — also called double conical, hourglass tube, or shaman's blower — was uncovered in Meigs County, Tennessee. Material was a dark-brown steatite with maroon streaks and mica flecks. The Mississippian-era pipe was 13½" long. (Hart, Gordon. "Shaman's Medicine Tube Pipe," *The Redskin*. Vol. 5 No. 4. October 1970, pp 112-113.)

Greenish bauxite was the material used for a large Mississippian pipe found in Ballard County, Kentucky, at a village site. Done as a crouching or kneeling human figure, the superb pipe measured 7¼" high, 4½" wide, and 5" long. (Perino, Gregory. "The Ballard County, Kentucky, Human-Effigy Pipe," *Central States Archaeological Journal*. Vol. 34 No. 2. April 1987, p 114.)

Fort Ancient pipe, Mississippian, broken, this half with portion of face showing weeping eye motif. Made of tan quartzite, this was a personal find of the owner in 1995. Adams County, Ohio. Dennis Link collection, Ohio. Unlisted.

Pipe-Tomahawks

Of all the white-made pipes that found favor with Indians, nothing was more sought-after or admired than pipe-tomahawks. Invented for the North American trade and for use on special occasions, pipe-tomahawks quickly became prestige items. Most important male Indians owned an example, and pipe-tomahawks were popular from the 1700s into the late 1800s.

Considered to be pipes and not weapons, pipe-tomahawks combined characteristics of the long-stemmed calumet pipe and the hafted metal-headed light axe or tomahawk. While the design marriage worked beautifully, it still created a pipe that was a bit heavy, and a tomahawk that was delicate compared with a true tomahawk or multi-purpose light axe.

Still, when the handle was properly holed the pipe portion worked quite well. And if nothing else was available a pipe-tomahawk could be used in violent conflict. In at least one case a white man was recaptured after being stunned by a pipe-tomahawk blow. For the rest of the man's life, his skull was missing a small round section where the pipe bowl had struck.

Pipe-tomahawks were made in England, France, Canada and in the American Colonies, later the United States of America. Some frontier blacksmiths were so skilled they could make a fine pipe-tomahawk from a section of rifle or musket barrel. In such cases the gun bore was enlarged to become the pipe bowl interior.

The heads of pipe-tomahawks were made of iron, brass or pewter, with better examples in iron and brass having a carefully inset lower blade of steel. Decorations on the head might include cut-out designs like hearts or stars, or the metal might be inlaid with bits of brass or silver. A few outstanding examples were made as presentation pieces to seal a treaty or secure friendship or reward the help of a chieftain. So treasured were some examples that they stayed in the same Indian family for generations.

Handles were usually of hardwood, drilled with a small hole that ran the length of the handle, with a right-angle hole that connected to the bottom of the pipe bowl. The handle, within the head, was sometimes given a thin wrap with leather to assure an air-tight fit. And the handle end at the head might be capped with silver or pewter for further decoration. At times, if the hole continued through it might have a metal take-out peg beyond the head as an aid in cleaning. The mouth end might be carved into a mouthpiece or have a metal extension.

Handle stem-decorations might include brass tacks and paint. Plains examples were often further decorated with wire or leather wraps and might have attached feathers, beads or braided horsehair.

Beginning in the 1970s collectors started to realize that pipe-tomahawks had been somewhat overlooked and prices began to rise quickly as better examples went into private collections. Not long after some unusual pipe-tomahawks appeared which were genuine example at first look only. Old heads were jammed into old tool handles or good old handles were pushed into the first suitable head that could be found. Generally the old pipe-tomahawk heads survived in one condition or another, and the real shortage was in original or at least truly old handle-stems.

Another, rather unusual, problem developed. For U. S. Centennial celebrations and other historic occasions, a few cities or organizations issued metal pipe-tomahawk heads and wooden handles to mark the event. The heads were solid-cast, using an authentic old pipe-tomahawk to make the mold. So while the form is correct, the method of manufacture usually is not.

Other examples available to the unwary collector consist of modern heads and modern handle-stems which are aged to resemble old and good pieces. Authentic pipe-tomahawk heads turn up surprisingly often, found on the sites of trading posts or along early trade routes. Most of these are heavily corroded and pitted. Some of these have been joined to old or old-appearing handle stems but the condition of the head indicates they do not belong together.

For those who would like to learn more about this fascinating subject, four books would be very worthwhile, and they are described below.

John Baldwin put out *Tomahawks/Pipe Axes of the American Frontier* in 1995, the same year a revised edition of *Indian Tomahawks & Frontiersmen Belt Axes* was published by Daniel D. Hartzler and James A. Knowles. In 1994 a reprint of a standard 1971 book became available, *American Indian Tomahawks* by Harold L. Peterson. Finally there is a small softcover called *Tomahawks Illustrated,* a 1977 production by Robert Kuck.

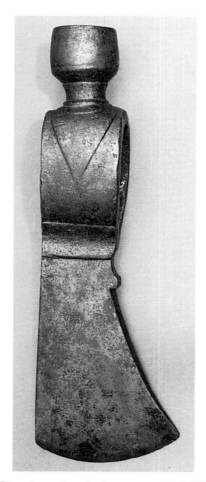

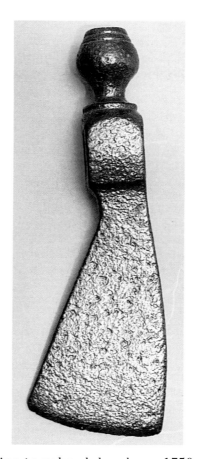

Pipe-tomahawk head, 8" high, English, ca. 1800. This trade-era piece is ex-collection Dr. Lyons and was found in Medina County, Ohio. Dave Summers, Native American Artifacts, Victor, New York. $375.00.

Pipe-tomahawk head, ca. 1750, 2¼" wide and 7" high. It has the typical pitted surface of trade iron that has been in the ground for many years. This example is probably Iroquois and was found near Greenwood, Massachusetts, in 1854. H. B. Greene II collection, Florida. $150.00.

Pipe-tomahawk, iron, ca. AD 1780. This early example measures 2½" wide and 7½" high. It is attributed to use by the Miami Indians, and came from Franklin County, Indiana. H. B. Greene II collection, Florida. Unlisted.

Pipe-tomahawk with missing bowl, iron, ca. 1770. It is possibly American-made and now measures 6½" high. Private collection, Pennsylvania. $300.00.

Pipe-tomahawk with missing bowl, iron, ca. 1740 – 1760. This is possibly a French piece and measures 5" high at present. Private collection, Pennsylvania. $400.00.

Pipe-tomahawk, ca. 1750 – 1780, iron head with silver disc inlay. This fine pipe is 7⅜" high and is English. Private collection, Pennsylvania. $1,000.00.

Pipe-tomahawk, ca. 1750 – 1760, iron head with hardwood stem/handle. This pipe is 7¼" high and is an English piece. Private collection, Pennsylvania. $1,200.00.

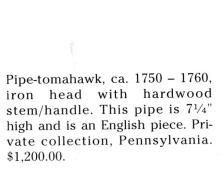

Pipe-tomahawk with missing bowl, iron, ca. 1750 – 1770. This iron piece, now 6" high, is English. Private collection, Pennsylvania. $300.00.

Pipe-tomahawk, top, #AK-81, 7½ x 18" with decorated stem. Ca. 1880 – 1900, this is a rare piece with a sand-cast iron head. It came from the Allegany Reservation, New York. The two other objects shown are very rare wooden forms used to make sand molds for cast-iron Pipe-tomahawk heads. Iron Horse collection. All museum grade.

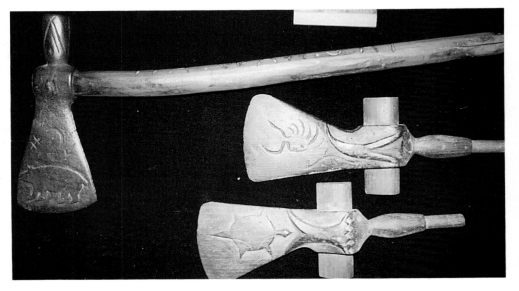

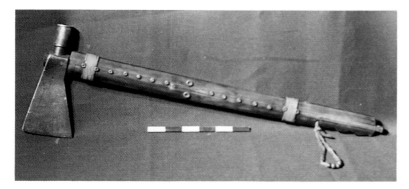

Pipe-tomahawk, high-bowl style, brass head, ca. 1890. This piece has a decorated handle/stem and measures 20" long. Western type. Dave Summers, Native American Artifacts, Victor, New York. $895.00.

Pipe-tomahawk, embossed bear image on blade, old but age uncertain. The wood handle/stem is about 14" long. Dave Summers, Native American Artifacts, Victor, New York. $750.00.

Pipe-tomahawk, historic, ca. 1810, iron head with short handle. The handle is ash with inset pewter and pewter mouthpiece. Overall length of this early piece is 9⅜". H. B. Greene II collection, Florida. Museum quality.

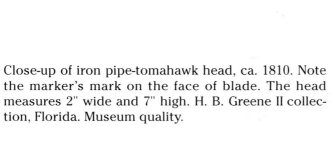

Close-up of iron pipe-tomahawk head, ca. 1810. Note the marker's mark on the face of blade. The head measures 2" wide and 7" high. H. B. Greene II collection, Florida. Museum quality.

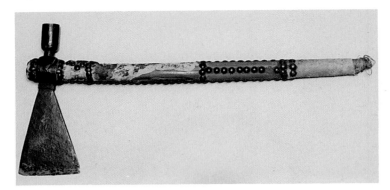

Pipe-tomahawk, historic and ca. 1860, highly unusual in having a copper head. The handle is ash and is decorated with trade cloth, sinew, tacks, and a beaded turtle. Overall length is 18". It is believed to have been made by an Indian in the Great Lakes area from native copper. H. B. Greene II collection, Florida. Museum quality.

Close-up of the copper pipe-tomahawk head from the Great Lakes region, the design derived from white-made iron heads. It measures 3¼" wide and 8½": high. H. B. Greene II collection, Florida. Museum quality.

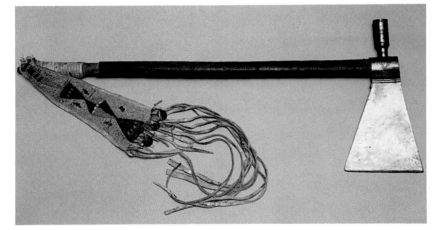

Pipe-tomahawk, historic, ca. 1860, ash handle with squared copper wire taken from telegraph line. The handle is further decorated with beadwork on hide flap terminating in bells and thongs. This excellent piece measures 24½" long and was collected from the Sioux. H. B. Greene II collection, Florida. Museum quality.

Close-up of head of Sioux pipe-tomahawk, which measures 4⅞ x 10¼". H. B. Greene II collection, Florida. Museum quality.

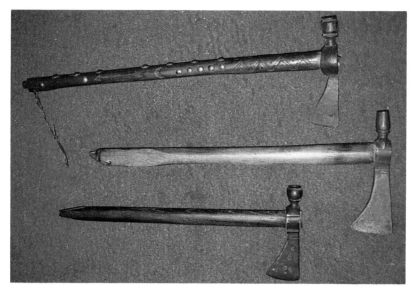

Pipe-tomahawks, historic period, ca. 1780 – 1830, with hand-forged iron heads and wooden handle stem. Size, middle example has a blade of 7½" and stem of 18". These are from Indian reservations in western New York. Top, #JP-15, brass tack decorations. Middle, #20, plain handle. Bottom, #RO-K/4, head with circular cut-outs in blade. Iron Horse collection. Each, $1,800.00+.

Pipe-tomahawk with brass head, original handle with brass tacks, head 5⅞" high and with edge decoration. This fine example is ex-collection Currie and from the Midwest. Len and Janie Weidner collection, Ohio. $3,500.00.

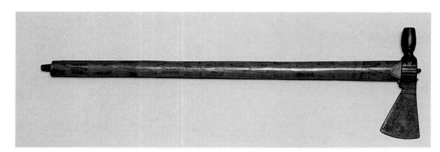

Pipe-tomahawk, historic period and ca. 1830. The handle is a file-branded replacement and overall length is 24". This graceful piece was acquired on a Chippewa reservation, Michigan. Hogan Gallery Inc., Naples, Florida. $2,500.00.

Close-up of Chippewa pipe-tomahawk head, with measurement 2½ x 7⅜". Hogan Gallery Inc., Naples, Florida. $2,500.00.

Sioux pipe-tomahawk, pewter head with beaded drop and geometric designs, ca. 1880. This excellent early artifact has a head 10¾" high, while length is 19" and the tab and fringe are 23". Sam Merriam collection, Oregon. $3,500.00.

Iron pipe-tomahawks, late 1800s. Top, 6⅜ x 25"; bottom, 7¼ x 21¾". Both have the wooden haft at the head end covered with rawhide and capped with a lead disc marked "US." The pipe-tomahawks are Omaha, from northeast Nebraska. Richard Krueger collection, Iowa; Sandra Krueger photograph. Each $1,500.00 – 2,000.00.

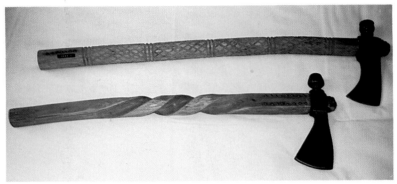

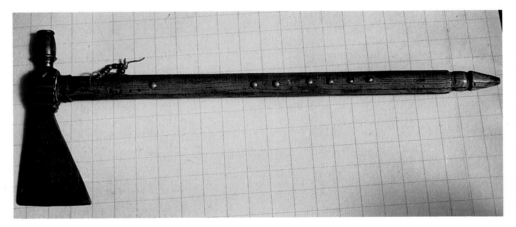

Pipe-tomahawk, Mohican, presentation grade with brass blade, ca. 1770s. The head is 8⅜" high and has etched designs with the British royal seal on obverse and a map of the Hudson River Valley on the reverse. Handle is hardwood with brass tacks and a short strand of beads on a leather thong. Overall length is 21½". Northeastern United States. Dave Summers, Native American Artifacts, Victor, New York. $2,950.00.

Pipe-tomahawk, scrolls and hearts design, brass head. This piece is ca. 1800 and has a wooden handle stem with traces of leather wrap and paint. It measures 7⅛ x 16¾" and is a style found in the eastern United States. Dave Summers, Native American Artifacts, Victor, New York. $2,900.00.

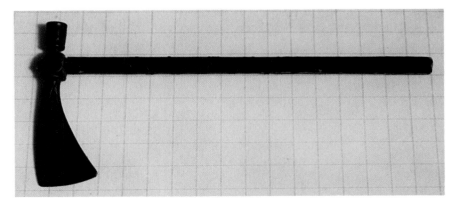

Pipe-tomahawk, Hunkpapa Sioux, ca. 1890 – 1900. The head is 8½" high and the piece is 22⅜" long overall. This fine artifact once belonged to Chief Flatiron, one of the Sioux chiefs with the Buffalo Bill show. Sam Merriman collection, Oregon. $3,000.00.

Early Southern Plains pipe-tomahawk, ca. 1840, with metal head and brass-tacked wooden handle with dangle. It is Cheyenne or Kiowa, and the metal head measures 7¾" high while the handle is 20¾" long. This piece has an austere beauty. Sam Merriman collection, Oregon. $4,000.00.

Pipe-tomahawk, Blackfoot, ca. 1880 – 1900. This has the spontoon type head and tacked ribbon-wrapped stem. A highly decorative piece, the head is 8⅜" high and overall length is 20¾". It came from northwestern Montana. Sam Merriman collection, Oregon. $3,500.00.

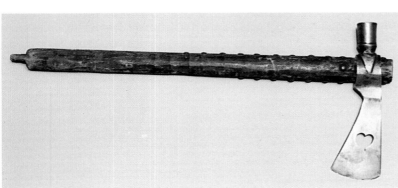

Pipe-tomahawk, blade with heart cutout, ca. 1850. The head is iron and handle is file-branded ash with brass tacks. Overall length is 18½" while the head alone is 2¼ x 7¾". This fine piece was collected from the Pawnee Indians in Kansas. H. B. Greene II collection, Florida. $3,500.00.

Close-up of Pawnee Indian pipe-tomahawk showing iron head with heart cutout. Head measurement is 2¼ x 7¾". H. B. Greene II collection, Florida. $3,500.00.

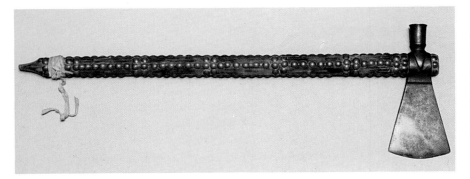

Pipe-tomahawk, historic and ca. 1840, file-branded handle with hide and brass tacks. Overall length is 24". This fine piece was collected from the Kaw Indians, Kansas. Hogan Gallery Inc., Naples, Florida. $3,000.00.

Close-up of Kaw Indian pipe-tomahawk, iron head measuring 3⅜ x 7⅞". Hogan Gallery Inc., Naples, Florida. $3,000.00.

Close-up of the ca. 1850 spontoon pipe-tomahawk head showing fine iron working and the pewter handle end cap. This head measures 1⅞" wide and 8½" high. H. B. Green II collection, Florida. Museum quality.

Pipe-tomahawk, historic, ca. 1850, spontoon type. This beautiful and important example has an iron head and ash handle decorated with pewter bands and stripes. Overall length is 25¼". It is reputed to be a presentation piece to a Delaware Indian chief. H. B. Greene II collection, Florida. Museum quality.

Trade Pipes

In-demand items made by whites for trade with Indians included pipes. Ceramic or pottery examples were inexpensive, attractive, and worked well. They were popular also because they were easily replaced if lost or broken.

The large numbers of complete pipes, damaged pipes, and pieces on historic Indian sites suggest that once such pipes became available they were widely and heavily used. Pipe styles are one way of dating such sites, since for many forms the place and at least general dates of manufacture are known.

Early white-manufactured pipes can be divided into two categories and there is much intermixing. These are pipes that were mainly intended for trade, often without stems for ease of boxing and transportation. When the pipes were received, Indians simply made the kind of stems they desired. This was also often done, by the way, with tomahawks, again because the heads alone were more compact and lighter in weight. The other category includes pipes used by Indians and whites alike.

Typical pipes were mold made of clay. A fine-grained white to yellowish to gray clay called kaolin was often used for pipes, and there were large deposits of this material in the American South. Trade pipes were also made from other metals, such as lead or pewter, plus some of iron, steel, tin, and copper. A few pipes were even made of silver and German silver.

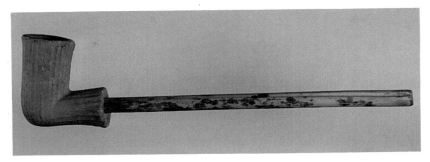

Historic pipe bowl, mold-formed light-brown pottery, 1¾" high. The old stem is made of Ohio River Valley cane and measures 6¼" long. Larry Garvin, Back to Earth, Ohio. $40.00 – 50.00.

Trade pipe, 1880s, mold-pressed pottery. This piece is 1⅝" high and was found in southwest Iowa. Richard Krueger collection, Iowa; Sandra Krueger photograph. $8.00 – 12.00.

Trade pipes, historic period, all three made from pressed-clay molds. All were personal finds by the collector in Pulaski County, Missouri. Collection of Bob Rampani, Bridgeton, St. Louis County, Missouri. Each $5.00 – 15.00.

Kaolin white-manufactured pipe (Dutch), with touchmark "EP," ca. 1700 – 1780. Used by the Iroquois, pipe #721 has a 3" stem and bowl height is 1½". New York. Iron Horse collection. $350.00 – 450.00.

Historic trade-era pipe, pressed and fired clay, with 2" scale. This interesting example was found near Boulder, Colorado. Lee Hallman collection, Pennsburg, Pennsylvania. Unlisted.

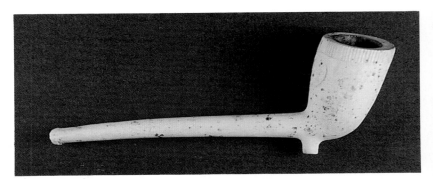

Early historic pipe, white kaolin clay, bowl with reeded top and impressed bowl side. This pipe measures 5½" long. Larry Garvin, Back to Earth, Ohio. $45.00 – 50.00.

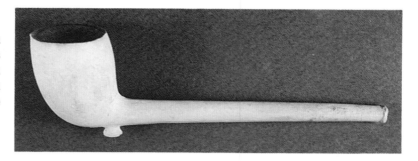

Early historic pipe, whitish-yellow kaolin 5" long. Such pipes are quite scarce, as most have the long and delicate stem broken in one or more places. Eastern United States. Larry Garvin, Back to Earth, Ohio. $35.00 – 40.00.

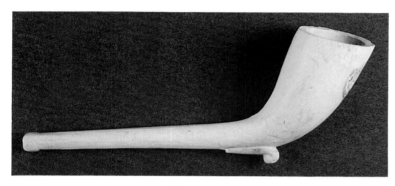

Early historic pipe, yellowish kaolin, with impressed mark on bowl front. This pipe, 4⅜" long, is in fine condition for a very old pipe. Pipes like this have been found on many historic Indian sites. Eastern United States. Larry Garvin, Back to Earth, Ohio. $30.00 – 75.00.

Historic trade-era pipes, various localities, all made of pressed and fired clay. Colors are light cream to reddish (bottom left) and gray (top right). Zell Adams collection, California. Each $10.00.

Trade pipe, early historic period, bowl only with faceted exterior, 1¾" high. Made of white kaolin, this pipe is from the Mt. Airy region of North Carolina. Larry Garvin, Back to Earth, Ohio. $35.00 – 40.00.

Trade pipe, brown kaolin, faceted bowl exterior, 2" high. Such pipes are a good time marker for historic sites because many styles have been firmly dated. Mt. Airy region, Surry County, North Carolina. Larry Garvin, Back to Earth, Ohio. $35.00 – 40.00.

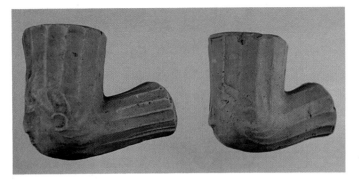

Trade pipes, two similar but not identical examples, tan porous pottery, each 1½" high. They both have a face at the bowl lower front that has been lightly impressed. Eastern United States. Larry Garvin, Back to Earth, Ohio. Each $35.00 – 40.00.

Early historic pipe, white bowl and brownish tan stem, top condition for age. This pipe measures 5⅛" long and the general type was used by whites and Indians alike in many areas. Eastern United States. Larry Garvin, Back to Earth, Ohio. $35.00 – 40.00.

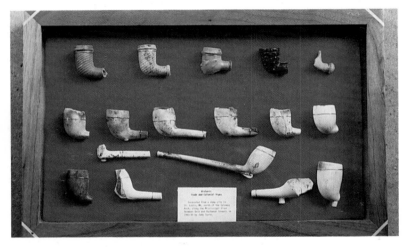

Historic colonial and trade pipes, pottery, excavated from a dump site along the Mississippi River in 1993 – 1994. Many different types are represented; from St. Louis, Missouri. Such well-displayed examples serve educational purposes. Collection of Bob Rampani, Bridgeton, St. Louis County, Missouri. Unlisted.

Contact period historic clay pipes, kaolin material, with scale indicating sizes. These came from a site in Lancaster County, Pennsylvania, ca. 1645 – 1665. Gary L. Fogelman collection, Pennsylvania. Each $40.00 – 60.00.

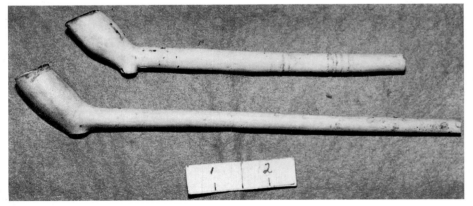

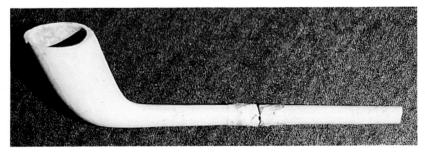

Trade pipe, kaolin, 5¼" long. It was made before 1779 and is marked with "T. Tippet" in a circle. The pipe in white clay is English-Seneca and from New York. Dave Summers, Native American Artifacts, Victor, New York. $50.00.

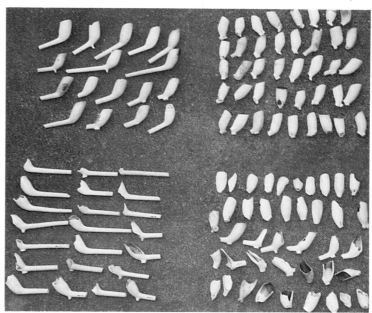

Trade pipe fragments, kaolin, all from the period 1640 – 1750. The white clay pipes consist of the following: 17 almost whole, 22 stems, 41 bowls, and 41 broken bowls. All are Seneca Indian, from New York. Dave Summers, Native American Artifacts, Victor, New York. Group $400.00.

Kaolin-type pipe but this example made of wood, rare, single ring on the bowl. Used by the Iroquois, this pipe is ca. 1750 – 1880. See measure for scale on #JF/10/23 which came from the Onondaga Reservation near Syracuse, New York. Iron Horse collection. $375.00 – 500.00.

Effigy early historic pipe, yellowed kaolin, white man's head for bowl, 4½" long. By the mid-1800s there was a proliferation of pipes in forms of people and animals. Eastern United States. Larry Garvin, Back to Earth, Ohio. $30.00 – 75.00.

Trade-era pipe, historic and ca. 1750, made of tinned iron. It measures 1¾" high and 5¼" long. The pipe is probably English or Dutch. Private collection, Pennsylvania. $175.00.

Trade-era pipe, historic period, made of brass with a heavy green patina. This ornate pipe is 2¼" high, 4" long, and ¾" wide. This specimen came from Massachusetts. Wilfred Dick collection, Mississippi. $400.00 – 600.00.

Collecting Pipes —
What to Look For

Anyone who wants to collect good Indian pipes needs to keep some things in mind. This is true whether the collection concentrates on or specializes in pipes, or whether the pipes are part of a larger and more diversified collection. Wide-ranging knowledge is important because pipes themselves are highly individualistic and there are countless unusual and one-of-a-kind examples.

Size is a main consideration and in general (other factors being about equal) larger pipes are preferred over smaller. This is because larger examples simply provide more quantity in terms of prehistoric artwork, and hopefully high quality as well. Larger pipes are more visually impressive and display with more presence, even impact. The rarity factor also comes in because there are more average-size pipes than large pipes.

As with most generalities there are exceptions. Miniature pipes are a collecting sub-field and here smaller can be better. Some pipes classes, like Hopewell effigy pipes, were never very large to begin with, and oversize examples would look somehow wrong or at least suspicious.

Still another aspect of size is the additional artistic accomplishment in making, say an 8" stem that is part of a Late Woodland steatite platform pipe. Such stems required extreme care in the making and extra-long drilling in the completion. Though some were perfectly done, others had a spot where the drill wandered off-course and broke through to the surface of the pipe.

Material is always of importance because it is the substance of the pipe itself. Good material, simply, makes a good pipe. Hardstone is generally considered better than softer material for a number of reasons, again speaking only of stone as distinguished from the various pipestones. Hardstone was more difficult and time consuming to work and shape, and it is obvious that the prehistoric craftsperson gave the pipe a great deal of work, care, and attention.

Most hardstone is highly resistant to weathering, compared with some limestones and coarse sandstones. The former can have some degree of surface disintegration, with portions of the original details being lost and the remainder left less precise. Sandstone can also wear away over time, especially if it is not the fine-grained, very compact form.

Hardstone also has several other characteristics important to the pipe collector. Many kinds of hardstone are colorful and attractive, adding these dimensions to the finished pipe. And hardstone usually takes and holds a good polish, one that often lasts literally for ages.

All this said in favor of hardstone, some softer grades of stone are also very desirable. These include the two great classes of materials used for prehistoric pipes, steatite and the pipestones. Both, compared with hardstone, were relatively easy to work. It is almost as if the earth itself, combined with time, created these materials to be ideal for pipes.

The collector quickly learns that some pipes were typically made of certain materials and seeks out such classic specimens. Even here some steatite, for example, is considered better than others, and some pipestone is preferred that has more color or mixed colors.

Pottery pipes are another matter, for here the material itself was created by the pipe maker, when clay was prepared and fired to hardness. Some pottery is more high grade than other ceramics, depending on the quality of clay, how well it was mixed and tempered, and how the firing went. In a sense, the pottery pipe is the result of more complex manufacturing, and some collectors appreciate this aspect.

Negatives for pottery pipes is the fact that they are rather fragile. Some pottery pipes also tend to crumble if not properly made or baked and require great care in handling. But, this is also true in a few cases with non-catlinite pipestone. Still, some areas of the country, like the Northeast and the Southwest, had many pottery pipes and collections in those regions reflect this.

Finish is several things, all important to pipe

collectors. Finish means the secondary but not minor touches, such as the detailing of feathers on a Hopewell effigy pipe or the scales of a fish effigy historic pipe in catlinite. It adds to the realism of figures and helps identify the species.

In the final stage of pipe making, finish is when the surface is ground smooth, followed by polishing. Such work makes the pipe more attractive and is the sign that at last the pipe surface is done. A few pipes were painted after being completed, but this does not seem to have been routine.

Finishing polish is welcome to pipe collectors, and has two aspects. One is the amount of polishing, whether partial or total (100%). Another is the degree of polish, whether light, medium, or heavy, and the greater the degree of polish the better.

Completion is whether the pipe has had all work it would normally have, including the drilling. (Of all prehistoric Indian artifacts, pipes need not only be finished on the exterior but the interior as well.) This means the large hole for the bowl and smaller hole for the stem should be present, and the two holes should meet. In other words the pipe should be capable of actually being smoked.

Some pipes made of ultra-hard material such as quartzite or diorite tend to be complete except for drilling. In some cases drilling was started, as indicated by depressions or cone-shaped pits in the appropriate places, or even by partial drilling. Such pipes are rarely as valuable as those in which the drilling has gone forward to completion. Evidently such materials worked fairly easily through pecking and grinding, even polish, but resisted drilling. One sees the same thing with quartzite for artifacts like boatstones and bannerstones where drilling was only begun.

Type is important to collectors, with some kind of pipes being more valued. For example, a collector of Adena (Early Woodland) cultural artifacts might acquire Adena tubular pipes and there would be half a dozen sub-types from which to select. In addition, examples would be available in fine-grained sandstone and pipestones, both materials typical of use by this mound-building people.

Some pipes are preferred, whatever the time-period or culture, because they are effigy forms. These not only are pipes, but small artworks of animals, birds, or humans that show how ancient artisans saw their world. And other pipes are sought because they have distinctive forms, like the sun-disc or the medicine tube.

Within the pipe-collecting field are sub-divisions or smaller collecting areas, and these are often explored. Certainly the most common type pipes gathered up are those in close geographic proximity to the collector. So, many specialize in pipes from their own state, being familiar with the prehistoric periods and materials commonly used.

Workstyle is related to some of the artistic features already mentioned, and it can be explained quite simply. Imagine for a moment that ten prehistoric craftspeople set out to make one kind of pipe from identical materials of the same size. This accomplished, the ten pipes are then compared in every way possible. Each, while similar in many aspects, will have individual differences.

How the pipes are the same and not the same constitutes workstyle. And while most ancient artistry was high, or excellent, some was merely good and some was quite average. Pipes do tend, however, to be nicely created, no matter when or where they were made.

Condition is key in more than one way, and can be quickly described as how nearly the pipe is today to when it was made long ago. As briefly mentioned in the material paragraphs, some pipestone deteriorates due to the twin forces of time and the elements. Other pipes were damaged during use or handling, and this may include chipped and reworked bowls and shorter stems, and much else.

Of greater frequency is damage to pipes brought about by agricultural equipment. Such damage varies from slight disc passes that mar finish or leave deeper lines or gouges to plow and planting strikes that badly fragment the pipe. Surface hunting, the collector is far more likely to recover bits and pieces of pipes after years of cultivation than unbroken pipes. Of course, the more recently received damage a pipe has the less value, both as a collector item and as an archaeological specimen.

Finally, appreciation of Indian pipes takes into account all of the aspects mentioned, a sort of artistic summing up. This can be hard to explain, but is nonetheless very real. If average collectors had three or four randomly selected pipes placed on a table, there would be little difficulty in selecting the best pipe — and even agreeing on the selection. Most combinations of traits or qualities are readily visible and decisions or judgments can be reached rather quickly.

Artistic matters in pipe collecting are vastly important, but another consideration is, dismayingly, gaining momentum. This new force is now to the place where it may be even more important than artistry. It is authenticity, determining whether a pipe is truly old and Indian-made, or a modern replica, reproduction, fake.

Experienced collectors are aware that, as with many other prehistoric artifacts, provenance is looked at more and more. Provenance is simply the documented story of where an artifact (here, a pipe) has been since it became known to the collecting world. Sometimes this includes find-data, who collected it and when.

An ideal provenance or pedigree would have a complete history, hopefully including major stopovers in old and well-known collections, especially those noted for quality and authenticity. All this, after all, is why prehistoric or early historic Indian artifacts in general and pipes in particular can bring high prices. Having been lodged in certain collections (or cabinets, as they were once called) is a sort of guarantee of authenticity, a form of cultural insurance.

Besides having been in important collections (or even museums) of the past, some pipes have been pictured in amateur or professional archaeological journals or books. Such documented exposure is very good, sometimes providing little-known information on the finder, origin, and so forth.

For years such an appearance has been a near-certain guarantee that the pipe so-pictured is undeniably old and authentic. No more. Some fakers are beginning to copy, in stone, a few of these pipes. Usually a very close copy of the pipe (yes, there are people today who can replicate in this manner) is offered, along with the original publication which featured the pipe.

There are two aspects, really, to having a good collection. One is the artistic aspect and the other is authenticity.

Top, medicine tube biconical pipe, steatite; measuring 12½", this is one of the longest of the type. The central ring has a zigzag mark around it and on the pipe side is an incised design resembling a turkey track. This extremely fine pipe has GIRS authentication number J3. The pipe has been pictured in Hothem's *Ornamental Ceremonial Artifacts*, p 130. Found in 1974, this pipe is from Jefferson County, Tennessee. Middle, a fine bird effigy Great Pipe in steatite with classic features. Bottom, Great Pipe, eagle effigy, black steatite, 10¾" long. With bird of prey talons on the feet, this image has all the features — head, tail, wings, feet, bowl, and stem plus condition — to be the finest of the Great Pipes. Most examples only have a few of these features. The pipe was found by R. W. Bronson and is ex-collection Edward Payne. It is pictured in Hothem's *Ornamental & Ceremonial Artifacts*, p 130. With GIRS authentication number L1, this pipe was found prior to 1900 in Washington County, Tennessee. Prehistoric art collection of John Baldwin, Michigan. All museum grade.

Fake Pipes — What to Look Out For

Indian pipes that, more or less, look old and good can be seen in many places. They turn up at flea markets, antiques malls and shops, auctions, shows, in collections, and in private (and even public) museums. Occasionally a great find of an authentic pipe is made at an antiques event or mall, but almost always such a find is made by an experienced collector who knows good from bad.

Often the purpose of pipe replicas or reproductions, in that they are not marked as modern, is to deceive the collector. The purpose is money, for major pipe types can produce hundreds, even thousands, of dollars.

Fake makers are getting better. Years ago, poor copies of pipes were turned out by machine and could easily be identified as not old. Today, fakers choose the correct materials and use ancient methods or at least finish the pipes using hand techniques. Then efforts are made to produce material patina, use marks, and surface deposits that appear to be like those on genuine pipes. Sometime a bit of honest-appearing unimportant damage is included at no extra cost. Some of these pipes are so well done they defy easy detection and need to be found out by those with knowledge picked up over the years.

Fakers know collector interests, and certain kinds of pipes are being made in large numbers today. Of course, some pipes such as those manufactured by Indians at places like Pipestone National Monument are perfectly legitimate and are sold as modern. The problem lies with those who make pipes that resemble ancient pipe forms as closely as possible in the hope that collectors will accept them as old. These pipes are made intentionally to confuse and deceive collectors.

There are many more fakes available than authentic pipes in the following type classes: Southern Great Pipes in steatite; Hopewell plain and effigy platform pipes in pipestone and hardstone; Woodland tubular effigy pipes in steatite; Mississippian sandstone effigy pipes; and, late prehistoric and early historic effigy forms in catlinite. This is not to say that other pipe types

in other materials are not being made, for they certainly are.

Collectors with many good pipes have learned to beware of certain things. If one pipe in a group of obviously bad pieces looks like it might be good, the chances are that it too is bad; it is simply a better-made fake. A dealer with bad artifacts likely bought for cents on the dollar and is unlikely to spend closer to what would be needed to obtain a truly good pipe.

Price is noteworthy. First, chances are that a genuine $1,000 pipe isn't going to be sold for $75.00. It happens, but not often. Another thing to ask yourself is, if a dealer or auction indeed has good pipes, why are they being offered to the general public instead of to collectors who (at least in theory) would pay much more?

Sometimes a fake pipe has several numbers on it, perhaps in different colors or styles plus a faded label or two. Supposedly from old but unknown collections, such marks can be added in a few minutes and really don't mean much. Keep in mind that there are collectors who recognize some of the better-known marks, so talk with such collectors about the authenticity of the marks themselves.

On fake pipes or examples that are questionable, what the maker did last might be checked out first. That is, the drilling should be closely examined. Is the drilling correct for the type of pipe? If a bowl was ground out, or gouged to a larger size, are the proper signs present? Are sizes accurate for the type? And do stem and bowl holes meet at the proper angle? A hole that has exactly the same dimension from beginning to end should be viewed with suspicion, as this is one sign of modern steel drill bits.

Short stem holes drilled with a flint tip will decrease in size. However, longer stem holes made with a copper drill will increase slightly in size as the tip flattens and begins to mushroom during drilling.

Is the pipe correctly finished? Much pipestone does not seem to patinate readily but may retain a high polish. Ohio pipestone, surprising for a fairly soft material, sometimes retains high polish even on a 2000-year-old pipe. Several advanced collectors have remarked that they have seen perfectly good pipes (again, of the Ohio pipestone so often used by the Adena and Hopewell) that look as if they were made yesterday.

One of the things fakers do is purposeful damage to a pipe. Knowing that pipes are often found with scars or breaks, they may artfully strike a fake pipe to take off part of the stem or a section of effigy or a platform corner.

If the pipe has been artificially patinated, this also serves to expose the interior stone and so "prove" the presence of age-induced surface coloration. The object is to make the pipe appear more genuine. At times a pipe may be burned, stained, or broken into pieces, with all the parts present or with a less-important section missing.

Experienced collectors look for the sheen and edge-rounding imparted to a pipe when used and held for years in a certain fashion. If the pipe has been in contact with the earth for centuries, it should show signs of such placement. This may be patination or staining or surface deposits or two of these or all three.

A person who wants to obtain good pipes either needs great awareness about what is being collected or must obtain solid information from one who truly knows. Collectors, fortunately, tend to be helpful in sharing knowledge when confronted with the common problem of fake pipes. Studying fakes doesn't necessarily help in identifying good pipes. But studying good pipes does help in detecting fake pipes.

While most pipe collectors can detect fakes fairly accurately, some examples are quite difficult and are in the questionable category. This simply means there are characteristics present that could nudge the pipe into either good or bad territory. Then, the best thing to do is get a consensus of opinion from several experienced persons. The knowledge of several people can sometimes settle the matter.

This gathering of experts method has successfully been used by amateur archaeological organizations such as the Society for the Documentation of Prehistoric America, SDPA. All collectors can also applaud a beginning trend in authentication which goes beyond (but does not replace) the time-honored technique of personal knowledge.

Scientific examination and testing can go beyond traditional detective methods and add new dimensions to determining new from old. A few skilled people are now, when necessary, subjecting surface deposits to testing. They can thus determine exact mineral or chemical compositions. High-powered microscopes are also being used.

A recent visit to an antiques shop in a Southeastern state was instructive. Among the coins, guns, and small antique items were approximately 40 "Indian" pipes. Half a dozen were made of pottery, while the remainder were stone of various kinds. Types represented included Great Pipes, mound platform pipes, medicine tubes, Cherokee pipes, and a variety of effigy forms. Materials were pipestone, steatite, catlinite, and unidentified stone. Of all those pipes, only one (a damaged bowl-type pipe) may have been authentic.

There are those who see the problem of fake pipes (and of fake Indian artifacts as a whole) as a minor, side issue. They feel that it is always buyer beware, and that fakes go to those who have not taken the time to prepare themselves adequately for collecting.

This is a short-sighted view that ignores the real issue, damage to the entire structure of collecting. Fakes cheat the collector. And fakes also misrepresent the past and insult the memory of the ancients who once lived in this land.

Decorated steatite elbow pipe in basic historic pipe form. Modern reproduction. Private collection. No value.

Large late Woodland or Intrusive Mound platform pipe. Modern reproduction. Private collection. No value.

Hopewell effigy platform pipe, frog image, probably in pipestone. Modern reproduction. Private collection. No value.

Hopewell effigy platform pipe, fish image. Modern reproduction. Private collection. No value.

Effigy pipe, raccoon in steatite. Modern reproduction. Private collection. No value.

Hopewell effigy platform pipe, bird image, probably done in pipestone. Modern reproduction. Private collection. No value.

Learning More About Pipes

The ideal state-of-being for knowledge about Indian pipes would be to have both a large, authentic collection of pipes and 30 or 40 years of experience in collecting. Barring this — and only a few hundred people would fit the descriptions — one simply learns as much about pipes as possible.

Museums are a good place to start. Both public and private museums abound in this country and far too few people take advantage of these educational resources. There is often a nominal charge to visit a museum, but this is reasonable income which helps maintain the facility.

Museums on the county and state levels usually have adequate displays of Indian pipes. This is a good way to see regional pipe styles and materials, providing the examples seen are authentic. And, for various reasons, the originals may not be on display and may be represented by replica pipes.

One of the side benefits of visiting larger museums is the association of pipes with other cultural material from the same Indian group and time period. This gives at least a hint of how pipes fitted into the overall lifeway, whether 200 years ago (Plains Indian) or 2,000 years ago (Woodland period).

Whenever the opportunity exists to tour one of the larger, important museums, by all means go. Besides many pipe examples, at these facilities can be seen dioramas and visual-education programs of different kinds, all instructive. Examples of such major museums are Field Museum of Natural History, Chicago; National Museum of the American Indian/Smithsonian, New York City; and (at a future date) National Museum of the American Indian/Smithsonian, Washington D. C.

Books are a primary source of information, and many titles on Indians have at least some coverage of pipes. It is unfortunately true that some of the best publications on Indian pipes — as referenced throughout this book — are old and out-of-print. The two-volume set by George West, for example, sells at well over $1,000 in almost any condition, and even the recent reprints are quite scarce and costly. Copies of this and a few other early publications may be studied in the rare book room of a large library. Sometimes they are also available via inter-library loan.

Archaeological society publications are a primary source of facts about North American Indian artifacts. These are of two kinds, journals for professionals and for amateurs. The latter are put out by, and directed toward, non-professional or avocational archaeologists, many of whom are collectors at some level.

Many states and regions have such societies and publications. A good way to learn more is to contact your state museum and ask about such organizations. It is no exaggeration to point out that amateur publications alone are worth the annual membership fee. The journals can be so valued by owners that year-sets are kept together and eventually hardbound for convenience and protection.

Shows specializing in displays of artifacts are held annually in much of the country. Artworks and artifacts usually include items from prehistoric through contemporary times. Notable events include those held at Pigeon Forge, Tennessee; Collinsville, Illinois; and, Louisville, Kentucky.

Not only will the visitor see many pipes, but books, magazines, and journals are usually available for further learning. These shows are educational experiences in many ways, indicated by the fact that people often come many hundred miles to attend.

Other collectors, met through the amateur organizations and meetings, are invaluable resources. Most are quite knowledgeable about what they collect and will readily share information. Those who specialize in pipes can be most helpful about what to collect, thus avoiding common mistakes (acquiring fakes, paying too much) often made by those just entering the field.

A good suggestion, one given the author by a noted collector, is to obtain broken pipes whenever possible. Whether in stone or pottery, these fragments are an aid in showing how pipes were made and what was done to the exterior and interior of pipes. While monetary worth for such pieces usually isn't high, the instructional value is priceless.

Final advice for the collector is to consider any pipe from two viewpoints. The first is artwork (and the many factors this takes in) and the second is authenticity (one thing only). The main way these two crucial considerations can be blended is through self-education, something we Americans are noted for. As one finds out along the way, good information builds a good collection.

Other Books By Lar Hothem

ARROWHEADS & PROJECTILE POINTS
Lar Hothem

Projectile points of American Indians have long been objects of interest to students and historians. This book has hundreds of photos, information about geographic origin, methods of production, sizes, 1997 values, and a special section on detecting fakes.

ISBN: 0-89145-228-1
#1426 • 5½ x 8½ • 224 Pgs. • PB • **$7.95**

INDIAN ARTIFACTS of the Midwest, Books I, II & III
Lar Hothem

These collector's handbooks are loaded with photographs of thousands of all types of artifacts found in the Midwest. They give the necessary facts about each item featured, such as important details, size, dates, location found, and of course, current collector values.

Book I • ISBN: 0-89145-485-3
#2279 • 8½ x 11 • 208 Pgs. • PB • 1996 values • **$14.95**
Book II • ISBN: 0-89145-615-5
#3885 • 8½ x 11 • 288 Pgs. • PB • 1997 values • **$16.95**
Book III • ISBN: 0-89145-782-8

COLLECTOR BOOKS

DOLLS, FIGURES & TEDDY BEARS

4707	A Decade of **Barbie** Dolls & Collectibles, 1981–1991, Summers	$19.95
4631	**Barbie** Doll Boom, 1986–1995, Augustyniak	$18.95
2079	**Barbie** Doll Fashion, Volume I, Eames	$24.95
4846	**Barbie** Doll Fashion, Volume II, Eames	$24.95
3957	**Barbie** Exclusives, Rana	$18.95
4632	**Barbie** Exclusives, Book II, Rana	$18.95
4557	**Barbie**, The First 30 Years, Deutsch	$24.95
4847	**Barbie** Years, 1959–1995, 2nd Ed., Olds	$17.95
3310	**Black Dolls**, 1820–1991, Perkins	$17.95
3873	**Black Dolls**, Book II, Perkins	$17.95
3810	**Chatty Cathy Dolls**, Lewis	$15.95
1529	Collector's Encyclopedia of **Barbie** Dolls, DeWein	$19.95
4882	Collector's Encyclopedia of **Barbie** Doll Exclusives and More, Augustyniak	$19.95
2211	Collector's Encyclopedia of **Madame Alexander Dolls**, Smith	$24.95
4863	Collector's Encyclopedia of **Vogue Dolls**, Izen/Stover	$29.95
3967	Collector's Guide to **Trolls**, Peterson	$19.95
4571	**Liddle Kiddles**, Identification & Value Guide, Langford	$18.95
3826	Story of **Barbie**, Westenhouser	$19.95
1513	**Teddy Bears & Steiff** Animals, Mandel	$9.95
1817	**Teddy Bears & Steiff** Animals, 2nd Series, Mandel	$19.95
2084	**Teddy Bears, Annalee's & Steiff** Animals, 3rd Series, Mandel	$19.95
1808	Wonder of **Barbie**, Manos	$9.95
1430	World of **Barbie** Dolls, Manos	$9.95
4880	World of **Raggedy Ann** Collectibles, Avery	$24.95

TOYS, MARBLES & CHRISTMAS COLLECTIBLES

3427	**Advertising Character** Collectibles, Dotz	$17.95
2333	Antique & Collector's **Marbles**, 3rd Ed., Grist	$9.95
3827	Antique & Collector's **Toys**, 1870–1950, Longest	$24.95
3956	Baby Boomer **Games**, Identification & Value Guide, Polizzi	$24.95
4934	**Breyer Animal** Collector's Guide, Identification and Values, Browell	$19.95
3717	**Christmas** Collectibles, 2nd Edition, Whitmyer	$24.95
4976	**Christmas** Ornaments, Lights & Decorations, Johnson	$24.95
4737	**Christmas** Ornaments, Lights & Decorations, Vol. II, Johnson	$24.95
4739	**Christmas** Ornaments, Lights & Decorations, Vol. III, Johnson	$24.95
4649	Classic Plastic **Model Kits**, Polizzi	$24.95
4559	Collectible **Action Figures**, 2nd Ed., Manos	$17.95
3874	Collectible **Coca-Cola Toy Trucks**, deCourtivron	$24.95
2338	Collector's Encyclopedia of **Disneyana**, Longest, Stern	$24.95
4958	Collector's Guide to **Battery Toys**, Hultzman	$19.95
4639	Collector's Guide to **Diecast Toys & Scale Models**, Johnson	$19.95
4651	Collector's Guide to **Tinker Toys**, Strange	$18.95
4566	Collector's Guide to **Tootsietoys**, 2nd Ed., Richter	$19.95
4720	The Golden Age of **Automotive Toys**, 1925–1941, Hutchison/Johnson	$24.95
3436	Grist's Big Book of **Marbles**	$19.95
3970	Grist's Machine-Made & Contemporary **Marbles**, 2nd Ed.	$9.95
4723	**Matchbox** Toys, 1947 to 1996, 2nd Ed., Johnson	$18.95
4871	**McDonald's** Collectibles, Henriques/DuVall	$19.95
1540	**Modern Toys** 1930–1980, Baker	$19.95
3888	**Motorcycle** Toys, Antique & Contemporary, Gentry/Downs	$18.95
4953	Schroeder's Collectible **Toys**, Antique to Modern Price Guide, 4th Ed.	$17.95
1886	Stern's Guide to **Disney** Collectibles	$14.95
2139	Stern's Guide to **Disney** Collectibles, 2nd Series	$14.95
3975	Stern's Guide to **Disney** Collectibles, 3rd Series	$18.95
2028	**Toys**, Antique & Collectible, Longest	$14.95
3979	**Zany Characters** of the Ad World, Lamphier	$16.95

FURNITURE

1457	American **Oak** Furniture, McNerney	$9.95
3716	American **Oak** Furniture, Book II, McNerney	$12.95
1118	Antique **Oak** Furniture, Hill	$7.95
2271	Collector's Encyclopedia of **American** Furniture, Vol. II, Swedberg	$24.95
3720	Collector's Encyclopedia of **American** Furniture, Vol. III, Swedberg	$24.95
3878	Collector's Guide to **Oak** Furniture, George	$12.95
1755	Furniture of the **Depression Era**, Swedberg	$19.95
3906	**Heywood-Wakefield** Modern Furniture, Rouland	$18.95

1885	**Victorian** Furniture, Our American Heritage, McNerney	$9.95
3829	**Victorian** Furniture, Our American Heritage, Book II, McNerney	$9.95

JEWELRY, HATPINS, WATCHES & PURSES

1712	Antique & Collector's **Thimbles** & Accessories, Mathis	$19.95
1748	Antique **Purses**, Revised Second Ed., Holiner	$19.95
1278	Art Nouveau & Art Deco **Jewelry**, Baker	$9.95
4850	Collectible **Costume Jewelry**, Simonds	$24.95
3875	Collecting Antique **Stickpins**, Kerins	$16.95
3722	Collector's Ency. of **Compacts, Carryalls & Face Powder Boxes**, Mueller	$24.95
4854	Collector's Ency. of **Compacts, Carryalls & Face Powder Boxes**, Vol. II	$24.95
4940	**Costume Jewelry**, A Practical Handbook & Value Guide, Rezazadeh	$24.95
1716	Fifty Years of Collectible **Fashion Jewelry**, 1925–1975, Baker	$19.95
1424	**Hatpins** & Hatpin Holders, Baker	$9.95
4570	Ladies' **Compacts**, Gerson	$24.95
1181	100 Years of Collectible **Jewelry**, 1850–1950, Baker	$9.95
4729	**Sewing Tools** & Trinkets, Thompson	$24.95
2348	20th Century Fashionable Plastic **Jewelry**, Baker	$19.95
4878	Vintage & Contemporary **Purse Accessories**, Gerson	$24.95
3830	Vintage **Vanity Bags & Purses**, Gerson	$24.95

INDIANS, GUNS, KNIVES, TOOLS, PRIMITIVES

1868	Antique **Tools**, Our American Heritage, McNerney	$9.95
1426	**Arrowheads** & Projectile Points, Hothem	$7.95
4943	Field Guide to **Flint Arrowheads & Knives** of the North American Indian	$9.95
2279	**Indian Artifacts** of the Midwest, Hothem	$14.95
3885	**Indian Artifacts** of the Midwest, Book II, Hothem	$16.95
4870	**Indian Artifacts** of the Midwest, Book III, Hothem	$18.95
1964	**Indian Axes** & Related Stone Artifacts, Hothem	$14.95
2023	**Keen Kutter** Collectibles, Heuring	$14.95
4724	Modern **Guns**, Identification & Values, 11th Ed., Quertermous	$12.95
2164	**Primitives**, Our American Heritage, McNerney	$9.95
1759	**Primitives**, Our American Heritage, 2nd Series, McNerney	$14.95
4730	Standard **Knife** Collector's Guide, 3rd Ed., Ritchie & Stewart	$12.95

PAPER COLLECTIBLES & BOOKS

4633	**Big Little Books**, Jacobs	$18.95
4710	Collector's Guide to **Children's Books**, Jones	$18.95
1441	Collector's Guide to **Post Cards**, Wood	$9.95
2081	Guide to Collecting **Cookbooks**, Allen	$14.95
2080	Price Guide to **Cookbooks & Recipe Leaflets**, Dickinson	$9.95
3973	**Sheet Music** Reference & Price Guide, 2nd Ed., Pafik & Guiheen	$19.95
4654	**Victorian Trade Cards**, Historical Reference & Value Guide, Cheadle	$19.95
4733	**Whitman Juvenile Books**, Brown	$17.95

GLASSWARE

4561	Collectible **Drinking Glasses**, Chase & Kelly	$17.95
4642	Collectible **Glass Shoes**, Wheatley	$19.95
4937	Coll. **Glassware** from the 40s, 50s & 60s, 4th Ed., Florence	$19.95
1810	Collector's Encyclopedia of **American Art Glass**, Shuman	$29.95
4938	Collector's Encyclopedia of **Depression Glass**, 13th Ed., Florence	$19.95
1961	Collector's Encyclopedia of **Fry Glassware**, Fry Glass Society	$24.95
1664	Collector's Encyclopedia of **Heisey Glass**, 1925–1938, Bredehoft	$24.95
3905	Collector's Encyclopedia of **Milk Glass**, Newbound	$24.95
4936	Collector's Guide to **Candy Containers**, Dezso/Poirier	$19.95
4564	**Crackle Glass**, Weitman	$19.95
4941	**Crackle Glass**, Book II, Weitman	$19.95
2275	**Czechoslovakian Glass** and Collectibles, Barta/Rose	$16.95
4714	**Czechoslovakian Glass** and Collectibles, Book II, Barta/Rose	$16.95
4716	**Elegant Glassware** of the Depression Era, 7th Ed., Florence	$19.95
1380	Encyclopedia of **Pattern Glass**, McClain	$12.95
3981	Ever's Standard **Cut Glass** Value Guide	$12.95
4659	**Fenton Art Glass**, 1907–1939, Whitmyer	$24.95
3725	**Fostoria**, Pressed, Blown & Hand Molded Shapes, Kerr	$24.95
4719	**Fostoria**, Etched, Carved & Cut Designs, Vol. II, Kerr	$24.95
3883	**Fostoria Stemware**, The Crystal for America, Long & Seate	$24.95
4644	**Imperial Carnival Glass**, Burns	$18.95
3886	**Kitchen Glassware** of the Depression Years, 5th Ed., Florence	$19.95

COLLECTOR BOOKS
Informing Today's Collector

4725	Pocket Guide to **Depression Glass**, 10th Ed., Florence	$9.95
6035	Standard Encyclopedia of **Carnival Glass**, 6th Ed., Edwards/Carwile	$24.95
6036	Standard **Carnival Glass** Price Guide, 11th Ed., Edwards/Carwile	$9.95
4875	Standard Encyclopedia of **Opalescent Glass**, 2nd ed., Edwards	$19.95
4731	**Stemware Identification**, Featuring Cordials with Values, Florence	$24.95
3326	**Very Rare Glassware** of the Depression Years, 3rd Series, Florence	$24.95
4732	**Very Rare Glassware** of the Depression Years, 5th Series, Florence	$24.95
4656	**Westmoreland Glass**, Wilson	$24.95

POTTERY

4927	**ABC Plates & Mugs**, Lindsay	$24.95
4929	**American Art Pottery**, Sigafoose	$24.95
4630	**American Limoges**, Limoges	$24.95
4312	**Blue & White Stoneware**, McNerney	$9.95
1958	So. Potteries **Blue Ridge Dinnerware**, 3rd Ed., Newbound	$14.95
1959	**Blue Willow**, 2nd Ed., Gaston	$14.95
1848	Ceramic **Coin Banks**, Stoddard	$19.95
1851	Collectible **Cups & Saucers**, Harran	$18.95
4709	Collectible **Kay Finch**, Biography, Identification & Values, Martinez/Frick	$18.95
1373	Collector's Encyclopedia of **American Dinnerware**, Cunningham	$24.95
4931	Collector's Encyclopedia of **Bauer Pottery**, Chipman	$24.95
1815	Collector's Encyclopedia of **Blue Ridge Dinnerware**, Newbound	$19.95
4932	Collector's Encyclopedia of **Blue Ridge Dinnerware**, Vol. II, Newbound	$24.95
1658	Collector's Encyclopedia of **Brush-McCoy Pottery**, Huxford	$24.95
1272	Collector's Encyclopedia of **California Pottery**, Chipman	$24.95
4811	Collector's Encyclopedia of **Colorado Pottery**, Carlton	$24.95
2133	Collector's Encyclopedia of **Cookie Jars**, Roerig	$24.95
3723	Collector's Encyclopedia of **Cookie Jars**, Book II, Roerig	$24.95
4939	Collector's Encyclopedia of **Cookie Jars**, Book III, Roerig	$24.95
1638	Collector's Encyclopedia of **Dakota Potteries**, Dommel	$24.95
5040	Collector's Encyclopedia of **Fiesta**, 8th Ed., Huxford	$19.95
4718	Collector's Encyclopedia of **Figural Planters & Vases**, Newbound	$19.95
3961	Collector's Encyclopedia of **Early Noritake**, Alden	$24.95
1439	Collector's Encyclopedia of **Flow Blue China**, Gaston	$19.95
3812	Collector's Encyclopedia of **Flow Blue China**, 2nd Ed., Gaston	$24.95
3813	Collector's Encyclopedia of **Hall China**, 2nd Ed., Whitmyer	$24.95
1431	Collector's Encyclopedia of **Homer Laughlin China**, Jasper	$24.95
1276	Collector's Encyclopedia of **Hull Pottery**, Roberts	$19.95
3962	Collector's Encyclopedia of **Lefton China**, DeLozier	$19.95
4855	Collector's Encyclopedia of **Lefton China**, Book II, DeLozier	$19.95
2210	Collector's Encyclopedia of **Limoges Porcelain**, 2nd Ed., Gaston	$24.95
1334	Collector's Encyclopedia of **Majolica Pottery**, Katz-Marks	$19.95
1358	Collector's Encyclopedia of **McCoy Pottery**, Huxford	$19.95
3963	Collector's Encyclopedia of **Metlox Potteries**, Gibbs Jr.	$24.95
1837	Collector's Encyclopedia of **Nippon Porcelain**, Van Patten	$24.95
2089	Collector's Ency. of **Nippon Porcelain**, 2nd Series, Van Patten	$24.95
1665	Collector's Ency. of **Nippon Porcelain**, 3rd Series, Van Patten	$24.95
4712	Collector's Ency. of **Nippon Porcelain**, 4th Series, Van Patten	$24.95
1447	Collector's Encyclopedia of **Noritake**, Van Patten	$19.95
1432	Collector's Encyclopedia of **Noritake**, 2nd Series, Van Patten	$24.95
2037	Collector's Encyclopedia of **Occupied Japan**, 1st Series, Florence	$14.95
2038	Collector's Encyclopedia of **Occupied Japan**, 2nd Series, Florence	$14.95
2088	Collector's Encyclopedia of **Occupied Japan**, 3rd Series, Florence	$14.95
2019	Collector's Encyclopedia of **Occupied Japan**, 4th Series, Florence	$14.95
2335	Collector's Encyclopedia of **Occupied Japan**, 5th Series, Florence	$14.95
1951	Collector's Encyclopedia of **Old Ivory China**, Hillman	$24.95
3964	Collector's Encyclopedia of **Pickard China**, Reed	$24.95
1377	Collector's Encyclopedia of **R.S. Prussia**, 4th Series, Gaston	$24.95
2034	Collector's Encyclopedia of **Roseville Pottery**, Huxford	$19.95
2035	Collector's Encyclopedia of **Roseville Pottery**, 2nd Ed., Huxford	$19.95
4856	Collector's Encyclopeida of **Russel Wright**, 2nd Ed., Kerr	$24.95
4713	Collector's Encyclopedia of **Salt Glaze Stoneware**, Taylor/Lowrance	$24.95
1314	Collector's Encyclopedia of **Van Briggle** Art Pottery, Sasicki	$24.95
4563	Collector's Encyclopedia of **Wall Pockets**, Newbound	$19.95
2111	Collector's Encyclopedia of **Weller Pottery**, Huxford	$29.95
3876	Collector's Guide to **Lu-Ray Pastels**, Meehan	$18.95
3814	Collector's Guide to **Made in Japan** Ceramics, White	$18.95
4646	Collector's Guide to **Made in Japan** Ceramics, Book II, White	$18.95
4565	Collector's Guide to **Rockingham**, The Enduring Ware, Brewer	$14.95
2339	Collector's Guide to **Shawnee Pottery**, Vanderbilt	$19.95
1425	**Cookie Jars**, Westfall	$9.95

3440	**Cookie Jars**, Book II, Westfall	$19.95
4924	**Figural & Novelty Salt & Pepper Shakers**, 2nd Series, Davern	$24.95
2379	Lehner's Ency. of **U.S. Marks** on Pottery, Porcelain & China	$24.95
4722	**McCoy Pottery**, Collector's Reference & Value Guide, Hanson/Nissen	$19.95
3825	**Purinton Pottery**, Morris	$24.95
4726	**Red Wing Art Pottery**, 1920s–1960s, Dollen	$19.95
1670	**Red Wing Collectibles**, DePasquale	$9.95
1440	**Red Wing Stoneware**, DePasquale	$9.95
1632	**Salt & Pepper Shakers**, Guarnaccia	$9.95
5091	**Salt & Pepper Shakers** II, Guarnaccia	$18.95
2220	**Salt & Pepper Shakers** III, Guarnaccia	$14.95
3443	**Salt & Pepper Shakers** IV, Guarnaccia	$18.95
3738	**Shawnee Pottery**, Mangus	$24.95
4629	Turn of the Century **American Dinnerware**, 1880s–1920s, Jasper	$24.95
4572	**Wall Pockets** of the Past, Perkins	$17.95
3327	**Watt Pottery** – Identification & Value Guide, Morris	$19.95

OTHER COLLECTIBLES

4704	Antique & Collectible **Buttons**, Wisniewski	$19.95
2269	Antique **Brass & Copper** Collectibles, Gaston	$16.95
1880	Antique **Iron**, McNerney	$9.95
3872	Antique **Tins**, Dodge	$24.95
4845	Antique **Typewriters & Office Collectibles**, Rehr	$19.95
1714	**Black** Collectibles, Gibbs	$19.95
1128	**Bottle** Pricing Guide, 3rd Ed., Cleveland	$7.95
4636	**Celluloid Collectibles**, Dunn	$14.95
3718	Collectible **Aluminum**, Grist	$16.95
3445	Collectible **Cats**, An Identification & Value Guide, Fyke	$18.95
4560	Collectible **Cats**, An Identification & Value Guide, Book II, Fyke	$19.95
4852	Collectible **Compact Disc** Price Guide 2, Cooper	$17.95
2018	Collector's Encyclopedia of **Granite Ware**, Greguire	$24.95
3430	Collector's Encyclopedia of **Granite Ware**, Book 2, Greguire	$24.95
4705	Collector's Guide to **Antique Radios**, 4th Ed., Bunis	$18.95
3880	Collector's Guide to **Cigarette Lighters**, Flanagan	$17.95
4637	Collector's Guide to **Cigarette Lighers**, Book II, Flanagan	$17.95
4942	Collector's Guide to **Don Winton Designs**, Ellis	$19.95
3966	Collector's Guide to **Inkwells**, Identification & Values, Badders	$18.95
4947	Collector's Guide to **Inkwells**, Book II, Badders	$19.95
4948	Collector's Guide to **Letter Openers**, Grist	$19.95
4862	Collector's Guide to **Toasters** & Accessories, Greguire	$19.95
4652	Collector's Guide to **Transistor Radios**, 2nd Ed., Bunis	$16.95
4653	Collector's Guide to **TV Memorabilia**, 1960s–1970s, Davis/Morgan	$24.95
4864	Collector's Guide to **Wallace Nutting Pictures**, Ivankovich	$18.95
1629	**Doorstops**, Identification & Values, Bertoia	$9.95
4567	Figural **Napkin Rings**, Gottschalk & Whitson	$18.95
4717	Figural **Nodders**, Includes Bobbin' Heads and Swayers, Irtz	$19.95
3968	**Fishing Lure** Collectibles, Murphy/Edmisten	$24.95
4867	**Flea Market Trader**, 11th Ed., Huxford	$9.95
4944	**Flue Covers**, Collector's Value Guide, Meckley	$12.95
4945	**G-Men and FBI Toys** and Collectibles, Whitworth	$18.95
5043	**Garage Sale & Flea Market** Annual, 6th Ed.	$19.95
3819	**General Store Collectibles**, Wilson	$24.95
4643	**Great American West** Collectibles, Wilson	$24.95
2215	Goldstein's **Coca-Cola** Collectibles	$16.95
3884	Huxford's Collectible **Advertising**, 2nd Ed.	$24.95
2216	**Kitchen Antiques**, 1790–1940, McNerney	$14.95
4950	The **Lone Ranger**, Collector's Reference & Value Guide, Felbinger	$18.95
2026	**Railroad** Collectibles, 4th Ed., Baker	$14.95
4949	**Schroeder's Antiques** Price Guide, 16th Ed., Huxford	$12.95
5007	**Silverplated Flatware**, Revised 4th Edition, Hagan	$18.95
1922	Standard **Old Bottle** Price Guide, Sellari	$14.95
4708	Summers' Guide to **Coca-Cola**	$19.95
4952	Summers' Pocket Guide to **Coca-Cola** Identifications	$9.95
3892	**Toy & Miniature Sewing Machines**, Thomas	$18.95
4876	**Toy & Miniature Sewing Machines**, Book II, Thomas	$24.95
3828	Value Guide to **Advertising Memorabilia**, Summers	$18.95
3977	Value Guide to **Gas Station** Memorabilia, Summers & Priddy	$24.95
4877	Vintage **Bar Ware**, Visakay	$24.95
4935	The W.F. Cody **Buffalo Bill** Collector's Guide with Values	$24.95
4879	**Wanted to Buy**, 6th Edition	$9.95

This is only a partial listing of the books on antiques that are available from Collector Books. All books are well illustrated and contain current values. Most of these books are available from your local bookseller, antique dealer, or public library. If you are unable to locate certain titles in your area, you may order by mail from COLLECTOR BOOKS, P.O. Box 3009, Paducah, KY 42002-3009. Customers with Visa, Discover or MasterCard may phone in orders from 7:00–5:00 CST, Monday–Friday, Toll Free 1-800-626-5420. Add $2.00 for postage for the first book ordered and $0.30 for each additional book. Include item number, title, and price when ordering. Allow 14 to 21 days for delivery.

Schroeder's ANTIQUES Price Guide

. . . is the #1 best-selling antiques & collectibles value guide on the market today, and here's why . . .

Schroeder's ANTIQUES Price Guide

Identification & Values of Over 50,000 Antiques & Collectibles

8½ x 11, 612 Pages, $12.95

• More than 450 advisors, well-known dealers, and top-notch collectors work together with our editors to bring you accurate information regarding pricing and identification.

• More than 45,000 items in almost 550 categories are listed along with hundreds of sharp original photos that illustrate not only the rare and unusual, but the common, popular collectibles as well.

• Each large close-up shot shows important details clearly. Every subject is represented with histories and background information, a feature not found in any of our competitors' publications.

• Our editors keep abreast of newly developing trends, often adding several new categories a year as the need arises.

If it merits the interest of today's collector, you'll find it in *Schroeder's*. And you can feel confident that the information we publish is up to date and accurate. Our advisors thoroughly check each category to spot inconsistencies, listings that may not be entirely reflective of market dealings, and lines too vague to be of merit. Only the best of the lot remains for publication.

Without doubt, you'll find
SCHROEDER'S ANTIQUES PRICE GUIDE
the only one to buy for
reliable information and values.

COLLECTOR BOOKS
A Division of Schroeder Publishing Co., Inc.